Great Games Need Great Leaders

This book brings together the knowledge and perspectives of numerous past and present games industry leaders and practitioners to form a clear picture of how leadership operates in a game development studio. It identifies the ways in which things are changing or can change for the better in the games industry and provides a set of tools for the reader to use in their own professional practice.

Embark on a journey with this book to understand how great leaders help make great games. These leaders embrace change through a broad set of skills intended to empower and nurture the teams they find themselves responsible for. Through the lens of three fantasy roleplaying classes – the Warrior, the Bard, and the Cleric – readers will understand the wide variety of skills and considerations involved in leading game developers well.

This book will be of great interest to anybody curious about or currently working in games development.

Matthew John Dyet is the founder and project lead of EverySecond Studio and a games lecturer at the SAE Institute in Perth, Western Australia.

T0384797

Great Games Need Great Leaders

Multiclassing to Lead Game Development Teams

Written by

Matthew John Dyet

CRC Press
Taylor & Francis Group
Boca Raton London New York

CRC Press is an imprint of the
Taylor & Francis Group, an **informa** business

Designed cover image: Lisa Rye

First edition published 2025
by CRC Press
2385 NW Executive Center Drive, Suite 320, Boca Raton FL 33431

and by CRC Press
4 Park Square, Milton Park, Abingdon, Oxon, OX14 4RN

CRC Press is an imprint of Taylor & Francis Group, LLC

ISBN: 9781032556642 (hbk)
ISBN: 9781032554464 (pbk)
ISBN: 9781003431626 (ebk)

DOI: 10.1201/9781003431626

Typeset in Minion
by KnowledgeWorks Global Ltd.

This book is dedicated to the 20,000 game developers who lost their jobs over the course of its writing.

Contents

Foreword

Let me tell you the biggest professional mistake I've ever made: allowing myself to achieve, at best, only three years of career growth in 11 years at a game studio. I just sort of floated through my duties, assuming if there was something else I needed to learn, someone would come along and teach me. I should've realised I'm the only one truly responsible for my own development, so that mistake's on me. But what didn't help was that exactly zero people at the studio were trying to teach me anything or provide me with growth opportunities of any kind. No mentoring. No coaching. And that's a failure of leadership.

I left fingers-on-keyboard AAA development in 2010 to do consulting in leadership and cultural improvement for game companies. I wanted to see people fulfilled at work instead of burned out and left to flounder like I was. Since then, I've taught leadership to game developers on four continents. I've written a book on leadership for developers. I've worked for $2 trillion worth of clients. (Admittedly, that one gig with Google skews the numbers, but still.)

Leadership is kind of my thing.

Imagine just my interest level when my friend Matthew phoned up to tell me he was authoring a book on sustainable and ethical leadership practices in the games industry. I've been a huge fan of the project from day one, and now here we are. He's done the research, held dozens of interviews, and wrestled with how best to present his findings, and I'm honoured to be writing the Foreword.

But it doesn't end with you reading the book.

The true end of teaching is to change behaviours. It's not just about sharing an opinion or imparting knowledge. When, through persistent investigation, one uncovers noteworthy data or superior practices, one doesn't just unveil the findings and sit back and say, "I'm sure you agree that's interesting."

Just sharing is not the goal. The goal is for things to improve. For the industry, the companies, and the workplaces to get better. For people to act differently. Knowledge won't do it, but actions will.

Good on Matthew for writing the thing. And good on you for reading it! But your role here isn't complete when you finish the last page. Get there, close the back cover (or whatever the Kindle equivalent is if you aren't holding a physical copy), and then go forth. Do something different. Ponder what's been shared and find a way to make your workplace, company, and industry improve.

Help someone become a better leader. Or become one yourself! These are the kinds of changes the author wanted when he set out to write this book. Bless him for doing it. Because it's what our entire industry desperately needs. And every change, at every level, matters.

Your change matters.

When I squandered years of my career, that was on me. But once you've absorbed all of the painstakingly gathered material within this book, will anything come of it?

That's on you.

Keith Fuller
Leadership Consultant, Founder of GameDevCoaching.com
Wisconsin, United States
January 2024

Acknowledgements

When I set out to write *Great Games Need Great Leaders*, I wanted to ensure that it was more than simply a representation of my own views on leadership in the games industry. This book needed to reflect the combined experience of leaders and developers who could amplify and reinforce the message. It is difficult to feel qualified to be a singular expert on a subject, and it was only through the insights and time provided to me by other people that this book was made possible.

Many of the people listed here were not able to make time to provide me with interviews, but their friendship and mentorship throughout the years have changed me and inspired me to do better. Their individual wisdom and experience have influenced my own leadership through their authenticity, and they inspire me to constantly find ways to do better. I would like to thank the following people for their contributions to this work: Anna Barham, Dr. Raffael Boccamazzo, Branden Buffalo, Jetha Chan, Alayna Cole, Amy Dallas, Luke Dicken, Amy Louise Doherty, Osama Dorias, Megan Fox, Keith Fuller, Jason Imms, Jonathan Jennings, Dr. Lakers Komaiya, Dr. JC Lau, Jean Leggett, Dr. Marija Koprivica Lelićanin, Emily MacMahon, Lazar Mesaros, Xalavier Nelson Jr, Chima Denzel Ngerem, Damon Reece, Liana Ruppert, Camden Stoddard, Anthony Sweet, and Zenuel.

Where I have quoted these individuals, I've included their role and place of work; however, this only reflects their position at the time of writing. Several of the people I interviewed moved to other businesses or were fired among the wave of industry layoffs throughout 2023 and 2024. By the time that you are reading, it's not unlikely that many of these people will have moved on to new positions in new places.

I would also like to acknowledge the support of the team at EverySecond Studio. While I was away focused on writing this book, they were able to keep things going by developing our first game, Omi Oh My AI. I am lucky to have had the opportunity to work with a team of such passionate and kind developers, whom I also considered friends Making games is hard, but they make it feel like the best and easiest job in the world.

Finally, I need to thank my partner, Mayghan Thon. In the time since I brought her to Australia from her family in the USA, she has had to suffer through me tending to what has been easily the busiest period of my life, but at no point did she ever stop supporting me. She is my stable ground and the ray of sunshine that keeps me going, and I could not have been more lucky to find somebody so sweet and patient to call my partner in crime.

Prologue

It is no secret that making games is hard. The games industry draws in people attracted to technical and artistic challenges who are passionate about the creativity involved in game making. Games fail and studios close for many reasons, but when you talk to game developers to get their stories, you begin to realise that there are recurring themes among their experiences. Most game developers have experienced poor leadership at some point in their careers. We expect it to be hard to make games, not for it to be hard to work with others.

Leadership in the games industry suffers from a unique set of problems. Obviously, poor leadership is not a problem unique to the games industry. Rather, the circumstances surrounding developing games create challenges for leading teams effectively. There is a feeling among many people in the games industry that these problems are unique to us, and so we must seek our own solutions. Worse still is the feeling that our current solutions are simply the best that we will get.

Games are developed by teams of skilled individuals from a variety of technical and artistic backgrounds. Each of these people brings their own expertise to projects that leaders must help navigate into a single, unified product. Rather than embracing the creativity of individuals, many leaders instead direct teams to meet their strict expectations. These sorts of leaders often end up micromanaging their teams.

Sister industries such as animation and film experience similar leadership challenges, and their solutions have contributed to informing the process of game development for decades now. Titles such as "director" and "producer" were taken directly from film, though the specifics of their roles and job descriptions have evolved with time. Initially the whole development process was pulled from film, but this rapidly changed to instead borrow from manufacturing and software development. Even terms such as "indie" were inherited from the

DOI: 10.1201/9781003431626-1

music industry to reflect the lack of a record label – or in our case, a lack of publisher.

This is just how the games industry has operated since its inception. We take concepts from elsewhere that come close to achieving what we want, and we use them to make games. Few concepts in the games industry are generally accepted as "best practice." The circumstances surrounding the development of one project will be entirely unique in structure and process from another project. The variety of interpretations of the role of leadership create drastically different working environments.

Valve and Bungie are both Seattle- based studios, both developers of well-known first-person shooters, and both best described as AAA game developers. Valve is self-described as a flat-structured studio, complete with visual aids, as demonstrated by their publicly accessible employee handbook (Valve Corporation, 2012). There are no hierarchies in Valve other than those its employees decide to create with their peers. Theoretically, it is an environment in which its staff are free to express their creativity and are entrusted with doing the work however they wish. Bungie, by comparison, is a studio of hierarchies. Their studio is made up of smaller strike teams, more commonly known as pods (Noseworthy, 2014). These strike teams are groups of five or so developers of mixed disciplines, made responsible for individual tasks and features, and report to directors who act as vision holders for their games.

An often-shared joke among developers is that nobody really knows what they are doing, but there's a grain of truth in every joke. These are drastically different approaches to games development. How can two studios in the same place operate in such drastically different ways? The answer is that the games industry is still searching for solutions, for the best and most reliable ways to make games and ensure success. In terms of creative industries, it is exceptionally young. We had to borrow our terms, techniques, and processes from elsewhere in order to exist. We could only secure financing if we worked within similar frameworks as other technical or creative industries.

Game developers need to be flexible. The circumstances they are expected to work in at one studio will be dramatically different at another. Even when working for major publishers, direct sister studios are prone to having very different ideas about the best way to make games. The unfortunate reality, however, is that many successful games are made off the backs of bad practices.

The games industry is prone to what is called crunch: excessive workloads and hours enforced upon game developers. Crunch is so well known across the industry due to its prevalence and the damage it has caused to the health and well-being of individuals. Few game developers will avoid having to crunch during their careers. Most of us will have a story about the nightmarish circumstances we were put through in the name of getting a game released on time.

Sometimes I wonder if the industry itself is not sustainable. People turn over in studios rapidly. There is a pace of work expected in a game studio that makes game careers exhausting. We aren't exactly saving lives here, but you often hear people in the industry saying things like "game devs are survivors' or 'every game dev has a heartbreak story" because we've all had projects cancelled, experienced massive layoff rounds, or worked on something with unreasonable timelines.

– ALAYNA COLE, DIVERSITY EQUITY AND INCLUSION MANAGER, SLEDGEHAMMER GAMES

Stories from inside game studios have become more prevalent as developers have started to take a stand against these sorts of practices. Writers like Jason Schreier have made their careers in investigative journalism, sharing the stories of game developers. But even with the added visibility, game developers still find themselves in repressive working conditions. A developer survey conducted by the International Game Developers Association (IGDA) in 2021 reports that a majority of game developers felt that there were unequal opportunities and treatment for people in the industry and expressed continuing concerns about unlimited and unpaid overtime (International Game Developers Association, 2021).

Work in the games industry is also not stable employment. Layoffs in 2023 and 2024 were particularly awful, with estimates currently sitting at over 16,000 people fired in the 12 months between February 2023 and February 2024 (Noor, 2024). By comparison, the video game crash of 1983 was estimated to have impacted just 3,000 game developers at Atari (Kocurek, 2015). However, neither of these events is particularly unique other than in their scale. Every year, game development studios lay off experienced staff in the hundreds as they cut costs, close projects, or shift focus to new ones. It is little surprise then that unionisation in the games industry is rapidly gaining momentum, with numerous new unions established in the last few years (Carpenter, 2023b).

There comes a time in the career of every game developer where they have to make a choice. They will look at other opportunities and either choose to leave the industry or somehow find a way to remain within it. That decision is only made easier when it seems clear that the industry has little respect for individual abilities or the need to balance their lives with their work. The events of 1983 are called a crisis because they not only impacted staff but also sales. By comparison, 2023 was a great year for people that play and sell games, but not the people that make them.

Brain drain in the games industry has the potential to mirror the effects of COVID-19 on the aviation industry if it is ignored. To save on costs, airlines chose not to train new pilots – instead primarily hiring from the air force or from their competitors. During the pandemic, airlines fired or offered early retirement packages to their pilots to reduce their costs in the face of fewer flights. These cost cutting exercises may have had short-term benefits but have created the long-term crisis the industry is now facing: they are unable to hire new pilots. The militaries of the world have been moving away from training in-cockpit pilots to training drone pilots for some time now, reducing the pool of experienced pilots available to the airlines. Combined with a lack of training programmes, the airlines now face a challenging reality: create training programmes that may take years to have results, or spend more money to offer higher wages to pilots working for their competitors (Murray and Green, 2021).

The games industry also lacks training programmes for staff. Investment in staff is minimal, with entry-level roles requiring years of prior experience. Once in that position, people typically find themselves needing to improve upon their skills in their own time. If they manage to develop their skills and remain, the pathway forward always includes the expectation of accepting some leadership responsibility. An individual may be an incredible artist or programmer, but they will inevitably be taken away from those tasks to lead others in doing them. Of course, these new leaders are unlikely to be provided training on their new responsibilities.

It really is no wonder then that many leaders find themselves frustrated at having to deal with people. They are no longer engaged in doing the thing they love.

> People really miss being on the tools. I've had to have a couple of quiet conversations where I've asked, were you thrown into this role as a manager? Now you're leading a team, do you really want this job? Because part of the job is making peace with the fact that you can't be on the tools all the time. Leadership is your primary role, it's to be there to be a people guide and coach them. If you find yourself always being sad you're not on the tools, you're not going to be showing up to people with your heart present. You'll just want to get it over with.
>
> – EMILY MACMAHON, LEADERSHIP CONSULTANT

University and college programmes training new developers are often staffed by graduates with little to no industry experience of their own. Educational institutions typically do not offer the competitive wages necessary to bring in experienced developers. The expectation of postgraduate study and a lack of respect for lived experience make it an unappealing career shift for most developers to make. Combine this with strict non-disclosure agreements, and the people training game developers are often left having to guess what modern tools, practices, and techniques look like.

It's not unusual to see gamers and game developers alike bemoaning the loss of skills we saw during the golden years of the Super Nintendo. Rollercoaster Tycoon is an often-repeated example, given that it was coded in a low-level programming language by a single game developer in order for it to run on the machines of the era (Sawyer, 2003). The skills that allowed projects during that era to overcome the immense technical challenges presented by limited hardware and software have largely been lost to the industry today. This is not because the new generation of game developers is any less skilled, passionate, or interested in working with interesting technical challenges. It is because the people that they could learn from have resigned or been fired.

> We lost the ability to make Damascus steel because the people who were responsible for it had either failed to pass it down, or passed it on to people who didn't care enough about it. Fast forward a few decdes and they found a master who had kept a written log of how to make Damascus steel. It was monumental for metallurgy. And now in order to preserve this art, they have burned Damascus steel into the de facto baseline for new metallurgists. They must learn how to create Damascus steel before they are ready to create anything else. And it's this thing that has kept this art alive. I think about that a lot when it comes to the things we're not teaching students. We teach them to be really good at solving tests, at filling this exact need, but not what it means to make games in a live environment that is volatile, that is unstable. The idea that we don't have a baseline for that yet.
>
> – ZENUEL, INDEPENDENT DEVELOPER, PREVIOUSLY OF STRANGE SCAFFOLD

This all impacts the quality of leadership in the games industry. Studio leadership is usually made up of people who have managed to stay employed long enough to see themselves promoted to the role. They have not been provided training on leading game development teams effectively by their educational institutions or by their employers. The leaders that came before them had the same problem. There are typically two ways leaders go from here. Either they see the role of leadership as a promotion and never truly embrace or learn the skill to lead. Or they choose to do better, teach themselves, and take on the challenge of trying to be better than their predecessors.

Leadership is a challenging and often thankless job. But it can also be an immensely rewarding job, one which enables us to empower the people around us to not just succeed in their roles but thrive as creatives. This style of leadership was the uniting thread that all the people interviewed for this book shared in common. It comes from a focus on the people around us and a desire for constant improvement. To truly lead others well, we need to accept that we are not in control of others at all.

If this sounds counter to your understanding of leadership, you are not alone. Many fresh new leaders step into the role with the best of intentions, expecting to bring order to the chaos of games development. These leaders are rarely remembered fondly as they are perceived as prescriptive and prone to micromanagement. There's no formula that guarantees success; there is no one-size-fits-all method of leadership. A recurring theme of many interviews was the challenging decisions that leaders often face. But some decisions should not be easy; it is necessary that we be challenged. Cold calculation is often a way to separate ourselves from the human cost of the decisions we make.

> Micromanagement is one of the top characteristics of intolerable bosses and of the bad boss. It kills creativity. We talk about managers, we need more coordinators. Those people who are accountable for their part of the work. We don't need rigid. The literature is saying those kind of bosses are being recognised as totally intolerable.
>
> – MARIJA KOPRIVICA LELIĆANIN, SAE INSTITUTE

The industry is rife with stories of studios with unsustainable working practices that are simply the expectation of staff. Many of the leaders at these businesses have gone on the record stating that they believe this is simply the way the industry needs to operate. That there is no art without some degree of suffering. Developers are privileged to be working in a job that is so fun. These sorts of backhanded comments hide the reality of employment in the games industry. Developers enter the industry with an expectation of a degree of freedom that few studios will allow them to have, with leadership that often treats them as expendable or a means to an end. There is at least some truth in the saying that people don't leave bad jobs; they leave bad bosses.

The games industry has a long way to go before it is the wonderful place to work that we want it to be. We are not just fighting against unrealistic expectations from publishers and players, but also against capitalistic forces that emphasise the creation of value above all else. It may be overwhelming to read all of this and to consider our role in what that change looks like, but as leaders, we have the power to offer some protection and empowerment to the members of our team. Change for the better is not out of reach, it can start with us.

HEARTBREAK

Getting a job in game development seemed like an impossibility for me. While I had good grades coming out of university, I had no experience and lived in one of the most remote cities in the world. I was lucky to be provided with an IGDA Foundation Scholarship in 2013 to attend the Game Developers Conference in San Francisco. In addition to providing me access to the conference, the scholarship provided me with a mentor and the unique opportunity to visit local developers like Double Fine and the now-defunct Three Rings Studio. It reignited my passion for game development and made me realise that getting a job working in the industry was not impossible at all.

I resigned from my web development job before I even left the conference.

About a year later, I would be hired as a producer by a small independent studio with a team of about a dozen people. It wasn't an easy job, and I didn't expect it to be. I enjoyed the challenges it posed as I tried to balance feature additions against the time and budget available to us. There were mistakes and missteps, and being new to the industry, I just figured these were to be expected. I'd read enough articles about studio closures and working conditions to feel well off.

But as time went on, it became harder to justify the sort of stress and heartache the team was put through as a direct result of our leadership. Time and time again, I'd highlight the negative repercussions of a decision, just for the choice to be made anyway. When things inevitably went bad, there would be apologies and excuses. "We should have listened" and "we couldn't avoid this outcome" became some of the most frustrating things to hear from our leaders. I worked on my communication, thinking that perhaps I just wasn't being clear enough in the information I was providing.

Our small team was funded by private investment. With a recent project having not made back the funds invested in it, the leadership was looking to hedge their bets on the next projects. Our initial plans were to work on several smaller, faster games to make the most of our funding – essentially, we would put our eggs in a few different baskets. We had been prototyping a few games for some time when leadership decided on working with an existing IP to try and secure a larger audience.

Plans changed quickly once we'd signed on with the IP holder. The contract stipulated a change of Producer to somebody the IP holder was familiar with. I was removed from the project. In the few months after I'd been replaced, the project had gone off the rails in a variety of creative ways, and studio leadership had asked me to step in to fix it. There were several issues: the team was still debating art styles, with a push from leadership to use expensive facial motion capture technology; deadlines for writing delivery, which the IP holder was responsible for, had not been set; and the IP holder was clashing with our narrative designer over word count and the description of their role.

Once I was back on the project, I set about trying to solve problems. Working with our art and animation team, I put together estimates on the time it would take to animate dialogue. This set the limits for how much could be written and spoken and made it clear that the purchase of the facial motion capture rig was a poor financial decision. The rig was purchased despite the advice and information provided. This had the additional impact of meaning that the funds that were designated for other projects were now gone – everything would be spent on this game. It was all or nothing.

Leadership asked me to sit down with the IP holder and the narrative designer to attempt to resolve the issue. I had no authority over the IP holder or the contract, and so my role was really just to get a sense of what the issue was and if it could be resolved. Together, the narrative designer and I presented the limitations of the writing. There was a clear lack of respect for the narrative designer or the value of their role, and so the meeting went poorly. I suggested that leadership needed to intervene and have a difficult conversation with the IP holder about their behaviour. Instead, they fired the narrative designer the following morning.

All of this compounded upon events in my personal life. I was in a long-distance relationship, and my partner had been admitted to the hospital. She had been suffering with shortness of breath for as long as we were together. After a particularly bad day, she went to get a check-up. Her doctor had sent her for a flurry of tests that would reveal an extensive blood clot running from her heart to her liver. Further tests revealed the cause was a combination of autoimmune diseases that complicated the treatment of the clot.

I was hopeful that it was treatable, and so I had chosen to remain in Australia to attempt to resolve the issues at the studio. My partner had been telling me to quit for months as she could see the negative impact it was having on me. Between the recent events at the studio and her time in the hospital, I finally chose to hand in my resignation.

The doctors would successfully remove the blood clot, only for my partner to get an infection. She passed away just a few weeks after I resigned.

The studio would declare bankruptcy before the end of the year.

I was lucky to be able to get therapy that would help me work through everything I was feeling in the months that followed. There was the grief of losing her and the guilt of not having done more sooner. But also an anger at the studio leadership that had made me feel so powerless. I stayed far longer than I should have out of a sense of responsibility to protect the team, but it came at the cost of my health and my time with a person I loved. I would eventually be able to come to terms with these feelings and forgive myself and the people who had failed me.

Over the years, I've looked back at what happened and tried to understand, but I have concluded that it's not really my place. I cannot speak to the reasons why our leadership made the decisions they made, or why they so often ignored the advice of staff. I think there was a lot of fear, and that they had their blinders on. There was a fixation on their individual circumstances or goals that repeatedly came at the cost of the team. They were not bad people, but they were awful leaders.

Poor leadership usually comes at a human cost. I do believe that my experiences made me a better leader, not because I had leadership to aspire to but because I had personally experienced the sting of when it was lacking. I figured out how I wanted to lead others by understanding the shortcomings of the leaders I had before. It's not a way I would wish for anybody else to find their leadership style. But reflecting on the choices they made and what I would do differently acted as a guide for my leadership in the following years. It informed a greater search for how I could avoid repeating the mistakes they made.

It was these experiences that created the desire to find ways to contribute to collective efforts to improve the games industry for all. It's a challenging problem to solve. Many of the people with whom I've spoken have chosen to take their experience into leadership training and consulting. Others have given incredibly insightful talks to work to inspire others to change. Everybody I spoke with has, in some way, given me mentorship to help guide this book into the product you are reading now.

The problem I found throughout my career was that these require a huge time investment to absorb. Every conference I went to, every person I met, every book I read – they were all immensely valuable. But it's taken me a decade to find myself at a point where I feel like I can qualify for everything expected of me as a leader. If we are expecting every leader in the industry to simply do their own research to improve themselves, and it takes this much work to figure out how, then it's little wonder that leadership in the industry is of the quality it is.

So when I eventually went on to do my Masters, I did it researching Games Industry Leadership. My objective was to begin to identify the collective qualities of leadership and to use these to create a model. But I did not want it to just be informed by the literature. If you have ever tried to research the games industry, you will know that there's not a lot. Unless you are looking for dozens of different design frameworks proposed by people who have never created a game, you are likely going to be reading literature from adjacent industries or consuming content from conferences.

What the games industry lacks in literature, it makes up for in shared knowledge through conferences. I have attended or found online some fantastic talks and presentations about managing teams, and people are speaking earnestly about their experiences. However, the unfortunate reality of these talks is that people rarely discuss failures – they simply cannot. Strict non-disclosure agreements in the games industry mean that it's nearly impossible to discuss failed projects openly, and few businesses are going to want to approve such a potential public relations disaster as their developers talking about how they mess up.

There is a degree of survivorship bias in most conference talks. They usually lean towards demonstrating great results, as this is often the only way to be approved by the business. They can often present poor practices that happened to pay off. Taking the advice of such talks at face value can inadvertently direct new leaders to attempt practices that will inevitably harm their teams. Do not let this undermine their worth however: they are invaluable to expanding our understanding of the industry and improving our skills. But we need to consume this information with a degree of scepticism.

It was my desire to have this book present a collective of experiences that did not need to be so sanitised. I wanted to be able to speak about my experiences and share the lessons that I learned from them, but I also wanted to avoid speaking like my experience described anything even close to the experience of an entire industry. Despite over a decade of working in games, I feel deeply unqualified to talk about games industry leadership. I could speak to singular skills and experiences, but I do not believe that I am some sort of image of the ideal leader. I've not met anybody who would desire to be placed on such a pedestal.

I chose to gather perspectives and insights from as many people in the industry as possible while writing this book. I wanted to present a diverse set of backgrounds: different genders, different races, different nationalities, different studios, and different roles. This isn't just about leadership in a big studio or a small one. It's not about leadership in Japan or America. These fundamental concepts were universal to every leader I spoke with. The circumstances, places, projects, and people changed, but the fundamentals did not.

Doing your own research and seeking further insight is essential. Even when you close this book and put it down forever, your journey as a leader does not end. There will be new processes, new challenges, and new thinking. You will want to make yourself familiar with all of it and embrace that sense of continuous self-improvement as a key component of your leadership. But we start this journey by ensuring that we have a firm understanding of the fundamentals of leadership.

That is the purpose of this book. To develop our understanding of leadership by bringing together research and the collective wisdom of over two dozen leaders from across the world. The majority of them are from the games industry, but I have also spoken with individuals with backgrounds in the military, medicine, and education. No matter their background, the thing that unites them is their care for people. They hail from all over the world, including the United States of America, Japan, the United Kingdom, Europe, and Australia. This book presents their stories, their quotes, and their anecdotes so that we may gain an understanding of what it takes to be a great leader in the games industry.

1.0

Leadership

When starting a new position as a leader, we may take up the shield and set our intentions for the protection of the team. We might place ourselves out in front of them, directing them to where you need them to go while protecting them from the unexpected. The team comes to rely on us for direction and protection. We are out in front, sword in hand, team at our back. We charge into danger on their behalf and hack away at the things that keep them from success.

Our mantra may be that we would never ask the team anything we would be unwilling to do ourselves. We work late nights in service of the game and the team, but we refuse to ask the team to do that themselves. By the time we finish that first game, we feel exhausted, but we are satisfied that we did everything in our power to protect and lead the team. We got the game out the door. We have successfully released a game, and that is no small feat.

But the team seems dissatisfied with our performance. We were so focused on their protection that they avoided bringing their problems to us, meaning we often got surprised by threats at the start of the project. We started being nosy in order to protect the team from threats. Control of the project was reliant upon us, as nobody could make a decision without our involvement. As a result, the team felt creatively stagnant.

We led from the front, removing the ability for people to go out seeking their own paths or more effective solutions. Without their input, we lead the

DOI: 10.1201/9781003431626-2

team down dead ends. Our constant need to jump to the defence of the team leaves the team feeling like you don't believe they can fight their own battles. They didn't feel empowered by our actions; they felt that we did not trust them.

This theoretical leader tried to do everything right. They had the team's health and well-being at heart and made it their responsibility to try to protect these things. But the reality is that for us to improve, we need to first let go of any preconceived notions that we understand what leadership is. Leaders are not just experienced members of staff. They are not just protectors, advocates, or vision holders. They are all these things, and they change based on the needs of the moment.

Leadership in the studio is responsible for two things: the business and the people. We may have a publisher, development partners, clients, or stakeholders. These are all specifically business concerns, however. We are responsible for all of them, and where they land on our list of priorities will depend upon our title and where we exist in the studio hierarchy. The people in our team are always equal in priority to all these business concerns.

Where many leaders in the games industry fail is by focusing more on the business than the people. We are never just developing a game for a business; we are also developing the people employed by the businesspeople work on the games we sell to maintain the business, and in return, the business pays the people. Ignoring one is detrimental to the other.

This failing, then, is likely the fundamental motivator for the focus on people that came with every leader I spoke to. We were not discussing how projects get made or how to balance budgets, these things change depending on our position and place in the hierarchy of a studio. The one thing that every leader shares in common is the people that they work with.

> There's a consistent leadership style among studios that treats it more like any other business. To make money, be profitable, hedge against risk, manage business and personal resources accordingly. There's a lot of focus on keeping stakeholders and shareholders happy so they keep funding games. It's valid and important, but at the moment I feel the pendulum has swung too far in that direction. Like, where's our culture? Where's the focus on mental health and work-life balance, and the hey, don't kill yourself crunching?
>
> – CHIMA DENZEL NGEREM, PRODUCER, ZYNGA

The reality of making games is that the individual games aren't the product; the people making them are. We might make a single great game, but it will likely be our last if we fail to maintain or support the people who made it. A team will only go on to make more great games if they work for a business that respects and empowers them. Our responsibility as leaders is not to make great games but to empower and retain the people that do.

It is telling then that so many leaders in the games industry discourage unionisation. I have spoken with leaders in the past who explained that this rose out of a concern for the employment of their teams. They were worried about reprisals by businesses or funding going overseas. There are absolutely challenges and risks involved with unionisation, but these things do not outweigh the value of a strong union presence. As leaders, we should be pushing to ensure our teams are cared for. This can only truly happen if they are empowered to hold their businesses and their leadership accountable.

Great leaders are not only willing to be accountable, they also actively seek improvement. They take action on the feedback they hear from their teams. They adjust their practices based on the input of others. This need not just be feedback about their personal performance, it could be feedback about the direction the project is taking or how things are being managed. Sometimes it is difficult to hear that feedback, but they have chosen a path of self-improvement. Every great leader is always learning what the best possible practice looks like and is improving upon their own skills and techniques. Great leadership is the sum of its parts.

The characteristics of leadership are universal. It's not attached to a specific role or position in a hierarchy. It would be incorrect to say that a leader is somebody who has command over others. A leader is anybody who chooses to act with self-awareness of how those actions may impact others. They are somebody whose behaviour inspires and motivates the people around them. They take responsibility for people, for projects, and for processes. Anyone can be a leader.

There is no one way to lead people in the games industry, however. The expectations of a leader in a publicly held AAA studio will be incredibly different from those of somebody leading a small indie team, to say nothing of the cultural differences depending on where it is they are leading from. Great leaders understand and adjust appropriately to their environment. The people and the projects change, and so the leader must be willing to change too.

We may find ourselves in a position where our options are limited. We have been given our own instructions from the leadership above us. Even if we disagree, we just have to enact it. It can be easy in such circumstances to feel powerless, to give up, and to walk away from the idea of improving our leadership when the people we report to are all too content in their own mediocrity. But today our team needs us to guide them out of the darkness so that we might be better prepared for that moment in which we have the capacity to avoid putting them in a dark place in the first place.

Great leaders are set apart by their adoption of ongoing learning and improvisation. Every tool or skill that we have at our disposal has examples of both good and bad ways in which it can be used. We can very easily make wrong decisions for all the right reasons. Taking on the responsibility of leading others does not mean that we are perfect or avoid failure, but that we embrace and learn from our failures. It is the only way we can grow as great leaders in our own right.

Working in the games industry means that every day is different. We work on creative products that have an immense variety of challenges and potential complications. We work with creative people who come from a variety of artistic and technical backgrounds. Leaders reside at the point between the project and the team, and so we need to have the capacity to work with both.

Multiclassing as a concept came about due to the need for leaders to be prepared for every circumstance. It is not enough to just be great at leading in just one way, we cannot just be a great protector of the team if we wish for them to be empowered to take creative risks. Protection is a great ideal, but we cannot only be protectors. We have the tools at our disposal, great leadership is knowing what tool is necessary in the moment.

This isn't a book of solutions to the unique problems we will experience throughout the course of our careers. It's a book of the characteristics that enable us to solve problems.

The only certainty that we have is that nothing is certain. We must be open and prepared to experiment with style and process to best serve the unique circumstances of our team and the project that we are developing. Many leaders that I spoke with referred to leadership styles such as situational leadership or servant leadership but heavily emphasised that these were just tools in their toolbox (Greenleaf, 1970; Blanchard, Zigarmi and Zigarmi, 2013). It is the fundamentals of these styles which we desire to achieve; changing in the moment, always in service of the people.

> I haven't really thought about myself as having a specific leadership style. It's like a bucket that I fill with rocks. The rocks are the fundamentals that I rely upon, the things that cannot change. The spaces between those fundamentals is like sand, it's flexible and made to fill the gaps. That space changes depending on the specifics of the circumstance, or the people I'm working with.
>
> – KEITH FULLER, LEADERSHIP CONSULTANT

I was expecting a variety of styles and perspectives to arise out of my research and interviews on leadership. Instead, I discovered that many leaders were gravitating towards specific traits with very little outside influence. Experience and practice within the games industry by those leaders who reflect and work on improving their practice lead to similar solutions. Perhaps it's just in the nature of game development that the appropriate response to change and the unknown is to embrace adaptability.

CRUNCH

To have a foundational understanding of leadership and its role in the games industry, we must also understand crunch. However, it makes for a particularly challenging subject to discuss as it is so poorly defined. Even among the leaders I spoke with, many of them had differing feelings and definitions of what crunch was. Without a clear definition, it may be easy to say that crunch is just another misunderstood tool in our kit of tools. But crunch has a human cost involved in it, and we need to be clear on the reasons why crunch should not be an option we are willing to entertain as leaders.

Crunch has been a subject of discussion for the last decade, with coverage generally presenting it as excessive overtime. There were some leaders I interviewed who responded as I expected with this simplistic definition; crunch (excessive overtime) is always bad, and we should never do it. But when pressed with examples of circumstances that other studios had experienced and had chosen to crunch, many leaders found it difficult to condemn their actions. If the choice was to keep the studio operating and ensure the ongoing employment of staff, and the only reasonable way to do so was an expectation of excessive overtime to get there, was that a trade worth making? A few leaders even saw value in the overtime and the way it had brought the team together during a particularly difficult period

The issue with defining crunch as simply being excessive overtime is that it does not capture the real issue. While discussing crunch with game developers, there are three recurring themes: overtime, overwork, and burnout. It's not unusual in any job to have a degree of overtime expected of you in your role: that you will work additional time if necessary to remain on top of your tasks. Defining crunch as just being overtime – even excessive – makes it easier to excuse. Overwork, by comparison, is a symptom of poor leadership. An overworked team is one that has been given more work than is reasonably achievable in the time allocated to them. Overwork can lead to needing to do overtime, but working overtime does not necessarily mean we are overworked.

Burnout is a symptom, not a cause. It is a feeling that may arise from crunch or any number of other negative circumstances in a studio. But unlike crunch, burnout is a particularly well-researched subject. The 2023 Game Developer's Conference titled "Occupational Burnout in Games: Causes, Impact, and Solutions" (Boccamazzo et al., 2023) explores a model of occupational burnout proposed by Dr. Christina Maslach and contrasts it against the stories of game developers working in the industry (Maslach, 1998). Dr. Maslach's model defines occupational burnout as the result of enduring overwhelming long-term stress and identifies six contributing factors that lead to burnout:

- Workload, the mismatch between what you are assigned to do and what you are sustainably able to achieve in a given amount of time.

- Reward, the mismatch between the effort you put into a job and what you get out of it.

- Control, the lack of control over your tasks and how you achieve them.

- Community, the lack of a sense of belonging or community in your workplace.

- Fairness, the perceived lack of trust, openness, and respect between you and the work environment.

- Values, the mismatch between the things that are important to you and the things that are important to your workplace.

So when it comes to occupational burnout, focusing on individual resilience and self-care without changing the system is a bit like suggesting people just need to learn how to swim better in a leaky boat. Learning to swim is great, but we have to fix the boat.

– DR. RAFFAEL BOCCAMAZZO, CLINICAL DIRECTOR AT TAKE THIS INC

If we define crunch simply as the excessive application of overtime caused by overwork, then workload is the clearest connection between burnout and crunch. However, it is clear from Dr. Maslach's identification of the factors leading to burnout that there are many other potential factors involved in the crunch. Game developers are typically not paid overtime, meaning that those hours spent crunching go unrewarded. The expectation to crunch is one that is dictated by leadership, leading to a lack of individual control over how the tasks are completed. The leadership setting those same expectations for crunch may or may not participate in or take ownership of the failure that led to crunch becoming necessary in the first place. If the place we workplaces value on people and work-life balance, then being expected to crunch is a betrayal of those values and of the studio culture.

It is possible then that the leaders who saw benefits in crunching were not actually crunching, they were working overtime. Dr. Maslach's model categorises burnout into three dimensions: exhaustion, ineffectiveness, and cynicism. All three of these dimensions must be true for a person to experience burnout. We may feel exhausted after a long workout at the gym, but we aren't ineffective or cynical. So a team working together to solve challenging problems and empowered to do so may not feel overwhelmed at the end of a long or challenging task. If we worked additional hours and felt good at the end of the tasks set before us, were we really crunching?

During my time at university, I worked with a friend on a project which we had drastically overscoped. I found myself asleep on the floor under my desk while he slept in his car. The following morning when the project was due to be presented, we found ourselves dishevelled but successful and proud of what we'd managed to achieve. That pride quickly turned to embarrassment as – unshaved and smelling like two-day-old university student – students from the school of music came to discuss creating soundtracks for our games. We left unscathed, but it made me quickly realise the importance of scope and taking care of myself.

It was somewhat ironic then that I ended up working on projects with that same friend that would see us repeating this kind of behaviour. But now it was not because we had misunderstood the scope. Presented with extremely tight deadlines on projects that paid well, we took it as a challenge. Now, instead of university desks, I found myself crashing on his futon after working well into the early hours on games.

Nothing about these memories is unpleasant to me. We were presented with a challenge, we accepted the challenge, and it had a clear deliverable and deadline. We made the call to work late hours to get the projects delivered. There was a real sense of satisfaction and pride when we got to see people playing those games and hear how pleased the business was with what we'd managed to achieve. We were working overtime, but we certainly did not feel that we were crunching.

Later experiences in my career would be far less positive. Working with a team well into the evening hours on projects that had been updated just moments before they were due to be submitted, only for them to break down and fail. We would stay back late, hammering away on the problem until we were ready to resubmit lest we miss our deadline. Just to hear back from our console partner days later that they had discovered multiple bugs with the build that would need to be fixed, and have the deadline pushed back. We would repeat these late nights over and over again for months as we worked to get the game finished within the limited budget and time that we had available to us.

I recall one morning where I woke up and broke down after the night before had caught up with me finally. Feeling a responsibility to the team, I still went into work.

In one case, we had made the decision to take on the challenge. We looked at the problem, measured ourselves as capable of the task, and we got it done. We delivered the project, and the stress ended. In the other case, it was a made necessary by leadership. At no point did anybody declare that we were crunching to get the task done; it simply felt like an expectation of us that nobody was willing to say no to. We were in it together as a team. Every time we went through that stress together, we quickly learned that any relief gained would be short-lived. There would be another push over the horizon, and we would be repeating the actions all over again. There was no satisfaction in delivering that project; it was just relief to be rid of it.

Looking at the examples of crunch in the industry, the uniting factor among all of them is not just the overtime: it is the human cost. This is a conversation that started back in the early 2000s with the story of the EA Spouse, Erin Hoffman. Posted on Livejournal in 2004, Hoffman describes the circumstances surrounding the employment of her partner who was working at Electronic Arts at the time. It paints a picture of a dysfunctional studio with a workload set on a schedule that would never be achievable in a reasonable timeframe. Developers would be expected to perform gradually scaling levels of crunch that would eventually require staff in the office 13 hours a day, seven days a week (Hoffman, 2004).

The story of the EA Spouse would thrust crunch into the limelight, but it would do little to change practice in the games industry. Fifteen years later, history would repeat itself at another Electronic Arts-owned studio. Bioware's Anthem would release in February of 2019 to a poor public reception, criticised for shallow gameplay and technical shortcomings. Just two months later, Jason Schreier would publish an article providing insights from the developers working at Bioware as to just how things went wrong.

Schreier's article details a studio in crisis, plagued by indecision and mismanagement. Anthem was in development for nearly seven years, a lengthy period of time even by AAA standards. However, despite this lengthy development the game did not begin to take shape until the last 18 months of development, as decisions got made and core concepts of Anthem's gameplay and narrative were finally solidified. Finally clear on what they were making, staff were required to crunch. For many it was too much, with some of the studio's most experienced developers leaving the company due to the oppressive working conditions. This was so prevalent that staff at Bioware referred to these lost coworkers as "stress casualties" – a term typically used to describe members of the armed forces who are unable to perform their duties due to exposure to operational stress (Schreier, 2019; APA Dictionary of Psychology, 2023).

There is this idea in art circles that great art comes from great pain, that art is unlikely to be good unless the artist suffers (Zara, 2012). Unfortunately, many industry leaders have seemingly adopted this same perspective. Under these leaders, crunch is treated like a workflow or process. They push to meet the deadline and requirements of the current milestone, and then they do it again and again until the project is finally completed. The people who remain at these sorts of studios tend to adopt a similar mindset of its necessity, or simply do not have anywhere else to go in order to support themselves or their families.

No piece of art is worth so much human suffering.

Crunch is self-replicating; doing crunch leads to more crunch. This is due to the fact that measurements taken of team output during crunch fail to be consistent. Our teams output the first time they crunch may be more or less than the next time they crunch. That period that you crunch for becomes unreliable data; the team, when pushed, can achieve this sort of output. But will they achieve that sort of output for long periods of time if we continue to push them? How much turnover and how many stress casualties are we going to suffer from along the way?

So what is a crunch? It arises primarily from overwork due to poor scoping of projects. It may arise from overtime if it is long and excessive enough. And it is not unlikely to create burnout due to the lack of control a crunched team may feel. Leadership can identify and avoid many of the problems that lead to crunch: read enough stories out of the games industry about those studios that crunch, and it is either not unexpected by the team or just a choice made by leadership. Crunch is not a tool; it is a failure of leadership.

We may find ourselves in circumstances in which asking the team to work overtime may be an option or even necessary. The key to making such a choice is the need for leadership to maintain control. It must be temporary, brief, and followed by an opportunity to recover. This isn't condoning or calling for overtime to become essential, but a reality of leadership and of making games.

If the room is on fire around us, the time to calmly escort the team out has passed. We are now in an emergency, and that requires acting with urgency and decisiveness. This is the time that we reach for the fire axe and direct our team with appropriate energy. We bark orders and push them to do whatever is necessary to get us all out of the building alive. As we stand outside and everybody catches their breath, the team will be understandably shaken by the experience. This is our time to step in, ensure their well-being, and take care of them. We give them the time necessary to tend to their physical and psychological well-being.

Overtime is our fire axe. It is survival. It is urgent and rushed, and the focus is on getting out of the building. If we find ourselves here, then quality is no longer our priority. We are not in a place where we can criticise the form of the person swinging the fire axe. When we find ourselves in an emergency, we don't blame our leaders for needing to put pressure on us to get out quickly. We blame our leaders for missing the signs that our building was a fire risk.

The fire axe is an emergency tool. When we reach for it, we must be doing so with the understanding that we are going to be damaging something. We are breaking the glass, we are hacking down doors, and people might get hurt. It is essential that we have tools at our disposal to handle emergencies, but this is never a tool we want to rely upon to get work done over long periods of time. We should rightfully feel bad if we need to ask the team to work overtime, but sometimes it is better than the alternative. The best we can do in some circumstances is learn from the experience and work to prevent it from happening again.

Leaders are not perfect. We cannot predict every issue we will need to face. But crunch does not come from a singular mistake; it comes from a long-term failure of leadership to identify or act upon issues within a project. It is our responsibility to watch for the signs and do whatever we can to ensure that our teams never need to endure such working conditions.

Fundamentals

The longer we lead people, the more difficult it becomes to define what exactly makes somebody a great leader. Our first inclination may be to say that a great leader is somebody who gets great results for the project and the team, but an answer like this just raises more questions. What are great results for a team? Is a project a great success based on reviews or meeting business goals?

We may be inclined to say that leadership is a trait. That it is something people are born to be, not necessarily shaped into. This assumption not only undervalues the learning and development involved in striving to be a better leader but it also excuses those people who lead their teams badly. As though they cannot help it, they just aren't born to be a great leader.

The truth is that great leadership is not a singular skill or moment in time. There are so many skills involved in leadership and so many moments in which those skills are tested, there is no real moment in which a person may be declared a great leader. The skills involved in leadership can be learned if we are willing to embrace growth and reflect upon our successes and failures.

If we ever do declare ourselves as great leaders, we have accepted stagnation. We are saying that at this specific moment in time we are as good as we will ever get. Every person I spoke to while gathering material for this book refused to declare themselves a great leader; it was an ideal they were striving for every day. They may perform well on a project and their team may appreciate their effort, but that does not mean that they try any harder to prove themselves a great leader on the next project. Just as an

DOI: 10.1201/9781003431626-3

artist is always looking for new ways to improve their art, great leaders are always looking for new ways to improve their leadership.

The journey to great leadership starts with three foundational skills: humility, accountability, and integrity. Without these skills, nothing else in this book is possible. They are not necessarily more valuable skills than any other that we will discuss, but they are essential to everything that we want to achieve through our leadership. Without humility, we cannot take accountability. Without accountability, we have no integrity. Lacking these foundational skills means being unable to embrace failure and understand the ways in which we need to improve.

These skills guide moral leadership. I hesitate to call this ethical leadership, as there is a difference between business ethics and people ethics. But we understand what immoral leadership looks like. It is blaming others for our failings and taking responsibility for their success. It is putting the interests of the project ahead of the interests of the people. It is the lack of integrity, humility, and accountability. We cannot be immoral leaders and also be great leaders simultaneously; these concepts are antithetical to one another. An immoral leader may achieve great project outcomes, but they are not a great leader of people.

> There's this dance between how do you be a compassionate boss, and how do you be a good business person? How do you be a good and ethical business person? How do you set boundaries?
>
> – JEAN LEGGETT, LEADERSHIP COACH

People are unpredictable. Creativity is unpredictable. Many leaders who care about the quality of their leadership fall into traps, wherein they try to control people to protect themselves and their projects from the unexpected. They build structures and processes to control the team and their output in ways that hamper creativity. Teams often become so reliant upon their leadership that nothing gets done without leadership in the room.

The reality is that it is necessary for leaders to embrace a little bit of chaos.

Unexpected opportunities can arise from change. It does not mean that we reject taking control, or that we let our teams run rampant with no processes or structures to define the ways in which they operate. It means that we know to try to find opportunities in the chaos. We can never create the perfect circumstance within which everything will go exactly according to plan, or the people around us act exactly the way we expect.

Coping with change and chaos requires improvisation, and it's a skill that flows through everything that we will discuss about leadership. There is no one way that we should act at all times, all of our skills require some degree of improvisation. Circumstances change, expectations change, projects change, and people change. They do not always change for the better, of course. It is our responsibility as leaders to know when it's necessary to improvise and when it's necessary to plant our feet and stand firm.

In Homer's Iliad, Ulysses makes a pact with his men. They are on approach to a stretch of water in which they know they will find Sirens, dangerous creatures with alluring voices that would lure sailors to their doom. But Ulysses wanted to hear their song. So he instructs his men: they are to put wax in their ears as to not hear the song, and he wants them to tie him to the mast. Under no circumstance are they allowed to take him down, no matter how much he begs or commands them otherwise. They sail past the Sirens and Ulysses struggles against his bonds, but his men keep him on the mast until they are safe (Homer, 1991).

This idea of the Ulysses Pact is one that is used often in medicine and technology today to capture the idea of making a decision during a time of strength to hold us accountable during a time of weakness (Spellecy, 2003). It also manages to capture many of the concepts we are discussing about morality. Ulysses identified that he would struggle to control himself during that time of weakness; he wasn't too proud to expect he could somehow resist the song: he had humility. In asking his men to not let him make a decision that would risk harm to himself or them, he had the integrity to tell them the risks and asked to be held accountable.

Anecdotes like this are excellent to see the ways in which we can act morally within our businesses. Our Siren song may be that looming deadline. We must have the humility to tell our teams that it worries us. If we value their time more than the project, telling them that we will choose them over meeting that deadline is setting an expectation for our integrity. It is telling them that we will have accountability for our actions. Then, if the moment comes that our deadline seems likely to slip, we need to find options that maintain our integrity: we cut the scope or push back the deadline.

Integrity is about consistency: we live our values, we do what we say.

Humility is about us: we are just a part of the whole, and we have a responsibility to it.

Accountability is ownership: we own our responsibility, and we communicate our failings.

We not only have a responsibility to our business, but we also have a responsibility to the team. Having integrity means being able to push back when the business asks us to do something that we disagree with. It means understanding what we value as leaders, and acting in accordance with those values. People are not willing to follow somebody that lies. Acting without integrity will quickly lose any sort of trust we have built. The goal is to be consistent between our words and our actions.

If we say that you are going to do something, we do it. Our words are our bond, and this is especially true of our values. If we tell our team that we don't want anybody to work overtime, we cannot stay in the office late. The greatest test and measurable example of our integrity is doing what we say, even when it hurts. Our choice in that moment is something that the team recognises. Having integrity when it hurts builds trust and respect. Failing to do so will lose it.

> Integrity is an inverse square law, like gravity. When there's a small difference between what you say and what you do, it's noticed less. When there's a big difference, it's noticed a whole lot more.
>
> – KEITH FULLER, LEADERSHIP CONSULTANT,
> FOUNDER OF GAMEDEVCOACHING.COM

It starts with not making promises we aren't willing to uphold later. If asking our team to work overtime to get the game done on time is something we are willing to do, telling the team that we value their time and their life outside of work just makes us a liar. They will remember our words when we ask them to work overtime, as our actions now are in contradiction to our words.

The point of the Ulysses Pact is to maintain accountability. If it is something that is challenging to even accept in a time of strength, we are going to be desperate to get out of it during a time of weakness. We particularly see this in terms of crunch, where team leadership gives their word that crunch will not be necessary for a project, but then the unexpected happens and – unwilling or unable to seek alternatives – crunch becomes necessary.

It does not matter if we have a good reason for it. We gave our word. We set the expectations. We failed to follow through on our word when times got tough. We failed to have integrity. The team will have every right to be angry with us. If overtime seems like a viable option to take during a time of crisis, do not promise the team they will not be asked to work overtime. What we are actually promising them is that there won't be a crisis, and obviously we cannot promise that at all.

Treating integrity as consistency, we are also able to apply it to other ways we lead. integrity means that we lead with fairness. It means that we would not ask the team to do anything that we would not be willing to do ourselves. It means that we would not punish the team for doing something we do. The old admonition of "do as I say, not as I do" does not make us an effective leader, it just makes us a hypocrite. We need to set the standard as to how we expect our team to operate, and we need to be beyond reproach in our actions reflecting our values and our word.

This means avoiding the risk of being seen to be playing favourites. Giving special opportunities to somebody within the team that we are friends with will be perceived as nepotism. It's not good for us or for our team member. This does not mean that we should avoid friendships at work or, worse, that we should hold our friends to a higher standard. It requires some integrity and self-awareness. Recognise that there will be a power imbalance between us and the people we lead, and we must be aware of that when we have friendships with our direct reports.

The best way to avoid any issues around these circumstances is to maintain internal consistency. We must separate the request or the expectation from the person we are speaking with. Consider what it means on its own. If we would scold an employee for not attending a meeting, but we would give our friend the benefit of the doubt, then it's important to decide on how we want to operate specifically and consistently. Will we only admonish people if they are repeatedly late? And if so, then we need to hold the people we are close to equally accountable to this expectation.

The team pays attention to how we choose to operate and will follow that as a guide to their own behaviour. If we work overtime, we are giving the team the impression that they should work overtime as well. I have heard stories from people in the industry working under especially talented or passionate leadership who consistently worked overtime, and the team followed suit. They remained in the office so long as their leadership was present. Their leadership cared about their team and about the project and would never ask the team to work overtime. But they didn't need to – the leadership choice to work overtime inspired the choice in the people that followed them.

Dealing with this circumstance does not mean reprimanding the team for working overtime. It requires humility to recognise that we made the mistake that inspired that behaviour. Then we take accountability for the failing. We stand up before the team and make it clear to them that we acknowledge that they felt it was necessary for them to work overtime as a result of our actions. We tell them how we intend to change our personal behaviour and then have the integrity to follow through.

This sends a message to our team that we care about this issue. We cared enough that we noticed that we were doing it; we were accountable for our actions and the impact they had on others, and we took the necessary action to make changes. These aren't just leadership qualities; they are qualities that we want to see in our team. A team that is unwilling to be accountable for its own failures is going to be dysfunctional at its core. The only way we will inspire that kind of behaviour is if we hold ourselves and others accountable.

> When people talk about wanting a job where they feel like they are changing the world, they go be a doctor or a politician or whatever they want to do. I just make video games. Am I changing the world? But then I remind myself that I'm getting to enable a whole bunch of people to do the stuff that makes them happy.
>
> – JASON IMMS, HEAD OF QUALITY ASSURANCE, KEYWORDS STUDIOS

Expressing humility is something of a transitional skill. It represents our ability to step back and understand our part in the whole scope of the project. If we look at our team and see ourselves as the heart of it, we lack humility. But humility does not mean we are powerless. If we look at our team and see ourselves as unable to help them improve, we also lack humility. We are not the centre of the universe, but we do have power over our world and responsibility for it. Humility is the wisdom to accept the things we cannot change and the courage and understanding to change the things we can.

Humility is having the modesty to see our role in the bigger picture and the pride to take full ownership of our responsibility. Being too modest means that we can discount the power that we have over the situation. If we are working in a team that is currently struggling, it can be too easy to waive our responsibility to improve the circumstances of our team. Too proud, and it can be easy to see ourselves as the only reason that our team is able to succeed at all. Their excellent work is seen as just an extension of our leadership, and we can take responsibility for their successes. Humility balances these two competing forces.

I want to call myself a servant leader, because that's what you're supposed to be in the military. That's what everyone wants to be. But what does that mean? It means putting the needs of the people you lead ahead of your own. That's a catchphrase really that people throw out there. But it means if it's a holiday, you're the guy pulling duty so the team can go home. It means giving them time off when it hurts. And it does hurt.

– CAPTAIN BRANDEN BUFFALO, NATIONAL SPACE
DEFENCE CENTRE, UNITED STATES SPACE FORCE

While nobody I interviewed prescribed a specific style of leadership, the concept of servant leadership was one that became a recurring theme. Originally proposed in an essay by Robert K. Greenleaf, the servant leader is somebody who uses the power of their role to protect and develop their team (Greenleaf, 1970). To do this requires humility, as we first need to accept that we are no longer the one creating the results with our own two hands. It's the team achieving results, our responsibility is to ensure they are enabled to do so with as little distraction as possible.

We will fail as leaders, and we need to have humility in those moments to be able to accept and own that. Perfection is not the goal of our leadership; that's simply unattainable. We need to be able to identify where we had the power to prevent or create a circumstance and how we failed to do so. If humility is our ability to identify our role in success and failure, then accountability is our ability to step up and say that out loud to others. Accountability is simply impossible without humility.

Accountability is personal. It means that it's not anybody else, you don't blame anybody else, you take it. The reason that's effective and people are affected by it is because it's a sacrifice. It's an ancient thing that is singularly human. You can see it in the animal world, but for humans they do complex levels of sacrifice. I could probably get out of this, but it needs to end. I'm going to step up and tell you why this happened, why it's my fault, and what I mean to do about it. That's a sacrifice. It's about them doing something for somebody else.

– CAMDEN STODDARD, AUDIO DIRECTOR, DOUBLE FINE

Accountability often means taking responsibility when the team has failed. This is one of the most challenging aspects of leadership that many people struggle to accept, as the team failing at doing something we told them to do is easy to deflect back on them. But we provide the team with direction and a vision for how things should work. The responsibility isn't necessarily in the execution; it is in the direction. We gave the order; the team simply followed it. As leaders, we are empowered in a way that our teams are not. We must be accountable for our power to prevent or avoid failure.

Not long after I set out to write this book, the small team I work with received an offer for additional funding. I had proposed the additional funding and this book with the expectation that only one would come through. So receiving the opportunity to do both, I was now having to decide if I would turn down the offered funds in order to focus on my book. I could not in good conscience say I could juggle both opportunities, but it wasn't just about me either. I didn't want to refuse the team the opportunity to get paid to do more of what they love.

I accepted the funding and hired one of my old students to pick up some of my responsibilities on the programming. I was clear with the team from the start that my time would be reduced, and I would do my best to enable them as much as I could. But my responsibilities teaching and writing absorbed far more of my time than I had initially planned, and as a result I had less time than I would have liked with them. While they continuously knocked it out of the park while I wasn't around, there were ways in which I could see the lack of direction and leadership was lending to a sense of lethargy in the team.

Recognising that this was my failing, I took responsibility. I reached out to the people who had provided us our funding, and made it clear that we were likely to be delayed in meeting our milestones. I also made it clear to the team that this was my responsibility, not theirs. But it was important to also set expectations, and I made it clear to them that it was likely we'd just be slow for a while before I was able to give the project more of my time, and that's okay. The worst thing I could have done would have been to say nothing and give the impression that I simply no longer cared about the game we were making.

There is that fear of making mistakes, but also that fear of asking because surely if they put you in this position, you know what you are doing. What I've come to learn is a lot of times, you get put in that position because there's nobody else. It's not necessarily that you are the greatest manager, you are the least bad candidate.

– DR. JC LAU, SENIOR ADVANCED PRODUCER,
PROBABLYMONSTERS

The people we lead will follow the example we set. If we set the example in our teams that we embrace failure and a desire to improve, it has the capacity to reduce their anxiety dramatically. No creative medium has examples where something was created right the first time, every time. We want to embrace this in our leadership as well. This isn't to say that we need to tell the members of our teams that we will fail, but that we own it when we do fail.

The projects we work on are not defined by our influence, but they are certainly influenced by us. It may be easy to say that people could just work better or harder without us present, but this is why servant leadership is so important a concept to understand. If we are not present, then we are not removing those obstacles that get in the way of our team doing their best work. We don't make the games. But we do make the games happen.

VALUES

As we lead others we make decisions about how we operate and make it clear what we care about. These are our values, and they give our team expectations to hold us accountable to. Writing a document to detail our values and providing it to our team isn't necessarily something you need to do (though it certainly doesn't hurt). Our values are not just a statement or a catchy phrase, but the things that we are willing to stand by and act on, even when it hurts. It reflects our integrity to stand for the things we say we care about, and it is just one of the many ways in which our teams will get a measure of our leadership.

Our values can be found in the things we care about that we consider non-negotiable. What do we value achieving, how do we value operating, and what kind of leadership do we value? The things we value could relate to the project, the team, the tools we use, or the kind of life we lead. I have met leaders who clearly value technology. I have met leaders who came from academic backgrounds and valued contributing to the development of knowledge and skills. I have met leaders who value closeness and friendship with the members of their team.

The things we want to achieve are broad and varied, and we usually say something about what we would like our legacy to be. It may be something we want to achieve individually, something we want a project to achieve, or for our team or business to achieve. The objectives we set out to achieve should not be about earning awards or high review scores, as these place immense pressure on a team to perform. More powerful values of achievement come from the things we have some control over as leaders. It may be an achievement to have a documentarian film the full production of a project, or for the next project to be completed without a crunch.

When it comes to the way we want to operate, we are talking about processes and the day-to-day operation of the team. Do we want people to feel free to come into work late and work their own hours? Do we value balancing life with work and ensuring that people have time for their families? Do we value flexibility or adherence to the process? Even if we do not have the power to change the hours our teams work or the tools they use, our values can be reflected in other ways. We can encourage them to take time off or negotiate some flexibility in their work.

The kind of leadership we value can be the most challenging to define. We want to avoid our value here being something like being a great leader, because as we have already discussed, what does great leadership look like? Instead, think about the ways in which we value being led. Do we value leaders who provide us with some creative freedom or leaders who give lots of mentorship and guidance? How can we act through our leadership that matches with the sort of leaders we would value having? We may value leaders who take a personal interest in our lives, and so we choose to take an interest in the lives of the people around us.

Finding what you care about is challenging. It takes time and reflection and is often something that we discover through our leadership rather than a decision we make as we become leaders. Even as somebody new to the leadership role, there are experiences we have had in previous roles or throughout our lives that have influenced our values. We just need to take the time to consider them and discover them.

Values are really about us as individuals and how we want to operate, and allow our team to hold us accountable. It sets the standard for our integrity. The risk here is if we set unrealistic expectations of ourselves. If we value being transparent with our team, does that mean being transparent all the time? We may find ourselves in circumstances in which full transparency is undesirable or even impossible without risking our roles or the well-being of our teams. So what is it about transparency that we value, really?

Our values are organic. They may change with time and experience, but we absolutely cannot betray them. There are some very good reasons why our values may change, but we need to be clear with our teams when these circumstances arise. We may value transparency and want to tell the team about something, but we do not have the capacity or freedom to do so. It's as simple as telling the team as much. It sends the message that we value transparency, but not when it risks our business or the employment of our team members. We have told the team we care about this thing, but we are not in a position to act on it as we would like.

I had decided early in my career that the crunch was simply unacceptable. I acted in such a way that I wanted this to be a clear value to my team, that I valued not having excessive workloads or unrealistic scope expectations, and that I would fight for them to prevent situations where crunch would be necessary. When the crunch did happen, it was a decision outside of my control. I told the team as much, that I would continue to fight against crunch where possible. But if the team needed to crunch in order to save all of our jobs, would I choose to instead close down the business?

The answer of course is that it is complicated. I value teams not being asked to crunch, but I also value them being a team. If it came down to a choice between crunching or closing the studio entirely, I would have to have to look at the reasons it became necessary to make such a choice in the first place. Is the business so broken that this is what it has become? At the very least, I would need to have an honest conversation with the team about the options. To make it clear to them that I do not want to ask them to crunch because I value not doing it, but I also value them having employment.

The team can and will see how we operate. They will internalise what we say and what we do, and they will form opinions about us as leaders as a result. If we tell them that crunch is something we will not accept them doing, but then choose it even in a moment of crisis to prevent them from coming to even greater harm, will the fact that we made the hard choice mean much to them? Even when we explain why it was necessary, they have reason to question our values. What other things do we say we care for that will so easily change in the face of external forces?

Is it really something we value if we are willing to compromise on it?

Today rather than saying I value not having to crunch, I would instead say that I value the team's health and well-being. I value minimising the impacts of a crunch on them if it becomes necessary for any reason, and ensuring that it is never ongoing for long periods of time. I value accountability and integrity should I fail to protect the team from a crunch. If it came to a decision to crunch at the cost of their health, or choosing to give something up about the game and deal with the fallout from clients or partners? I would absolutely choose the latter option. The team needs to know that I will go to bat for them in this respect, and that I intend to be responsible for the repercussions either way.

As you read this book, you may find that certain chapters resonate with you. When you find yourself resonating with such chapters, make a note of them. You may find yourself fond of concepts like protection and well-being, and this could reflect that you value ensuring the team can balance their work with their lives. Perhaps you particularly like authenticity and transparency, and this may reflect that you value leadership that is not just honest to the circumstances but also to themselves.

Much of what we are discussing is not just skills, but the things that the leaders I spoke with valued. You will often find this reflected in the places where individual leaders see their quotes and stories shared. Each of these leaders has been on their own journey, and along the way, they have discovered the skills and traits they value above others. As we are starting our leadership journey, it is not unusual to find inspiration in the people you admire and the things they value. We aspire to the example their leadership sets for us and start to find our own values along the way.

Multiclassing

It's not easy to learn to be a great leader. If you have read any content on the subject of leadership, you will have quickly found that there are so many differing perspectives on the subject. Despite the huge amount of material out there on leading people, it can be really challenging to find good ones that are also useful to us as game developers. Much of these resources are very broad or very specific in the skills they cover, or the kind of leaders they are targeting their content to. As a new leader, it can make the skills required feel somewhat impenetrable.

There is some truly excellent material out there on leadership, but they can feel irrelevant to us. Part of my journey in putting together the content for this book was to engage with the content that seemed unlikely to hold worthy advice for us in the games industry. I expected that I would find overlap with how we operate and what we want to see change, and I was not disappointed. One of the books I have read that has earned a place on my shelf is about leading veterinary teams, appropriately titled Oops, I Became a Manager (Newfield, 2020). This is a book which deals with similar challenges that we face in the games industry such as building trust and empowering people to do their best work. The work could not be any different, and yet the problems that arise out of working with people are the same.

There is a perception in the games industry that our unique circumstances at the intersection of art and technology mean that we have nothing to learn from elsewhere. We have unique considerations that mean that the job often requires improvisation, but this does not mean we have to start with nothing and improvise our way to a leadership style. We have so much that we can

DOI: 10.1201/9781003431626-4

learn from other industries that would improve the way that games are made if we only took the time to understand them at a fundamental level.

> We have a problem in the games industry where people in general don't take leadership as seriously as it should. There's a lot of different reasons why, but one of those is that we really do feel special. We feel different than other industries. In some ways we are, and in others we're not. The problem is this feeling of being special is a double-edged sword. It is a thing that actually makes us make really poor decisions. We think that the process of making games is so different that we have very little to learn from other industries.
>
> – OSAMA DORIAS, LEAD GAMEPLAY DESIGNER,
> BRASS LION ENTERTAINMENT

When I set out to write *Great Games Need Great Leaders*, my intent was to remove the barriers to understanding what leadership is about. I took the time to do research and talk to leaders from the games industry and elsewhere to provide a springboard. This book is intended to kick-start your leadership journey. Once you close this book, you will have a better understanding of the fundamentals, and know what you want to start learning next. It is my hope that even if you are simply curious and do not work within the gaming industry, that you will find something insightful in these pages.

This book is not about tools or processes. These things change, and they change often in the games industry. Effective leadership does not come out of spreadsheets or game engines; it comes from us. It is how we choose to act and interact. How we care for ourselves and others in high-pressure environments. Leading game development teams isn't about making games, it's about leading the people that make games. These concepts are timeless, you should be able to keep a copy of this book on your desk and still find it relevant in the next 10 or 20 years.

During the process of gathering perspectives and information for this book, all the leaders I interviewed for this book explained the value of their skills and experiences in stories and anecdotes. A recurring theme from these was the idea of the classes of heroes in fantasy roleplaying games. They were an effective way for leaders to discuss and understand the great breadth of their skills and became a recurring theme throughout our discussions.

Much of the skills discussed in this book are often referred to as soft or transferable skills. These skills are soft in that they are about dealing with human concerns, and transferable in that we bring them with us into every workplace. Skills like this are not like learning 3D modelling or how to make a brilliant spreadsheet, we don't use these skills in every job. These skills describe our ability to communicate with one another, manage our time, or solve problems.

We need to be able to value these skills as active and part of our jobs, not a passive trait that people simply do or do not have. Part of the reason these skills are undervalued in the games industry is due to our focus on tangible outcomes. When we make a 3D model or a spreadsheet, we are creating something tangible. It can be challenging to see how our actions as leaders create tangible outcomes when the results of our actions may be filtered through individuals or take months to appear in a project.

When we set out with a team to make a game, it can be easy to become fixated on the outcome of the product or the tools that we use to make it. But it is bigger than that. Making a single game is akin to completing a quest: we gain experience, we level up, and we choose the tools we want to carry on to the next adventure. The thing we retain when we go from quest to quest is never the sword we wield; it's the experience we gain. We're not just developing games; we're also developing ourselves. Multiclassing is a way for us to understand how our skills and actions contribute to creating tangible outcomes.

Anecdotes like this resonate with us in a way that dry descriptions of the skills never could. It only takes a passing familiarity with roleplaying games and the fantasy genre to understand what the classes represent. Multiclassing is about the broad spectrum of skills required of us as leaders. It's not about the tools we wield or the quests we go on, but the ways in which we are prepared to improvise for every challenge that we face. As we explore the skills involved in being a leader, we will often come back to some repeating concepts:

- Archetypes, the specific class of skills that we are multiclassing into.

- Attributes, the key characteristics of those classes.

- Alignment, the way we use our skills for good and not for evil.

The archetypes are a selection of classic fantasy classes: the Warrior, the Bard, and the Cleric. When we talk about multiclassing, we are specifically talking about the need for leadership to "spec into" the skills and qualities of each of these archetypes. Each archetype does not represent a style of leadership, but rather a broad area of unique skills and principles that – taken together with the other archetypes – make great leadership in the games industry. There is no moment in which we are just exercising Warrior leadership. We want to balance the Warrior with the Bard and the Cleric. Each of these archetypes is a valuable and important skillset on its own, but it's only by using them together that we can begin to become great leaders.

It is to be expected that you may read about one of the archetypes and see yourself in it. Even once we build on our leadership skills, it's not unusual to see ourselves as exemplifying one of the archetypes more than the others. If you got your start in leadership from a role in the industry where you were performing a duty, it's not unusual to see yourself in the Warrior, the archetype that's all about doing, achieving goals, and getting into action. You don't stop being a Warrior as you learn more about leadership; you simply start levelling up the skills of the other archetypes.

Attributes describe the core characteristic that each of the archetypes focuses on. Roleplaying games typically have a variety of attributes, but we are focused on three in particular: Constitution, Charisma, and Wisdom. We do not want to be the leader who invests all of their experience into a singular attribute, especially if it is not one of these core three. A leader must be able to remain in the fight for a long time, to motivate and communicate with their team effectively, and to have the wisdom to know when and how to act.

Understanding the attributes highlights the need to multiclass. A leader with plenty of charisma may be great at motivating a team, but do they have the wisdom to know when their actions are manipulative? A leader may have the wisdom to be self-aware and caring for others, but they are of no use to a team if they do not have the constitution to stick it out when times get tough. We will develop a better understanding of the importance of these attributes as we explore each of the archetypes and their unique skills.

Alignment allows us to examine how a skill can be used for good or evil. Every archetype, attribute, and skill can be used for or against the team. It helps us to carefully separate the difference between a healthy use of a skill and one that your team may come to resent us for. The unfortunate reality of leadership is that many people end up leading teams and leveraging these skills for personal gain. These leaders usually lack integrity and tend to take actions that are selfish or even sociopathic.

Great leaders act with intent, but so do the evil ones. There is a theory in psychology called the Dark Triad, first proposed by Delroy L. Paulhus. This is a concept in which there is some connection identified between Narcissism, Machiavellianism, and Psychopathy. Despite being individually distinct personality types, the theory of the Dark Triad was proposed to account for this overlap between the different qualities (Paulhus and Williams, 2002). It's unfortunately not unusual to see these personalities surface among leadership types.

We want to ensure that our actions are aligned with good. The Light Triad, proposed by Laura Johnson in her masters' thesis, encompasses a group of positive personality traits. Specifically empathy, compassion, and altruism (Johnson, 2018). We are working with people, and that means our leadership must be people-focused. We need to value the dignity and worth of everyone, understand that they are not just on the team to achieve our objectives, and believe in them.

These concepts act as a guide to our leadership journey, and we will return to them often. Through the archetypes we can develop a better understanding of the breadth of skills required to be a great leader. The attributes will allow us to examine the underlying characteristics that we need to develop. And we will examine the ways in which our skills may be used for good or evil through the lens of alignment.

2.0

The Warrior

It's not unusual in the games industry for there to be a bit of a fixation about the things the leader does, rather than the things they are responsible for. We are an industry of doers, and so there is an expectation that leadership is also active and working on the game somehow. This may be why people gravitate towards the warrior as their first archetype. They focus on the project and fight to achieve success, diving into circumstances to protect the team and to fend off potential risks.

The warrior is the person who is often juggling work in their key area of expertise with the needs of the team. It's easy to understand why these skills become the first real draw for those people who are new to the idea of leadership, because what exactly does a leader do all day otherwise? A minimal understanding of what a leader does exactly can lead to an over-emphasis on the project outcomes, rather than tending to the team working on the project.

It's not unusual, even among the most experienced leads, to see them also working on content for the game. Watch any episode of Double Fine's documentaries, and you will usually see its studio head, Tim Schafer, hard at work writing the narrative for their games. Watch for long enough, though and you will see and hear how the rest of the team wants their leader to be more involved to provide them with guidance and input (PsychOdyssey, 2022).

Being an active contributor to the game while also leading it is not a bad thing. Tim Schafer recognises and owns it whenever he has locked

DOI: 10.1201/9781003431626-5

himself behind the door to his office to write for too long. But this kind of balancing act is one we can only be capable of through introspection and an understanding of the full breadth of our responsibilities. It requires an understanding of when we need to step away from our desk and do something that may feel less productive than the creative work.

Tasked with continuing creative work compounded by a lack of leadership training, the majority of new leaders will simply prioritise their creative work over their responsibility to lead others. Many leaders only go so far into the key skills of the warrior as seems reasonable atop their existing creative work. To truly embrace our roles as leaders, however, we need to get away from our desks. We need to interact with the other members of our team and provide them with the leadership they require.

It is not unusual for new leaders to have a misconception about the responsibility of leadership. Focusing only on the skills of the warrior and ensuring the project can be the best it can be, we can easily find ourselves not really leading at all. The code being written or the art being created cannot be led; it is the people creating these products that require leadership. When we are promoted to leadership and told we are responsible for guaranteeing the quality of those things, our port of call is not our desk to get to work creating them. Instead, we are responsible for the people generating that art and code, so that we might ensure the quality of their output.

This misconception is largely due to a culture fostered by the majority of the games industry that cares less about leadership and more about content. Those people who have been in the industry for some time to find themselves promoted to roles of leadership are prone to sorts of behaviour that prioritises their personal additions over the leading of teams. It is much easier to measure our individual contributions to code or art than it is to measure our impact on the people around us.

The warrior leaders who do choose to become more involved with the team often fall into a trap. Stepping away from their desks and understanding the responsibility of their role to ensure the quality of work done, they become prone to micromanagement. These leaders swoop in and direct the team towards specific practices they believe will achieve the best possible outcomes. They understand their responsibility to do the thing they are leading. If they are the lead programmer, they assume responsibility for all code created.

Many warriors are rigid leaders as a result, using their experience as a blunt weapon on the people around them. This type of leader quickly turns into a dictator, the warrior's evil aligned sibling. Disinterested in the people around them, the dictator fixates on specific outcomes or processes. They dictate the how, but never the why. Rather than seeing the members of their teams as individual contributors, they are seen as a means to generate results. The dictator spends their time adjusting the output of each individual team member to ensure the level of quality they desire, and this is enforced through rigid rules and outcomes.

Unfortunately, the people who work with dictators are prone to becoming dictators themselves. It becomes an expectation that this is simply how the industry operates: that the best results are only achieved with a firm hand and rigid structure. This sort of micromanagement kills creativity and destroys trust, as a team does not feel that their skill is respected.

Just because we have the power to tell other people what to do does not mean we should exercise it. There are, of course, moments when firm guidance may become necessary for effective leadership; the skill is in being able to identify those moments.

The dictator is born out of a misunderstanding of what the attribute is at the heart of the warrior. Dictators believe that good leadership is defined by strength: the capacity to bash through any problem, to wrestle their way out of any situation. They believe that they can be excellent leaders just by being at the front of the party and that their strength and experience will guide their team to success. But the leader who has invested only in strength will find themselves unable to use most of the key skills and tools available to the warrior that make them outstanding leaders.

Leaders who invest primarily in strength tend to burn out quickly as it becomes obvious that they cannot fight their way out of every situation. It's not enough to be strong. The warrior is absolutely a front-line leader, up there in the fray with the team. But rather than being defined by their strength, they are defined by their constitution. The warrior is defined by their longevity and ability to remain in the fight for long periods. They have the capacity to take hits, to be the first person in and the last person out, and to still be standing at the end of the job.

This sort of fortitude isn't just physical; it is also emotional and mental. With constitution, the warrior can take risks that their Strength based counterpart never could. It's only through a willingness to take risks that we can have the courage necessary to build trust in our teams. Simply protecting them is not enough, they need to feel like we respect their abilities to get the job done and that we trust them to overcome challenges and achieve greatness without our influence.

We need to be able to take a few hits in the course of our leadership. The warrior and their constitution give us the capacity to remain standing no matter what we may face. This capacity to remain in the fight for long periods of time is essential to our ability to lead. The skills of the warrior are some of the easiest to learn and most satisfying to exercise in comparison to the more soft and squishy skills of the Bard and Cleric. Being able to surpass the skills of the warrior is our first test as we develop a greater understanding of leadership.

A warrior is a leader who recognises the value of the people they are working alongside. The protection they provide is not just about giving the team the space to succeed but also about enabling the members of their team to do their best work. Rather than wielding their experience as a bludgeon, it becomes a guide to empower and mentor the members of their team towards better outcomes. It is this dedication to achieving outcomes through the empowerment and protection of the members of their team that defines great warriors.

Acting

I had done the math, looked at our burn rate, estimated how quickly we'd get tasks done. None of it was good news. It was clear that we'd never be able to hit our milestones, and that something drastic needed to change about our plans for the project. We could reduce scope, we could redirect budget, there were options. The worst possible action we could take would be inaction. So I called a meeting with our CEO, and discussed the situation with them. I presented them the figures, walked them through just how much money we were spending every month, and compared that to the finances we had been allocated. I printed out all the figures and made pretty charts to make it easy to read and see what I saw. I showed them the burn rate of our team, how much work we were completing week to week and how it was falling short of the lofty goals we'd been set.

All through the conversation, the CEO was silent. They politely nod their head, but that was about it. The silence was worrying me. There were points at which I wondered whether or not they even truly understood just how dire the circumstances were, or if all of the presentation of figures and charts demonstrating the how bad the situation was just being interpreted as pessimistic fearmongering. I'd been right about these things before and had not come nearly as prepared when I tried to tell our leadership that something needed to change. I was confident in my maths and my presentation, so I was not at all prepared for what they would say when they finally chose to speak.

"Just do your best."

Those words lingered with me for a long, long time. I was angry coming out of the meeting at the implication that the team weren't already going above and beyond. Giving them the benefit of the doubt, it may have been some misplaced expression of faith in our ability, But I am very sure that it was simply to avoid the difficult truth. They had created this plan and had put us on that path with no other options, no space to deviate, no plan B. We had the money we had, we had the time we had, and we had the scope we had. To change any of it would mean some uncomfortable conversations with stakeholders about cutting scope or getting additional funds. So the team would simply have to do more.

– ANONYMOUS

When Spider-Man gets his superpowers, he spends a great deal of time misusing them. He isn't particularly heroic; he is often prone to choosing self-satisfaction over using his powers for the benefit of others. When his actions lead to him bringing harm to the people he loves, he is told that with great power comes great responsibility. You may read this as Spider-Man needing to be responsible with his powers as power is corrupting, and that is certainly accurate. But I believe there is another accurate reading of this advice he is given: that his power gives him a responsibility to act. He has been empowered to act in a way that few others are able to, and choosing selfishness or inaction is to be irresponsible with his power. This is a theme you often see repeating around the character as he is thrust into choices between the greater good, or himself, and the people he loves.

Accepting a leadership role is to accept some amount of power over a project and the people working on it. That power you hold is something that few people in your business hold, and it gives you a responsibility. That responsibility is to act. This may sound simple, but it's one of the first places that many leaders in the games industry find themselves tripping up.

Coming from a background of creative work, it can be easy to wish to spend your time focusing on that well into your time spent as a leader. But a leader who is fixated on their own creative tasks is one who has chosen not to wield the power they have been given. They may choose the best or most interesting tasks for themselves and spend their time focused on their art. Through inaction, they are irresponsibly wielding the power of leadership.

To truly embrace leading people, we need to accept that we have power that they do not. It can be all too easy to fall into selfish behaviours when given the potential to lead. It may seem to be an opportunity to direct a project or team to take a direction you would prefer to see, and this is certainly something that you are empowered to do. But doing this blindly means ignoring the immense experience and expertise of the people for whom you have been made responsible. In order to use those new powers you have been given and to act responsibly, it is important to understand the ways in which they can be used or abused.

PROCESS

When we find ourselves placed in a position of leadership, it is usually by way of our experience. We've gotten to lead teams because we were really good at some other task. But we cannot allow these previous experiences, processes, or skills to dictate the way that we are going to lead. We need to be able to let go of the responsibilities we were previously accountable for, and embrace the new journey we are on. This starts with accepting that leadership experience is very different from experience making games. We have no experience leading people yet.

Maybe you have experience with a project going so far off the rails that you decide the solution is to more tightly document and track the process of development. You only need to be a little experienced in game development to recognise just how painful a circumstance this may be to work under: constantly pushed to spend your time documenting your work and checking in to ensure that you are on track and that the team is well-informed about the state of the project. Is documenting and sharing information a bad thing? Of course not. But unless we allow your team some room to breathe, we will absolutely be described as the leader who micromanaged everyone.

Our experiences then need to act as a guide for best practices, and we need to be prepared to change. An unfortunate reality in game development is often that the people promoted to leadership positions are those least prepared to change. A decade of experience becoming an expert in a singular role does not translate well to leadership. It can create leaders who spend all their time looking over the shoulders of their reports, telling them to do things differently – the way that they would do it.

These are leaders who were used to doing things their way. There is a process or technique to the work that must always be adhered to. Obviously, there is a reason for these expectations, sometimes good ones. But we must recognise that everybody works differently. There comes a point at which stringent processes can be actively detrimental to the quality of work we expect from our teams. We either need to clarify why the expectations exist where they are necessary or provide our team with the space to do the work their way.

This was a frustration expressed, particularly by those with a background in programming. There may be ways to write code that are more efficient, or allow us to better prevent the bugs that could arise in our work. But we need to be able to explain this to our team members, and let them build the skill to do it on their own. Many leaders fail to express clearly and respectfully why these things matter, and do not give their team the space to improve.

> Technical leads expect precision, which is a problem when they have difficulty articulating why things should be done a specific way. It's a real problem for those technical leaders who lack communication skills.
>
> – JONATHAN JENNINGS, GAMEPLAY ENGINEER II, OWLCHEMY LABS

Our experience is not a bludgeon; we do not pass it on by beating our team over the head with it. The members of our team do not share our perspectives; they have not learned the lessons we have learned, and they do not care about the things we care about. If we try to enforce these things upon them, they will either begrudgingly do the task as we demand or just reject it entirely and look for work elsewhere. In order for the members of our team to understand a solution, they first need to know what problem it is solving.

We help our teams understand problems and their solutions through mentorship. We want to guide them to an understanding of why the lessons we learned are important, rather than dictating the outcome to them. The objective here is not to make the game better but to help them avoid the mistakes that we made or saw made throughout our careers. But we also need to be willing to hear them out if their different experiences have led them to a completely different solution to the same problem.

Solving problems is really what lies at the heart of all tools, processes, and practices. When we are trying to help the team understand why something matters, start with the problem it solves. Why does it matter if everybody writes their variables and functions the same way? Because if you need to pass your code on to somebody else, they need to be clear on what it does. Why does it matter if somebody works in Blender rather than Maya? Because we invested in specific customisations and workflows to suit our specific needs.

If or when our experience or tools come into question, don't take it personally. This is an opportunity to reflect and consider what the justification is for how we get the work done, and to embrace change if there is a better way. Often, there are processes and tools that we use because, well, it is just the industry standard or it seems like the right thing to do.

A story I often hear is one about young producers just making their start. Straight out of their studies or first small projects, they have heard much about how good Agile is. Now they have been hired onto a team to manage a project, and Agile seems just the tool for the job. The team is getting together morning and afternoon to do stand-ups; there's a designated scrum master; sprint tasks are set at the start and are not allowed to change mid-sprint, playable builds are developed and iterated upon constantly.

And the team hates every moment of it.

The scrum master pulls aside a programmer after they create a bug task mid-sprint and resolves it before the sprint ends. They explain that this isn't something they are supposed to do; it's not how the process works. And so team members rapidly start to resent the process. Agile is dropped, and it's declared a failure. The team will then go on to claim Agile or the process just wasn't working for them and will prefer no process at all.

The problem is not that a process is somehow inherently bad, but that not every process works for every situation. A stringently dictating process causes unnecessary friction in an already complex environment. We want to use our experience and the processes we are familiar with, but we need to be prepared to adjust when they do not work exactly as expected. We all know that games are hard to make. So why would we expect that we could capture every potential circumstance within the realm of a process taken straight out of the box?

I tailor my leadership style to the people. It's about making the process work for the people, not the other way around. The process is the easier thing to change.

– MEGAN FOX, FOUNDER, GLASS BOTTOM GAMES

Agile was selected for use in the games industry due to the similarities between programming for games and programming for software, but that's about where the similarities largely end. Most pieces of software are not creative artistic products. Agile is particularly challenging to use for artists, who often find themselves grating against the prescribed iterations they do more organically. There are certain expectations and certainties around software development that make rapid prototyping and testing a reasonable expectation within the Agile framework, but a substantial challenge in the development of games.

This is not to say that software is simple, but that software is predictable with methods of best practice. In comparison to most software, every game is experimental and undocumented. The scope of work required to develop an Agile-style rapid prototype will fluctuate dramatically from game to game. This unpredictability makes it unwise to expect the same outcome every single time. Many game developers choose to test individual components of their games with the understanding that any feedback is likely to change. Games are the sum of their parts, after all.

I don't want to sound like I'm picking on Agile. It is a convenient example that highlights the point: best practice depends on the circumstances. Agile is an excellent methodology for the development of software with its user stories and iterative processes because the desired outcomes can be achieved with mathematical consistency. Agile methodologies can propose loops of infinite iteration to achieve outcomes because the outcome is measurable in software development. Very little about games is predictable, measuring fun and engagement are immense challenges.

The iterative loop is so dangerous in game development because games are not just software; they are art. Art is never truly finished. Teams with a blank cheque and no pressing delivery schedule can and will just work on a game forever if given the chance. Stories about the development of games like Duke Nukem Forever or Mass Effect Andromeda should be seen as a warning about the risks of infinite iteration. For years now, the games industry has been using Agile's iterative loops with Waterfall's firm deadlines to limit the number of iterations, but this too is an imperfect process.

The reality is that everybody is still figuring out how to make games effectively. This is not due to any lack of how games are made or what makes them great. It is because how each game is made and what makes it great is something that we must discover with time. The creators of truly excellent games and franchises can go on to make absolute duds, and not at all because they were bad at their jobs. They understood what made their previous games great and learned those lessons while those games were made. They just never really figured out what needed to be different.

We see this a lot with many creatives. They do exceptional work and make exceptional art until they think they have found the formula. They lose their humility. It becomes true in their minds that any product they are attached to in the future will be equally as successful as it was in the past. But experience and process do not guarantee success. The theme I see in teams with repeat success is that the real champion of that success is the team. Great leaders only remain great when supported by great teams. This requires that we maintain our humility and that we respect and trust the people around us. We cannot entrap ourselves in the shadow of how things were done before.

Processes and experience are tools that are invaluable to guiding games to success. The problem with tools is that when we like one or use it for long enough, every problem looks like one that tool can solve. The right tool to use is the one that is necessitated by the team and the game that we are currently developing. You may have an amazing motorboat, but if we are going down white water rapids, we would be better served by a kayak.

> What is it we are about to do? What sort of river are we going down? What sort of supplies and tools do we need? The river is powerful, there will be rough rapids. People will get hurt if you are not properly prepared.
>
> – CAMDEN STODDARD, AUDIO DIRECTOR, DOUBLE FINE

The process is just a vehicle that gets us to a destination. If we set out on a journey and are stricken by a storm, we don't blame the boat for having sails. If we set out on a kayak and your river leads out to sea, we don't blame the kayak for getting tossed around by the waves. Understanding how to identify the waters we are navigating comes with experience. Once we understand what we are up against, we can make informed decisions about the most appropriate tools and supplies to take for the journey. If we know ahead of time what sort of waters we are navigating, we can plan ahead of time to change vehicles. We always want to be using the right tools at the right moment.

People tend to hate a tool or process because it was used in a situation it was never designed for. Conversely, they may love a tool or process specifically because it was used under perfect circumstances. Obviously, changing processes part way through our journey is going to be an expensive and difficult thing to do, and we want to avoid that. It's up to us as leaders to be able to identify whether a total change of process is needed or if we just need to stow the sails until the storm passes.

We can always just change the process if we need to. If parts of the process simply do not work for us, we can choose to stop using those parts of the process. We must seek out feedback and listen to the members of our team when they have legitimate issues or concerns about the way we are choosing to get work done. Express a desire to improve, to make the process work for them. We want our tools to help enable our teams to find success, not to put up barriers to it.

It's understandable to feel challenged by the idea that we need to let go of experience and processes when moving into a leadership role. These are the things that most likely earned us our position as leaders. When we are good at our trade, people respect us for our skills. We are recognised and remembered for how well we performed the craft. But leadership is its own craft; it is its own skill that people will respect us for doing well. Nobody in our team will remember our leadership fondly because of all the time we spent creating art or enforcing processes.

Our team will remember us for how we led them. We will earn their respect through skilful leadership, by not being beholden to processes or the way that things used to be done, and by expressing trust in those around us to do their part. Where previously we may have been masters of the blade, we must now show a willingness to carry the torch instead. Lead others to their own mastery, shed light on the path, and trust that the people we lead will strike down the monsters we face as a team.

PERSPECTIVE

I knew a leader with many years of experience in the industry who had found themselves in a leadership position on a team. They were a very good example of the Warrior; clearly interested in the safety and health of their team and the issues that they were facing, but perhaps a little too invested in being a "strong" leader. This person's responsibilities included all of the technical concerns of the project; the language the team would write in, the game engine that would be used, and the technology that they would invest in. It was clear that their primary interest was in ensuring the team excelled in these aspects in a way that did not come at a cost to the team's well-being, but they had not yet explored the other aspects of leadership outside of the Warrior.

Despite their interest in and taking responsibility for the health and well-being of the team, a project they worked on experienced a disastrous series of failures that would negatively impact everybody on the staff, well outside of the programming department. There were a variety of reasons for the events that would befall this team, but key among them was a lack of consideration for the impacts of a technological decision by this lead. They did their job, by all accounts: they advised on the purchase of software and hardware that would be used in the development of the game by the art department. This purchase was necessary for the vision they had for how the team would manage technology in the future.

Either through a lack of consideration or a lack of understanding, this decision had drastic flow-on effects. The already overwhelmed team would be saddled with the technical debt that came with a lack of understanding of how to use the new software and hardware. Time was limited but needed to be dedicated to training staff on how to use the new tools and workflows. An already tight budget was tightened further by the decision, leading to the project quickly going over budget. Rather than solving a problem faced by the team, the technology introduced a new set of issues that the team was ill equipped to deal with, blowing out the project scope.

This software purchase would solve a singular, specific problem on the project. A problem that was in the way of achieving the vision that had been established. As this was a technological solution to the problem, this leader had taken centre stage as the authority best informed to make the choice as to whether the technology should be purchased. Where this turned into a failure of leadership was in the inability to get some perspective on the decision. Was the team prepared or have the capacity to use this hardware? Just how much budget did the project have remaining, and how would this decision impact it? Could the vision for the project be achieved in some other way?

Game developers often talk about this idea of the staff that are in the trenches: the space where the creative work gets done. In the trenches we only have so much space to focus on the threats directly ahead of us. There is a degree of tunnel vision that comes with working in the trenches, an obscurity to our surroundings as our priorities are to complete the task directly ahead of us. The leader is no longer down in the trenches; they are in the war room.

Get off the dance floor and onto the balcony

– JASON IMMS, HEAD OF QUALITY ASSURANCE,
KEYWORDS STUDIOS

We need to be able to see everything happening and understand the threats that our team cannot see around the corner. We are responsible for making decisions now that will put people in danger. The only way for us to make informed decisions is to understand the terrain ahead by getting our heads out of the trenches. The trenches are no longer the place we live and breathe; they are a place we visit to provide assistance and seek perspective.

As we embark on our leadership journey, it's likely that we have come from a background in which we have had clear objectives. We have been goal-oriented, focused on overcoming the tasks set out directly in front of us. We created art, made music, wrote code, and identified bugs. Our outputs were clear and measurable. This sort of outcome-oriented focus allowed us to excel when we were set on tasks alone, but it will rapidly hamper our ability to lead teams. Rather than standing toe to toe with a singular problem and overcoming it with our wit and expertise, we are now leading a group of people in their own individual battles. It can be easy, then, for a leader from this sort of background to continue to focus on the fight.

We need to understand every variable we can in order to make informed decisions for our teams. This is impossible to do while we are still in that mindset of overcoming the immediate issue ahead of us. We need to be able to put our past behind us in order to give our leadership the focus it requires. Our duty now is to care for the people around us and to dedicate ourselves to ensuring that they are well equipped to become excellent creatives in their own right.

At the core part of your job, yes, you are supposed to navigate the business. But no one person has the experience or the knowledge on how to do that alone. That's a shared thing. But what you can do as an individual is protect your team and speak up when shit is going down.

– LIANA RUPPERT, COMMUNITY MANAGER,
PREVIOUSLY OF BUNGIE

Developing our perspective actually requires that we develop two separate skills: having perspective and seeking it. Having perspective requires the decision to pull ourselves up out of the trenches and start getting an understanding of the broader circumstances taking place around us. This is a learned skill, particularly if you come from an existing background in the games industry performing technical work. You will feel the desire to be down in the trenches, as that is where you have spent your time throughout your career. But it is an essential choice to make to get up from our desks and start seeing the bigger picture.

Once we can have that perspective outside of the trenches, we can start to seek perspective. We will absolutely lack the full context of specific issues in the trenches and the specific level of detail that our team has. The danger that comes with having our heads out of the trenches too long is that things may feel less urgent, and the danger may feel less present. Seeking perspective will help us supplement our broader perspective with more specific information.

These two skills go hand in hand; they complement one another. It becomes much easier to have perspective when we are actively seeking it. This is a balance of maintaining an understanding of the big picture events taking place around us while also knowing when and where to assist our teams in those small-scale battles they face.

Making uninformed decisions without seeking further information is a quick way to become responsible for cataclysmic failures within our team. We are responsible for ensuring that we are well informed about every decision that we are responsible for making. It is not the responsibility of others to prove us wrong, or to step in and prevent us from making mistakes when we set ourselves on the path to make poor decisions. We must be accountable for our decisions and the ways in which our actions may impact the team. We can only do this by ensuring that we are well informed and have perspective at all levels of our team.

As we seek perspective, we want to seek diverse opinions. Consider a circumstance in which asking staff to work overtime for two weeks is a viable solution to a problem. To ensure that we are making informed decisions, we go and speak with several team members and hear that they have no issues with that. Who did we speak to? How many of them had children? How many of them had plans they were frustrated they would need to cancel?

It can be easy to assume that, because most people we spoke with had approved of a decision, it would be a reasonable choice to make.

But it is critical that we seek input from people that can provide different perspectives, for the same reason we seek perspective in the first place. This is also one of the many reasons that the games industry as a whole has begun a push for a more diverse staff: to seek new perspectives that make for better informed creative works.

Seeking perspectives is also a balancing act; however, we must be able to make decisions in a timely manner. Spending all our time doubting our choices and seeking further input delays a choice being made. Sometimes we must own the unpopular choice and its outcome when there are no good options available to us. These sorts of decisions may often create anxiety within a team when it may have been better to just rip off the band-aid and get it over with.

Consider how a looming budgetary problem could cause immense stress for a team. Budgetary problems that require projects to be cancelled or staff laid off are very often complex and multifaceted circumstances that the team does not need to be subjected to. Transparency is admirable, but the way in which we choose to communicate the information is critical. We do not want to have to subject them to the challenge of making a decision about the employment of their peers. Sometimes the best thing we can do under such circumstances is to consider all the information available and make the decision that has the least damaging impact on the team.

> The reality of leadership is that we're often not privy to the information that leaders were made aware of. Sometimes you are in a lose/lose situation. If it's a decision between some of us being unemployed or all of us being unemployed, I am going to have to pick some of us.
>
> – KEITH FULLER, LEADERSHIP CONSULTANT, FOUNDER OF GAMEDEVCOACHING.COM

We are not just balancing our responsibility to the team but also our responsibility to the business. We can never just choose one over the other. Consider a circumstance in which our business is facing financial woes. The options put before us are to fire staff or to cancel a project. The least damaging choice on the surface may seem to be cancelling the project, but we absolutely must investigate further and get some perspective to understand the full ramifications of both choices. If the project is near completion, is it something we can afford to cancel? What staff do we need to lose specifically, and what are they responsible for? We cannot allow ourselves to assume which choice is the least damaging to our team.

Responsibility to the business may feel like it is just about ensuring the business remains profitable, but this misses the point. A profitable business can take risks and keep staff employed. The long-term health of the studio may be more reliant upon the income of a project than the skills of a team, and we may be faced with the challenging choice of the short-term employment of a group of staff or the long-term survival of the whole studio. An unprofitable business lays off staff and cuts benefits to try and stay afloat, which harms the team we want to protect. The reality is that we cannot protect the team without the business, but a truly broken business may be better off closed than open and continuing to harm staff.

Teams are often laid off by leadership that lacks the perspective to understand the value these teams bring. Developers working in quality assurance are often the first to lose their jobs due to a lack of understanding from leadership about the value they bring to a project. Without understanding the work that people do, leaders make misinformed decisions that negatively impact the long-term health of their businesses and teams. Paradoxically, these leaders are often especially focused on the financial output of their studios that their actions cause long-term damage to.

> If you are asked to reduce head count or budget, you may look at who is least likely to upend projects or who will have their lives impacted upon the least. You may choose to fire the people who are not supporting families. But then this risks getting close to discrimination. If you are sat down with the bean counters and told to bring the budget under a certain number, you're likely to be asked to cut the most expensive people on the team - the ones with the most experience.
>
> – KEITH FULLER, LEADERSHIP CONSULTANT, FOUNDER OF GAMEDEVCOACHING.COM

Our leadership needs to ensure that the business is doing more than achieving financial goals. It needs to ensure that the staff can thrive, so the business may also thrive. Current executive leadership in the games industry is ambitious and wishes to see their businesses thrive, certainly. But they lack the perspective or the desire necessary to understand how their own businesses work. In Jim Collins' book Good to Great, he details the businesses that managed to build themselves into prosperous institutions through not just ambition but humility (Collins, 2001). Focusing on just the current game or survival of the team prevents the more long-term perspectives that create future success and stability. Great leaders create great businesses, great businesses enable great teams, and great teams continue to make great games.

This is all high-level stuff, and thankfully, we will not be making decisions about the ongoing survival of our studios on a day-to-day basis. Typically, our perspective will influence the priorities of the work our team engages in. One interviewee I spoke with talked at length about how leadership had repeatedly refused opportunities to spend resources improving their game. Leadership had instead directed staff to the development of new projects, claiming that players would grow impatient if time were dedicated to working on improvements. Developers close to the gaming community saw the opposite as being true, with players desperate to see improvements to the game's existing systems. The lack of perspective from leadership harmed their game and the team developing it.

Often, the reason for such failures comes down to a lack of respect for the roles that are bringing this information. Roles such as community management and quality assurance do not get the respect they deserve from leadership at an executive level or in other departments. We need to respect the value that every person in our business brings to the work we are doing together. If we do not understand a role, then go out and seek that understanding. We cannot, for a single moment, assume somebody is somehow less valuable or expendable in the grand scheme of the work we do.

Games are giant and complex. A decision made by one department can very easily have flow-on effects on others. Even if we do not lead those other departments, it is negligent to not actively seek out other perspectives and information before making a decision that may negatively impact our teams or peers.

If accepting the need to get away from your desk and stop doing the thing you are good at seems too hard, then that's okay! If the thing that you enjoy doing is exercising the skill that you have become good at, and it is all that you are interested in doing in the future, then I encourage you to step back from leadership. Do not accept that offer for a leadership role. Embrace the skill you have developed fully, and do not treat leadership as any other promotion. While there may be opportunities to sit down and exercise that skill during your day-to-day, it will no longer be the primary experience that you have while working at the office. Your priority will shift from being about creating things at your desk to instead being about seeing to the needs of your team and of your business.

> It takes a level of maturity where you understand that I am not here to get what I want, I am here to help my company achieve their goals by helping my team achieve theirs.
>
> – OSAMA DORIAS, LEAD GAMEPLAY DESIGNER,
> BRASS LION ENTERTAINMENT

Choosing to continue focusing on your personal skills comes at the cost of both the business and the people around you. They miss out on our guidance, and we are perceived as negligent. There's no shame in embracing that skill as your primary area of interest; the industry has a need for great developers as much as it needs great leaders. But you must make the choice as to which of these things you desire to be, rather than trying to continue to be both.

It's a great failing of the games industry that leading people is treated as a step in the progression of a skill, rather than a whole new skill of its own. To choose to accept that leadership offer is to choose a new path. Embrace the idea that – in many ways – you are going to be starting over. Work on your perspective by taking the time to step away from your comfort zone and begin to explore. Spend the time speaking with the members of your team and those outside of it, and develop your understanding of the circumstances that your business currently finds itself in. As you find yourself responsible for decision-making, stop and consider the urgency of it. If there is an opportunity to gather perspectives to inform yourself, do so – even if you feel you know the right call to make already.

PROTECTION

During one design meeting, we ended up off-topic, discussing the potential ways in which we could visualise growing plants in our game. The artists saw it as a visual medium and argued that they could model and animate the plants by hand. The programmers saw it as easy shader work, arguing that writing code to visualise the plants would allow for reuse and take less time overall. The reality of the situation was that this was still very early in development, and we were getting caught on semantics: the best team to do the task was going to be the one who had the most time available for polish. So that's what I told them. I suggested that the growing plants needed to be delegated as a polish task, given they were not essential to gameplay.

At the time, that call was informed by advice I'd been given. There was a prevalent idea that a producer should not care about the quality of the game at all. Our priority as a producer was ensuring that the game got done on time and under budget. And at this early point in my career, I was doing just that: I assessed the situation, saw that what we were discussing would not contribute to us getting the game completed on time, and stepped in. I was motivated by a desire to ensure that we could prioritise the tasks that I perceived as being far more important to getting the game done.

In hindsight, I can see that I made the right call for the wrong reasons. If I had not suggested delegating the task to polish, it was possible that the team would go away from the meeting focused on this idea of cool growing plants. They may prioritise the development of that over everything else on the project. The focus on visual pop and polish that early on could very well have put us behind schedule, and being put behind schedule could have risked the team having to crunch. I was thinking more about the risk to the product than I should have been thinking about the risk to the team.

Protection is about taking actions that protect the team, often from themselves. We take actions that ensure our team has the safety necessary to do their jobs in peace. We protect them from outside sources such as partners, stockholders, clients, or even the gaming community. We also protect them from themselves, intervening when it's clear that they may be making more work for themselves than is achievable. Protection is navigating stormy waters and avoiding icebergs that have the potential to sink the ship.

> You are recognising, accepting, and taking on the role of a protector. You have to protect and provide for the people that have faith in you to navigate this ship.
>
> – LIANA RUPPERT, COMMUNITY MANAGER,
> PREVIOUSLY OF BUNGIE

This isn't a matter of choosing between the quality of the game and the experience of the team. Protecting the people around us at the right time gives them the opportunity to do the work to make better games. Protection is admirable, and we should absolutely consider it among our top priorities in our roles as leaders.

Choosing to protect the team requires some degree of selflessness. We are choosing to spend some of our energy to ensure that our team has the capacity to do what they need to do. But it is important that our protection of others does not come at the cost of our own well-being. We need to be able to step back from a situation when it is more than we can handle. We are still working in a team, and often we will need to delegate some responsibility, even protection. Choosing to protect our teams does not mean that we make ourselves into a meat shield.

Knowing when to protect ourselves and others is an excellent opportunity to lead by example. The people that report to us may not always have the power to protect themselves or others from outside forces, but they can be encouraged to look out for each other. It creates an environment in which mutual care is seen as an essential part of the process. That the people on our teams are recognised as the critical component to getting great games made. This comes back to the idea that the people on our projects are the product that our leadership fosters. We can find new sources of income and make new games, but it's immensely difficult to replace the specifically cultivated skills that the members of our team have brought with them.

> There's this catchphrase in the army: Mission first, people always. It should probably be reordered as people first. I can replace tanks, I can rebuild turrets or artillery pieces, I can get new uniforms. But I can't replace the person.
>
> – CAPTAIN BRANDEN BUFFALO, NATIONAL SPACE DEFENCE CENTRE, UNITED STATES SPACE FORCE

It will not always be easy to choose to protect our team. There will be pressures on us that will make the safety of our team a secondary priority. If these circumstances ever arise and the option feels viable to us, it is a sign that something has become dysfunctional somewhere in the business. It might be pressure or an expectation from leadership above us to push the team to crunch for months in order to meet a deadline.

The potential risks and benefits always need to be carefully examined before we ever choose to place the team in danger. Sometimes it may feel necessary. In these moments, it may be easy to say, "it's just a few months of overtime and then we are done." These kinds of choices tend to define the culture of our studio in the long term, to say nothing for the impact upon the trust the team has in your leadership.

We can, however, also become overly protective. Consider a circumstance in which you have a new member of the team that has just recently joined. They are still early in their careers and are largely unproven. They have been reliable, but it is clear that they are looking for opportunities to prove themselves. Being a leader who cares about their team and wishes to protect them, you take this member of the team under your wing and do all you can to ensure that they have the time and space they need to grow. During a discussion about tasks, they express interest in trying their hand at a high priority and challenging piece of work. Wanting to ensure that they do not bite off more than they can chew, you tell them to let one of the more senior members of your team do the task.

In this circumstance, you may have unwittingly disempowered this member of your team. They expressed an interest in taking a risk, but seeing them as still being new and inexperienced, you step in to protect them from themselves. It's important to consider the circumstances surrounding the risk they have expressed an interest in taking. If it is a period of relative stability and failure wouldn't put anything at risk, then this may be an opportunity to skill up a member of your team. These sorts of opportunities are rare, and it's important to enable people to seize the moment when our teams can safely take risks.

Being overprotective isn't necessarily an evil-aligned version of the skill. It often comes from a place of selflessness, out of a desire to see our team members thrive. But without chances to take risks and push themselves, the members of our team miss those all-important opportunities to grow as people or as game developers. It's likely that this individual would not thank us for your looking out for them, especially not when it was a risk they were willing to take for themselves. To them, we have just shown that you do not trust in their abilities and are unwilling to take a risk with them.

The reality of protecting others is that we will never truly be able to defend our team from every threat they face. Leaders that attempt to stridently prevent risks become frustratingly immobile. They are unwilling to shift from their foritified position for fear of inadvertently letting something through that harms the team. Those leaders who exercise the skills of action can often become rather focused on themselves and their power. It becomes their responsibility to protect the team from all sources of risk. They may even begin to see it as necessary to protect the project from the team, that the team is somehow a risk to their vision. We cannot just protect the team; we need to identify and balance both risks and opportunities.

There is also a cost to us that comes from being overly protective. We may have the constitution to step in and tank those risks on behalf of our team, but eventually we will fail, and they will be unprepared to deal with the result. When this happens, we may blame ourselves for the team coming to harm. This makes it all the more important to give them opportunities to grow; we need those chances to lower our defences and regain our stamina.

We must ensure that the protection we offer the people on our teams does not stagnate their creativity. There is no creativity without a willingness to take risks. Creatives desire to explore unknown spaces and see what they find to make something new and unique. It is a matter of balancing our willingness for risk against a desire to ensure the team can do their best work. We can only do this if we can identify the difference between risk and opportunity and accept the need to have some flexibility to allow people to do challenging work. The only way our teams will be truly prepared for the future is if we allow them to grow as individuals.

> There's a point where you can protect people too well, to the point that they don't realise they are in the midst of a hurricane. And that is actually harmful to morale because they are oblivious. Then those changes feel like they are coming out of left field because you've not told them they are in the middle of a hurricane.
>
> – LUKE DICKEN, SENIOR DIRECTOR OF APPLIED AI, ZYNGA

Of course, there are examples when protecting somebody from themselves would be well justified. If a new member of our team were wanting to take responsibility for a core part of the game at a particularly critical juncture, it may be necessary to tell them no – even when we know that they won't thank us for it. In these moments, we need to step back and consider the request in the broader circumstance of the game's development.

And then when we make the decision, we need to communicate clearly to this person the reason why we cannot allow them to take that risk.

Perspective is immensely important to protect and enable the people around us. It can be easy to see any sort of risk as, well, a risk. But what are the opportunities involved with that risk? We must ask ourselves if this is an opportunity for a member of our team to fail and learn without risking themselves or the project. This requires that we shift our perspective on protection to be less short-term and more long term.

Consider the example of that new team member. If they take responsibility for that challenging task, what will be the flow-on effects? Do we have the capacity at present to have somebody else step in and help them complete it if things go wrong? Is it something that the game can do without if it does not work out as expected? Do we currently lack the capacity internally for tasks like this, and could this team member benefit your team in the future by taking responsibility for similar tasks?

Longer-term thinking can make it much easier to make these challenging decisions about whether something is a risk or an opportunity. We can and will make the wrong call about whether something is an opportunity or a risk, of course. But remember that the goal of our protection is not about preventing any risk; it's about creating the capacity for our team to succeed.

Leaders prioritise the protection and well-being of their team from inside and outside sources while also allowing them the space to take risks and grow. Over time and with experience, we will better learn to identify those risks and opportunities or improvise in the moment. Protection is a prime example of a skill with which we will grow throughout our career as leaders.

Protection is a key skill of the Warrior that we will only improve upon with a greater understanding of the other archetypes and their skills. Protecting others requires you to use all of the skills at the Warrior's disposal, certainly. But truly good use of the skill requires more. We need to know your team, to know yourself, and to be able to reflect upon your feelings in the moment to understand whether choosing protection is the right call to make. There is no circumstance in which we keep our shield always raised.

Do not let this focus on the risks of protection discourage you from working to protect others. The benefits of protecting your team outweigh the risks of it being done poorly. It is my belief that a desire to protect your team for the right reasons is always correct, even if it does not necessarily end the way we would like. We can only learn from those experiences and do better the next time the choice arises.

Protection is just one of many skills which can go poorly even when performed with good intent. This does not mean you do not exercise the skill, but that you must be aware of the potential ways in which you may harm the people you are trying to protect. Reflect on how your protection may be perceived by the team, and allow yourself to provide them with opportunities and low-risk tasks that can grow their skills.

Allowing the team to take risks creates opportunities for them to grow their capacity for success. For them to grow and develop their skills, you need to empower and enable them. This requires courage, flexibility, and mutual trust. Keep in mind the importance of protection as we move on, but work on avoiding those negative aspects of the skill. Remember that as long as you keep holding up your shield to protect the team, they will never gain the experience necessary to grow. Sometimes the best way to protect your team is to hand them the sword.

CHAPTER **2.2**

Enabling

We have what are called troop schools that train special skills, like airborne school, air assault, pathfinder, ranger. They'll give you badges, special identifiers, and valuable skills that make you better at your job. But they are all time sinks. The amount of requirements that the Army says that, hey, you have to do these things to be proficient at your job and meet the qualification required more training days that were available on the calendar before you deploy. And that didn't include any of the special troop schools. So how do you get the time to do them? How do I get a badge that shows I am a cool Airborne soldier? How do I jump out of planes when I don't have enough time to do the basic stuff? That's a constant balance, but that's a leader problem, one hundred percent.

So in my last unit in the Army I was a Battalion Operations officer and the Battalion Fire Support Officer. At the same time. Very busy jobs. I'm responsible for all the operations and planning for the Battalion. But I really wanted to go to Airborne school. It was my dream to go to Airborne school. I've always wanted to go, and people used to make fun of me because I would always talk about it. But the Airborne school was on the fort where I was stationed, so I was convinced. I was like, I can walk on next week. I can go to Airborne school.

It's three weeks long. It takes me out of the fight for three weeks. That means I'm not here doing my job. And my commander at the time is just like, go for it. Go get your Airborne wings. Have a great time, do your thing. That's leadership. He assumed the risk that we are going to have to survive for three weeks without Branden. We'll figure it out. He allowed me to

DOI: 10.1201/9781003431626-7

develop myself in a way that probably doesn't mean much for me career wise. I'm probably never going to jump out of a plane again, but it was great career satisfaction for me.

– CAPTAIN BRANDEN BUFFALO, NATIONAL SPACE
DEFENCE CENTRE, UNITED STATES SPACE FORCE

Nobody is trying to get a job in the games industry to be told how to be creative. They recognise the challenges involved in making games, and they have invested in their skills to end up in the job they are in. A good leader recognises the value that their team bring not only from their skill, but also from their unique perspectives and experiences. A singular person does not make a game great; it takes a team.

Enabling our team is all about giving them space. Not just the space to succeed, but the space to fail. Enabling others requires surrendering some degree of control, to put aside the very specific concepts we have in mind and how we imagine them getting done. This is really what makes it so scary to enable the people around us. You have to have the courage to invest in your team, trust that that they will return with something close to what you imagine, and the flexibility to embrace other perspectives and solutions.

The leader who lacks courage usually fails to get the trust of their team. Their vision becomes inflexible. It is a destination that they are trying to navigate their team to achieve, with the sort of specificity that requires they arrive on the stipulated street corner at the given time. In order to meet our teams part-way we need to be able to embrace the idea of 'close enough', and allow them to figure out how they get there. We are giving them the flexibility to turn up anywhere on the block, not just at the given street corner.

Fear is a major factor in poor leadership, and it usually arises at this point where we are asked to trust and enable the teams we work with. It's not unusual to find those leaders who like the idea of letting the team do their best work, but simply are unable to execute it in practice. They feel it their responsibility to guide and direct the project, and to ensure that the outcome is successful. But this thinking is still in that acting mindset. You are not solely responsible for making the game great. We need to step beyond that protective mindset in order to fully commit to courage.

Much of this requires thinking well outside of the project. Stepping from acting into enabling is to take that leap into the recognition of the people that we work with. What are their individual motivations and desires? What experience do they have that could benefit the work we are doing? Are there ways they want to grow that could have short or long-term benefits to our work that we can encourage and provide them the capacity to do?

Enabling isn't just about making people feel better about their jobs. If we can step past the idea of acting and protection being the point where our leadership ends, you can act like an umbrella. Give people the safety in which they can take risks and find ways to get even better outcomes than we would ever have been able to imagine on our own. We can grow their capacity for success, and improve our odds of victory.

COURAGE

Among the skills I've come to value the most highly over the course of my career, courage is one which takes a special place for me. This has been a practice I started primarily while I was teaching game development students, where I found that being vulnerable and expressing courage in them to solve problems and achieve the task paid off in ways I never could have predicted. I have seen some quiet, low-confidence students simply flourish as a result of expressing your belief in their capacity to succeed, and giving them the space to try.

One student I've taught stands out as a prime example to me. Surrounded by young men, she did not have the confidence that she was a good programmer. Providing her assistance in the early stages of the unit mostly involved helping to foster her curiosity and understanding. Rather than teaching her how to resolve specific problems, I would show her my process for solving a variety of problems. Unlike her peers, she had identified that coding was a particularly challenging skill for her, and was struggling to do it effectively. She clearly lacked confidence, but was trying to overcome that perceived weakness. She was not hesitant in asking for assistance to solve problems.

This unit involved students developing their first larger scale game in teams, and I had a process. The unit was hands-on in that students would pitch and collaborate to design and develop their games. Rather than specifically guiding every element of the process or, our role as facilitators was to teach the students the tools they needed to succeed. For the first half of the unit, I would provide them with tools and reinforce the lessons about problem solving. For the latter half, the training wheels would come off. They would be expected to operate on their own for the most part, unless they were having some very strange and specific problem.

And so it was the case with this student as well. For the first half of the unit I would come provide her with assistance, and she would thank me for the help after we solved the problem together. When we hit the half-way point, I changed tact. She asked me for assistance, and I came over to have a look at the problem. Rather than walking her through problem solving it, I asked her questions about the problem she was having, and what she thought the source of it was. She rattled off some ideas, and I told her that she had everything she needed to start finding the solution her-self. I reassured her that if she couldn't figure it out in the next half hour, I'd come over and give her a helping hand to show her how to do it.

The first time I did this she was very clearly uncertain. But within 10 minutes, she called me back over to show me that she'd found the solu-tion. The next few times she would ask assistance we'd talk through the problem, and then she'd have that 'aha' moment during our discussion as she realised what she needed to change. The final few weeks she didn't need me at all. I would come over to check on her progress, and she'd instead demonstrate the latest problem she'd solved.

> It's like taking the training wheels off of the bike. I like being there around the bike, but you are just giving them the space to try and fail on their own. But they know you are there to catch them if they need.
>
> – DR. JC LAU, SENIOR ADVANCED PRODUCER, PROBABLYMONSTERS

I'm very sure that she caught on to exactly what I was doing in my sud-den change of strategy, but it was clear that she appreciated what I did. She understood that I was providing her with the tools she needed to no longer require my assistance. What I'd taught her was independence. If she was reliant upon the assistance of a senior or a lead every time she had a problem, she would struggle to be hired. She needed to know how to solve problems, while also feeling confident in her ability to ask questions.

It doesn't really take much vulnerability as a teacher to give students the ability to succeed or fail on their own. But I apply the same exact concept to the leadership of my own team. Right around the time I started writing this book, our team received an offer for funding. I knew this would pose an issue since I was already working full time, I could not do that and also accept funding. And so I hired a programmer to help supplement my work, one of the recent graduates from the program that I teach. I gave her a lot of freedom, and she excelled above and beyond my expectations. She is now wholly responsible for the programming on the project, allowing me to focus on leadership and project management.

For many leaders, the idea of handing over your work to somebody else to complete is like passing over your baby. It's a mindset that we desperately need to get away from. It is essential that we allow ourselves to be vulnerable and to entrust the people around us with some responsibility for the work. It's immensely unhealthy to assume full responsibility for the success or failure of a project. While this often comes from a place of care for the project and for the team, neither benefit from our inability to share the load. If you are unwilling to let your team get results or find solutions on their own, they and the project will both experience stunted growth.

> I understand the point of view that you need to be strong, but you have to be able to pivot and set yourself aside. All the great leaders I really admire from George Lucas to Alexander the Great to Alexandria Ocasio Cortez crave being around people smarter than they are, they seem to share that in common. They know they are not going to come up with all the brilliant ideas. It's hard to be a good lead because sometimes you have to be like, this is where we're going. And other times you have to be like a sieve and go, that's beautiful, let's do that. In the past I have wanted to do the big cutscene sound effects or whatever, and I'm getting to the point where I'm trying to let my team do what they are supposed to do. My role has been not necessarily about protecting them, but allowing them in an arena where they flourish and help.
>
> – CAMDEN STODDARD, AUDIO DIRECTOR, DOUBLE FINE

I give these examples to provide some specific insights for us as game developers, but the subject of courage is one that has been discussed at length by numerous others. You will often hear it referred to as vulnerability. I use the term courage, because it is the end result: in order to express courage, we must accept vulnerability. Brene Brown's work is easily the most cited resource among all of the people interviewed for this book, and it is usually from this material that leaders in the games industry first engage with the concept of courage through vulnerability (Brown, 2018).

The resources on courage and vulnerability do not end here. In The Advantage, Lencioni discusses the connection between vulnerability and the need to establish trust (Lencioni, 2012). Erika Andersen's Leading So People Will Follow frames courage and vulnerability as generosity instead: sharing power, sharing what we know, sharing reward, and providing the necessary resources for success (Andersen, 2012). Good to Great by Jim Collins is a challenging read thanks to its choice to establish new terminology to describe its subject matter of how leadership turned around businesses, but you will find that the concept of vulnerability and courage is a recurring theme throughout its pages (Collins, 2001).

The reason I provide so many examples is because this concept of courage can be challenging. At face value it may sound highly unusual to bring vulnerability into the workplace if you do not fully understand the concept. But the idea of vulnerability and courage have less to do with the emotion and more about trust and having a willingness to accepting risk. It means making yourself and even the project vulnerable in the name of building trust and enabling creativity.

> Brennan Lee Mulligan is a comedian, he does all this D&D stuff on TikTok and it's hilarious. But he's like, are you going for greatness? Or are you just trying to avoid disappointment? And I'm like, damn, I need to be going for greatness. Because otherwise if it's just you don't disappoint, you are never winning. It's just failure, and then… not failure.
>
> – AMY LOUISE DOHERTY, CREATIVE DIRECTOR, ARCH REBELS

Having worked in the industry for some time now, it's my belief that most people working on videogames experience some sort of impostor syndrome. This is a feeling of incompetence, particularly when compared to our peers (Langford and Clance, 1993). In Australia and New Zealand there's a term called tall poppy syndrome, the feeling that people that are too successful will end up criticised (Peeters, 2004). Work alongside other game developers for long enough and you begin to recognise this push and pull: the desire to prove themselves capable as they contrast their abilities against those of their peers, while also not wanting to go too far lest they get cut down. While Australia has this culture and terminology, I've spoken with enough game developers in the course of writing this book to see that it's a running theme even among the immensely skilled and experienced people I have interviewed.

Courage and empowerment offer a way in which we can start to push back against this tendency for our peers to feel self-doubt. Even you may have impostor syndrome, it's immensely common among creatives who have embraced the need to improve and aspire to better outcomes. We want to be able to encourage constant improvement while also reinforcing our trust in their abilities as a professional. Courage is an excellent way to press back against these feelings. Give people the time to not only encourage their risk taking, but also to praise their successes honestly and earnestly.

> Do I give you a fish, or do I teach you to fish? I can do both. If you are starving, I'm going to give you a fish first. You're no longer starving, you get out of the immediate crisis, and I can teach you. But there's no point trying to teach somebody to fish on an empty stomach.
>
> – DR JC LAU, SENIOR PRODUCER, PROBABLYMONSTERS

In many ways, vulnerability goes hand in hand with the concept of protection. Where Protection assumes that we are reducing external risks, Vulnerability assumes that we are giving the team the capacity to take risks. This does not mean that we lower our guard, it means that we are giving them the opportunity to grow. To use specifically gamey terms, our teams need to be given the chance to get in the fight if they are to gain experience. We are not choosing to blindly thrust our team into danger, we want to protect them from it. Vulnerability and courage then is about giving them the opportunity to take a risk and grow themselves while we keep a watchful eye.

Courage and vulnerability may seem like unusual skills for the Warrior, but it comes back to our focus on Constitution. As a leader, having courage means having a willingness to take risks; to allow the members on our team some autonomy, and to empower them to take responsibility for elements of the project. This is something a leader who is primarily interested in Strength will particularly struggle with, they cannot cope for long with risks. Courage simply presents too many dangers to themselves and to the project without much clear benefit. So the high Constitution leader succeeds where they do not, able to invest more energy into concerning themselves with growing the capacity of their team and ensuring they have the capability to be autonomous.

There's nothing inherently wrong with auteur leadership. There are people who set up their companies that way. But I believe it comes at the cost of peoples happiness. We are a creative field, and people come into this field because they have passion. They want to own a thing. They want to have positive results and get positive feedback from the work they do, and if you don't have leaders who are serving that intention by giving you clarity on execution and feedback, what you have is a very negative effect on the people that you lead.

–OSAMA DORIAS, LEAD GAMEPLAY DESIGNER, BRASS LION ENTERTAINMENT

To understand why courage is so important a skill, consider the alternative. The leader who lacks courage inevitably tends towards micromanagement. This absence of courage could come from a low sense of self-confidence, a lack of trust in the team, or any number of things. Unwilling or unable to allow members of their team to take ownership or responsibility for their work, these leaders are constantly looking over the shoulders of their team to ensure that the work is getting done to their exact imagining. Their direction can often be frustratingly paradoxical: they expect work to be done in specific ways, but tend to not provide clarity on how or why.

This then breeds a reliance upon the presence of leadership. Decisions cannot be made about how to progress without the lead in the room, and so work becomes sluggish and slow. These sorts of projects tend to be creatively stagnant, or speak with just a singular voice despite a team having been responsible for its creation. It is the video game equivalent of hiring a composer to write a song that sounds like one that already exists. The unfortunate reality is that many of the industries celebrated leaders both past and present have fallen into this trap of running a mediocre creative dictatorship.

Vulnerability is difficult to come by, because it requires self-confidence. You need to live a life independent of what others think. It's needs to not be superficial bravado. Truly self-confident people can be vulnerable.

– KEITH FULLER, LEADERSHIP CONSULTANT

Embracing courage also allows us to avoid the danger of being over-protective. As previously noted, there is a point at which we could defend your team so much from outside sources that we would be perceived as lacking trust in their abilities. Courage allows us to protect, while also reinforcing clearly to the members of our team that we do trust them to get the job done. We want them to feel safe, but free to do what they need to do.

We previously discussed the idea of a new member of our team expressing an interest in taking on a challenging task. We talked about how being overly protective of this individual would disempower them, risking them feeling as though we were not confident in their abilities. Having courage in this circumstance would then mean enabling this member of our team to take responsibility for the challenge, our responsibility is simply to provide them with a little oversight and assistance. We don't want them to feel abandoned, either. We need to check in now and then to make sure they are progressing and do not need any assistance.

But we can also possibly take this further. As a leader, we should be building our familiarity with each individual member of our team. What are they good at, what do they need to work on, what are their interests? If we can identify that they have a particular skill that could be used or further developed by having them engage with more challenging work, then don't wait for them to ask for permission - approach them and check if they would like to take that opportunity. This is advocacy and empowerment, and is the next step from simply having the courage to allow others to take risks.

> It's about giving them the tools and space they need to be the best they can be. To do what they need to do. Sometimes it's enough to just do well enough. But you want to create space for them to be the best they can be.
>
> – JASON IMMS, HEAD OF QUALITY ASSURANCE,
> KEYWORDS STUDIOS

Checking is important, as the worst possible thing we could do is dictate to this person that we want them to take on additional responsibility when they are not prepared to do so. This is why understanding who our team members are are and what their capabilities are is so important. We do not want to go delegating responsibilities to members of our team who are not equipped to do the task. If they are a brand new member of the team who just joined, then we are taking small risks to build their confidence while also building upon our own.

The worst piece of advice I could give you would be to just go out and start taking risks. We're being brave, not stupid. So it is essential in the act of choosing courage that we do so with a solid understanding of the risks and the potential outcomes. Measure the pros and the cons. We do not need to document this every single time we need to be brave, just think ahead to the potential outcomes. If the result of a risk is that we are set back a couple of days when we are still years out from release, then chances are that it's a risk worth taking. Knowing what risks to take and when to take them is a learned skill that you will develop throughout your leadership journey.

Courage isn't so much about risk or giving the members of our team the opportunity to take a chance. It's about giving them the capacity to fail safely. We take on the risk so that they do not have to. We do so on the understanding that they may not be able to achieve what we or they hope to achieve, but we have made the estimation that the risk is worth the reward. If something goes wrong it will be our responsibility and not theirs. We are not asking the members of our team to jump out of a plane without a parachute.

> Risk is all commanders, one hundred percent. No one can assume risk except the commander.
>
> – CAPTAIN BRANDEN BUFFALO, NATIONAL SPACE DEFENCE CENTRE, UNITED STATES SPACE FORCE

Sometimes we will know the members of our team better than they know themselves. I have worked with people who were only as brilliant as they were their sceptical of their own abilities. These individuals would be unwilling to take on any sort of risk without encouragement. Often what they need is a small push and our outside influence. Our willingness to be vulnerable, to express trust, and to empower them to get the task done will build upon their own confidence. With time and our support, we can hopefully enable them to see the same capacity for success within themselves.

Look at the people around you and be willing to take a risk on them. Help them find the confidence to overcome the tasks they are capable of completing with the benefit of your respect and confidence in them, and they will repay it in kind. If you can begin to exercise vulnerability in this respect, I believe you will find that it can have a particularly immediate effect on the quality of the work you and your team achieve together.

The most valuable risks worth taking are the ones that develop our people. These risks don't necessarily contribute to the project or guarantee more sales, they build on the potential of our future success. Investing in the members of our team in this way is invaluable to building trust for when we need it the most. It is a long-term investment in the success of our business and - more importantly - the success of that individual as a game developer and human being. These sorts of opportunities are rarely forgotten easily, and they pay off in unexpected ways. Make your people great, and making great games together becomes that much easier.

CHANGE

Every we time we work on a game we are dealing with forces of chaos. Our projects are prone to constant change. Things will go wrong and we will need to deviate from original plans. Simple tasks are for some reason far more complicated than originally assumed. But it doesn't end there, as we also contend with the unpredictability of people. The members of our team have their own needs, their own styles of work, and their own lived experiences outside of our projects. Projects and people are unlikely to give us a consistent experience from day to day, and so a big part of our role becomes managing change.

Trying to manage change by restraining it is a mistake, however. There are leaders construct walls around people and projects to try and prevent them from changing. They use processes, practices, constraints, deadlines, anything that makes it easier to control change. These are all valuable tools to us that we use in the course of our leadership, but we do not want to use them to restrict the project or people. Our objective is to manage change, not to prevent it.

> The implicit assumption that change is bad is at the hear of inflexibility and a lack of resilience. If I'm flexible, I can recognise that change isn't bad and choose to embrace it.
>
> – KEITH FULLER, LEADERSHIP CONSULTANT, FOUNDER OF
> GAMEDEVCOACHING.COM

Working on creative projects with creative people means that we must be willing to embrace change. Creating too much structure hampers creativity. Strict deadlines that focus only on the execution of a task restrict the ability to explore solutions. Sometimes this may be necessary or even reasonable depending on the task, but it can have dangerous flow-on effects. We may cause problems such as technical or creative debt as our desire for efficient work prevents our teams from finding effective solutions.

Cyberpunk 2077 is a game developed by CD Projekt Red which released with a slew of technical issues. Such were the games problems that it was pulled from the PlayStation store shortly after release (Taylor, 2020). In an article for Forbes, Jason Schreier spoke with developers at the studio who described how the game came to release in such a poor state. Having worked on The Witcher 3 previously, much of the technology required to develop Cyberpunk 2077 already existed. However, it had some important new additions that needed to be created along the way: customisable characters, driving, first person shooting, and an online element not dissimilar from that seen in Grand Theft Auto 4.

The issue faced by the studio was that the goal had been set to develop the game in the same time taken to develop The Witcher 3. It was clear to developers that this was an unrealistic expectation. There was no clear plan on how they could reach that deadline, with one person in the studio stating simply that they would "figure it out along the way." Combined with a leadership change mid-project that completely overhauled the gameplay vision, staff were quickly working overtime hours despite being told it would not be necessary (Schreier, 2021).

Compare this with the situation at Bioware a few years earlier as described by Jason Schreier in an article for Kotaku. During the development of Mass Effect: Andromeda, the team had settled upon a vision that was originally laid out by the developers of the original Mass Effect that included procedurally generated planets and space flight. The team worked on numerous prototypes to try and prove this concept. Questions arose as to how they would implement Bioware style storytelling into a game with such procedural generation, though this was never really answered. The team had settled on the idea of falling back on the galaxy map used in previous Mass Effect games if their procedural generation plans didn't pan out.

Three years into development of the game a decision had still not been made about whether the team would stick with procedural generation or not. Prototypes had done little to convince them that it was possible. By the time leadership had made the decision to rescope and abandon a fully generated universe the project was already in full production. The storytelling team had suffered due to a lack of decisive direction, and this was only compounded upon by the late-stage decision to not go ahead with procedural generation. Faced with only 2 years to get the game finished, the Bioware team too ended out having to crunch to get the game done (Schreier, 2017).

The result of both of these situations was largely the same, the games released with substantial issues. When comparing the circumstances however, there is a clear difference: where the CD Projekt Red team had lacked the time to explore solutions and were pushed into strict structures to achieve outcomes, the Bioware team had an entirely opposite problem with a lack of direction and decisive action. Both projects ended out relying upon crunch to get the games completed, with both teams reporting that it didn't really benefit the projects or get things done any faster.

What these projects demonstrate is the importance of setting reasonable constraints. We want to be able to provide our team with clear left and right limits that give them some flexibility on the outcome while also limiting the range of outcomes available. If our constraints are too tight, the team will be limited in their creativity. Too loose, and the team will end up in places we do not expect.

> What you're actually doing is giving constraints. Rather than saying we're going that way, say we're going between here and here. Anything between those two goal posts, and you'll score your goal. This combination of this is our goal and this is the limits of what is acceptable allows people to play within that and, if your timeline allows for it, if your budget allows for it, allow them to make as many mistakes within those as possible. Because even when they are wrong, they'll learn from that and sometimes, they'll prove you wrong too. You will find people are going to be a lot happier working with you, you'll get more quality work out of them. You've taught them not to follow specific instructions, but how to solve problems, to identify what those problems are, and that's going to make them better at their role. It's going to give you less work in the long run. That's better for everybody across the board.
>
> – OSAMA DORIAS, LEAD GAMEPLAY DESIGNER,
> BRASS LION ENTERTAINMENT

Neither constricting the possibilities nor leaving them wide open benefits our teams at getting the work done. We need to be able to identify when it is necessary to provide the team space to explore, or to direct them down an already familiar path. We require structure and process to meet deadlines and financial expectations, but we also do not want to dictate so much that we hamper the team or the creative work. The challenge of change management is the fact that there's no one way in which we should be approaching these situations.

In these moments we want to improvise based on our experience or past research. It is an immense benefit to our leadership to have had previous experience with similar circumstances that can guide our hand. But even the most experienced developer won't have gone through it all, and for these circumstances we want to engage with the stories of other game developers. Attending conferences, talking to peers, or reaching out to mentors are all important to our ability to improvise effectively. Have we seen or heard of something similar to this situation? What decision was made then, and how did it go right or wrong as a result? How can that guide our decision now?

Wargaming is an important component of military training and the preparation for officers for command. Faced with a problem, participants of a wargame must make decisions using their best judgement. A military officer will learn in the field, most certainly, but failure under these circumstances won't mean the loss of dozens of soldiers. They can test their theories, improvise solutions, and learn by doing.

Game jams are probably the closest analog we have in the games industry. We set out to create a product in a limited time frame, and cross many of the same issues we would face on a full-scale project. Faced with just a few days or weeks to get a task done, we tend to think more about the project than the people working on it. Unlike a wargame, we are less concerned about minimising friendly casualties.

There is a space for game jams that are more like wargames in that they are less about the result and more about the decisions made to get there. Faced with a limited time frame to get a product done, can we do so without compromising our values or principles? Using the tools and processes that we would typically use in the process of making our games, do we identify any issues that we should be aware of going into a larger project? How do our teams feel about our leadership under these circumstances when the pressure to succeed is high?

Without these experiences, many leaders try to tank changes. They stand firm and refuse to negotiate upon their vision in the face of adversity. But the reality is that our vision is a fuzzy and flexible objective that may be met through any number of means. Our objective as a leader is not to manage change by ignoring it or controlling it, but by adjusting our trajectory to ensure that the team end up as close as possible to our stated goals without destroying everyone in the process.

There are two skills involved in change management: resilience, and flexibility. Resilience is the term we typically find referred to in literature on leadership. It defines the leader who bounces back from failure, who is willing to accept change. I dislike the term, however, as it brings to mind that leader tanking change: feet planted, shield raised, resilient in the face of change. Many of the leaders I spoke with shared this opinion, preferring the concept of flexibility. That they could explore alternatives: their vision could be adjusted, and the processes changed to suit the needs of the moment.

Originally, I felt that these two skills were the same thing. But while there is some overlap, I believe that flexibility may be something unique to game developers - and likely creatives in general. A manager at a bank or retail chain needs to be resilient when faced with change: they need to be able to ask what the alternatives are, and manage their emotions when things do not go as planned. But a leader in the games industry must also be flexible. We are not working in absolutes; we are working on creative projects with creative people. We are exploring to find solutions. Flexibility is a dedication to the destination, not the path taken getting there.

> The way I describe my job is tap dancing in the eye of the hurricane. The hurricane is blowing around me and it's going to move, so I need to make sure that I stay in the eye of it as it moves around.
>
> – LUKE DICKEN, SENIOR DIRECTOR OF APPLIED AI, ZYNGA

When need to be both flexible and resilient while we're in the fight. Change comes at us quick and often like a flurry of punches, and we need to have the flexibility to duck and weave. We aren't giving up the fight, we're simply adjusting our expectations in the moment. But when we inevitably take that hit, we need to be resilient. We need to rely on our constitution to stay standing and manage our feelings in those moments things inevitably go wrong. We manage change with flexibility, we manage failure with resilience.

Good change management is knowing when to be flexible, and knowing when to be resilient. Much of this comes down to our personal experience, but we should also be turning to our team for their guidance. It is easy to get so lost in the noise while leading others that we only rely upon ourselves, but our teams are experts in their own right. They have their own experiences that they can use to help us guide our decisions when we have the opportunity to explore the alternatives.

We need to pay attention when the team tells us that something will be challenging or potentially impossible. Hand waving that problem with an expectation that the team is being dramatic or will figure out out is the point at which a disastrous outcome is all but ensured. What do the team need to assure success? What barriers do we need to remove in order to enable them to get the task done?

If we are asked how soon we can travel from our home to the local store, we will probably be able to provide a relatively accurate estimation. There may be a car accident or some other unknown event on the way that could throw off our estimation, but the odds of this happening are low when it's not that much time in the first place. But if we are asked how soon we can travel from our home to another country, it is a lot more challenging to estimate accurately. Even with departure and landing times, all it takes for our journey to be delayed is a single, minor point of failure to make our estimation inaccurate. Our time of arrival will be drastically different. If you have ever done international travel, you know first hand that these points of failure are not uncommon.

Plans are worthless, but planning is everything.

– KEITH FULLER, LEADERSHIP CONSULTANT, FOUNDER OF
GAMEDEVCOACHING.COM

We don't stop making plans just because tasks are more complex. We still rely upon estimations on what time we will arrive in a foreign country so that we can plan how we're going to get to our hotel, or what time we might check in. But we don't make these plans hinge upon that outcome occurring at exactly that time. It's just a bad idea to make plans about how we are going to step of the plane and be in an important meeting

10 minutes later. So why do we make such strict plans around how, when, and where specific work will be delivered?

Obviously we are not always the people responsible for setting or enforcing deadlines. Our role is about ensuring that we are ready to meet those deadlines by changing the route that we intend to take there. We need to avoid unnecessary layovers if our travel time is limited, and we have places to be. It may look possible on paper, but it is important that we account for the potential failures along the way. Allowing for those opportunities to fail reduces pressure on the team immensely.

If we are dealing with a project with a vast scope and years of development time, we will have to deal with many points of failure. In engineering these are called Single Points of Failure, or SPOF's. They are points at which a single thing going wrong means that the whole mechanism fails. NASA's James Webb space telescope had 344 individual failure points, each one representing a risk of the whole project failing (Wilcox, 2021).

Applying this concept to a five-year game development project is an exercise in genuine terror. Just how many single points of failure exist in the average games development?

Unlike engineering, we aren't dealing with precise measurements. We have room to manoeuvre, and we should take the opportunity to do so wherever possible. This is why change management is so key to our leadership. We do not want to inadvertently become a point of failure. Our projects can bend, they do not need to break.

Large projects will have an equally large number of points of failure. We typically break these projects up into milestones to better track and ensure success. If we look at our plans and failing to meet a single milestone spells out disaster, then something already needs to change. The team needs to have opportunities to fail and change direction without the whole project falling apart at the seams. This can be challenging to accept when we're working at such immense timescales and scopes, but experience will make it clear that change is inevitable. It shouldn't be punished or mean the end of the project when it happens.

> The leads job is to point the direction of where the team is going, and then to move mountains out of their way.
>
> – OSAMA DORIAS, LEAD GAMEPLAY DESIGNER,
> BRASS LION ENTERTAINMENT

Reflect upon the scale of the work we are doing. If we are working on a project that has limited time or a minimal scope, we are dealing with less potential points of failure and less risk of unexpected change. These projects benefit from tight schedules and scaffolded processes to ensure delivery, with time and freedom dedicated only to solving the most pressing unknowns. The longer a project is, the more necessary it becomes to provide some flexibility to seek outcomes. But we still need to provide the team with clear limits and constraints to guide their work.

TRUST

Trust seems to be hard to find, particularly in the shadow of a global pandemic. Forced to work from home for months or years, game developers released some of the best games in a decade. Leadership must trust that their employees were getting tasks done while being unable to keep a constant watch over their shoulders. Since the pandemic has been declared over, developers have been ordered back to the office. Leadership may attempt to sell this idea and its benefits as a good thing, but developers see it coming from two places only: the need to make use of the expensive offices that businesses have paid for, and a lack of trust in the output of staff working from home.

This is then only compounded upon by upheaval as studios lay off staff. Being fired is one thing, but a lack of care or empathy in the act is another. Staff laid off from Bungie in October 2023 had their employee credentials and building access revoked in the early hours, many before they had even been told that they had been fired. The layoffs took place at the end of the month, following a corporate norm in the United States of layoffs occurring at such a time to sever coverage of employee benefits that are renewed monthly. According to insiders at Bungie, this did not include their health insurance - making them an exception in the case of many of the other layoffs (Carpenter, 2023).

In July of 2022, Bungie was purchased by Sony Interactive Entertainment (Peters, 2022). Stressed by the potential loss of the independence for which they had fought so hard, leadership reassured their staff that the deal would not result in layoffs or restructuring (Grayson, 2022). Not even two years later, and the atmosphere in the studio following the layoffs has been described by developers as "soul-crushing." Feeling understandably betrayed by leadership, one anonymous person from Bungie told IGN "folks still there are very much feeling 'us vs them' between leadership and its workers. That trust has been eroded" (Valentine, 2023).

There is an impression among many of the interviewees I spoke with that developers are unfairly punished for choices they never made. Leadership takes risks or chooses a path - often against the advice of staff - and the business finds itself in a position that it can no longer operate effectively. Instead of taking responsibility for the situation, many leaders blame the environment that they have found themselves in as they lay off their staff. This isn't just a betrayal of the trust of those that lose their jobs, but also of the people that remain. They lose faith in the ability for leadership to take them in the right direction. It creates a feeling that people are expendable, so long as it serves the bottom line of the business.

> You have to protect and provide for the people that have faith in you to navigate this ship. You are the captain of the Titanic, you are the one that they have to just blindly place their trust in. That what you are doing is in their best interests. There's these levers you have to pull before you ever do layoffs. Have you taken off your bonuses? No? Do that first. Have you taken a pay cut? No? Do that first. Then maybe you can reach for the layoff lever.
>
> – LIANA RUPPERT, COMMUNITY MANAGER,
> PREVIOUSLY OF BUNGIE

Sometimes the unfortunate reality is that layoffs are necessary. Business deals fall through, partners go bankrupt, games take longer than expected or do not perform as well as we hope. Trust isn't so simple as just keeping people employed, but making it clear that we have done everything in our arsenal to act in the best interests of the business and the people that it employs. It is about having integrity, and being true to our word and our values. A business that states that they value their team above all else needs to find ways to protect that team above all else.

People have long memories. Leadership at Bungie promised that there would be no layoffs or restructuring as a result of the Sony purchase. The layoffs that staff would experience not two years later may have had less to do with the Sony purchase and more to do with the state of the game, but there is still a feeling of betrayed trust. This feeling is only compounded upon when staff get the sense that the game is in a state due to no fault of their own.

Trust is one of the five dysfunctions of a team as described by Patrick Lencioni. In fact, it is so essential to the running of effective teams that it is the foundational dysfunction. From the absence of trust come the other dysfunctions: a fear of conflict, a lack of commitment, avoidance of accountability, and inattention to results. The team that lacks trust work to protect themselves and care little for the outcome of the project so long as they are safe. They stop sharing information with one another, working to make themselves irreplaceable. It's unlikely that we will find any creative spirit in the team without trust.

Losing trust can be permanently damaging due to the challenges involved in building trust at all. When I pressed every interviewee on this, it was clear that there was no real solid answer on how to build trust. Everybody I spoke with hesitated to some extent. They talked about the need to build a relationship with their team, and to be aware of how they feel about them. There is no systematic way to build trust. After all, if it is clear to others that you are just going through the necessary motions to get trust, why would people ever really trust us?

This is one of those areas of the leadership in which we must embrace the chaos of people. Building trust requires action, and it will require varying amounts of time. Some people will be slow to trust. There may be some negative experiences with their previous leadership that we need to work through, or a particular level of independence and oversight that they desire that we will need to provide them with. Others may be blissfully quick to trust. We may just click with them on an emotional level and find that trust comes easily.

Do not misinterpret trust for respect. Say we work with a leader who has an impressive history working in the games industry, who has developed major successes. We may start the relationship with this person having a great respect for their experience, but what reason do we have to trust them? Even if they have led those teams that experienced those successes, without our direct experience with this person it may be difficult to trust them. We may be quicker to trust, but it is unlikely that our relationship begins with any unique amount of it.

> Do you trust somebody successful without a relationship with that person? You may respect them, but you do not trust them yet. They have not yet executed with regards to you. So operating within the same space is a consideration in establishing trust. You have to make deposits in my trust account, to be prepared for the times you need to make a withdrawal.
>
> – ANONYMOUS

Social science has identified a variety of types of trust, though the ones most useful to developing our understanding are contractual trust, competence trust, and goodwill trust. Contractual trust is essentially the expectation that we will operate within the terms of our contract. It is trusting that somebody will act within the terms of what they agreed to do (Markovits, 2015). We want trust which is more intimate and builds relationships, which brings us to the concept of competence and goodwill trust.

Consider the leader with the impressive track record in the games industry. Do we trust their competence? Their involvement in a lot of projects does not mean that they were responsible for those successes, but that they were at the very least present for them. And so before we can trust their competence, we must experience it. This is why we may be quicker to trust this individual: we have heard about their experience, and now we have seen first-hand that they can back up. We have developed a trust in their competence.

This level of trust may be good enough, but it is not particularly intimate. As a leader, we desire to trust in the competence of our team. But our team needs more than that from us. Somebody may be competent, but do we trust that they will act in our best interests? Where competence trust is about effectiveness, goodwill trust is about morals. Competence does not necessarily mean that we would be willing to make the difficult decision when the time called for it if it protected and nurtured the team. Truly intimate trust comes from a belief that the person we are working with has our best interests at heart (Maresch, Aschauer and Fink, 2019).

> It was hard to get trust in my old position. I was new to the business, I had trust from those higher up than me but not those lower. A lot of people questioned why I had the ear of our leadership. I only really gained the trust of others through accomplishments. Trust at my current job is more like that, it is absolutely about showing competence and skills. You earn trust by doing. Proving to people why you are necessary, why it has to be you. They have to imagine what it'd be like if it wasn't you and hate that idea.
>
> – ANONYMOUS

With this in mind, we can begin to understand how to build trust. Examining our role as a leader, we are the person whom the members of our team see as being the one wielding some degree of power. The team answer to us, and we can direct them. It is an expectation that we have a contractual obligation to the business and will operate in the best interests of it. We will ideally build trust about our competence through the course of our time with our team and demonstrating informed decision making. But we have the power to invest in goodwill immediately. Whether we have just joined a new team or a new employee has joined our existing team, being the leader means that we are the one with the power to invest in goodwill. The members of our team will look to us and watch where and how we use our power, and whether it benefits them.

The ways in which we use our power to invest in goodwill while in a position of power is how those around us get a sense of who we are and what we value. Our success as a leader will define our perceived competency, and how we choose to act will define our perceived morals. An incompetent leader can still have the trust of their team if they have demonstrated that they have the integrity to do what they believe is right, but it's much harder to trust a leader who is competent but immoral. This is why goodwill is so important to games leadership. There will come a point where things will get hard, competency will be hard to guarantee, and we will require the team to trust us in order to follow us into the unknown.

> I was taught early on by one of my commanders that there's certain events in your life that only happen once. Your kid only has their first birthday once, you only have that anniversary once. The unit will still function without you for a few hours or a day. So go take that time with your family, because little things like that mean a lot.
>
> – CAPTAIN BRANDEN BUFFALO, NATIONAL SPACE DEFENSE CENTER, UNITED STATES SPACE FORCE

It may be strange to imagine that goodwill is somehow more important than competency when it comes to trust in the games industry, but it is the nature of the work we do. Games are not developed based upon absolutes. We are working in an environment in which things are constantly changing and shifting. Competency may be essential in medicine where we want to ensure we get the correct treatment, but the emphasis here is on the word correct. There is no specifically correct way to lead, to make a games, or to be creative. We may be willing to tolerate a poor bedside manner in a doctor who we are only going to see once or twice, but most people will desire a doctor they can trust more intimately if we are going to see them often. We will see our team often, we do not deal in absolutes, and so our bedside manner is immensely important to them.

Trust is an extension on the core concepts of leadership: integrity, humility, and accountability. Doing the hard thing when times are easy means that we are prepared and practised when times are hard. We reinforce our skills around our ideals during these easy times and create the example to our team of how they can expect us to operate in the long term. We start how we intend to continue. Their trust in us will not be truly tested until those moments in which things become truly challenging, and we have to make the hard decisions.

Everything that we have discussed so far and will discuss will contribute to the building of goodwill with the members of your team. Choosing to be vulnerable and take a chance on a member of your team is a choice to invest trust and goodwill in them. You've made that exchange of trust, and they may or may not choose to invest it back into you at some point in future. People will have higher or lower thresholds before they are willing to trust you. The point isn't to become needlessly methodical in where we put our trust, but to remember that this isn't a currency.

In fact, it is important that you allow trust to evolve as a genuine human exercise. By approaching this idea of trust in a particularly businesslike fashion, expecting it to be truly transactional, your team are likely to reject you as manipulative. It is essential for trust to be genuine unless you are trying to build contractual trust. We want a similar sense of trust that we have built up with our close friends or family, the kind of trust where we freely offer our help and assistance because we care about them. We offer to help move their couch because they need help and it is the right thing to do. You do not buy integrity or goodwill. You do not invest trust on the expectation you get something in return.

Trust is most certainly transactional, but it is also organic. Let it grow through your actions and your deeds. Dedicate yourself to your leadership, to serving the members of your team, to achieving great results without a human cost, and you will gradually build the trust your team holds in you. Consider the necessity to gain the trust of the people in your team without the need to interrogate their willingness to trust you in this moment. You need to trust that they will trust you when you need them to.

3.0

The Bard

Popular for their roles in fantasy as charismatic entertainers, the bard is probably the easiest to understand of the different archetypes. The bard uses their charisma to influence and inspire the people around them. It's not difficult to imagine how this would work for a leader in the industry or why these skills are particularly important. And yet, many leaders don't tend to invest much of their energy into building their bardic skills. The ability to communicate with others is perhaps seen as something that is unnecessary as a leader, only necessary if you need to convince or negotiate with the people under your command. It's easier to see the benefit of this kind of charisma when the people that you are influencing can have some sort of external negative impact on the project. And so many Warriors stick to their protective nature of being purely brute force.

The role of a purely communicative class as a leader may seem strange at first. The idea of the Warrior as a leader seems sensible; they are guardians and protectors of their team. It's not hard to imagine that they are well respected for their prowess. Take a moment, however, and turn your mind to the kinds of characters that we place in our videogames. Is Link a great leader or just a great Warrior? Is the Master Chief a great leader, or just a great Warrior? The thing that usually unites the Warrior archetype is this stand-alone, face down all threats type of character that encapsulates a gaming power fantasy. Mass Effect's Commander Shepard is not a great leader because they are particularly strong or have powers the rest of the people around them do not. Instead, Shepard's superpower is their ability

DOI: 10.1201/9781003431626-8

to communicate. Their mission sends them face-to-face with unknowable threats that – somehow – they manage to unite the greater galaxy to stand against. Yes, no matter what class you choose for your character in Mass Effect, Commander Shepard is a bard.

Where the focus of the Warrior is on the project, the bard is interested in the role of others in achieving collective success. The Warrior is a reactive archetype, good at responding to events that it can see coming but prone to attempting to solve all problems alone. The bard thrives upon prevention through teamwork, rallying allies or influencing individuals to take action. The energy you would have expended defending your team from and outside source of influence never needs to be expended at all if you invest your energy into convincing that outside influence to see things your way. You can protect the team from themselves by communicating with them to help them see that the risks they are taking are unnecessary.

It's hard to discuss the bard without discussing their key attribute: charisma. It's my belief that a good part of the reason that many leaders don't see the value in investing themselves in charisma is due to a perception of it being somehow manipulative. Influencing others may sound like you are getting under their skin and getting them to do what you want without even really understanding the value of it. And this isn't untrue: if you fully invested yourself in the Bardic skills without taking the time to improve yourself as a Warrior or a Cleric, you could fall into a trap where your abilities are only manipulative. But this is why we're not investing in the bard on its own. The bard's skills are some of the most powerful and influential among all the archetypes, but they need to be healthily balanced with the Warrior's Constitution and the Cleric's Wisdom.

It can be easy to misinterpret that charisma is all about manipulating or leading others to see things your way, but these are just ways in which charisma can be used. Rather, I believe that charisma is all about communicating with people. You can be the most charismatic person in the room, but you need other people in the room with you to make use of your ability. This means that the bard is usually a people pleaser, somebody keen to keep those around them in good spirits and to remain in their good graces. This keeps the pure bard leader from being openly manipulative unless they are willing to absolutely burn bridges, which is likely to be another very good reason why there are not many bard leaders in the Games Industry.

Of course, these points also highlight just how easy it is for the bard to be aligned to evil. There's a reason inside of fantasy roleplay settings that the bard tends to be aligned to chaos or neutrality, it is very easy for the bard to manipulate and mislead, and this is usually done for their own selfish benefit. This kind of bard often treats the people around them as puppets that can be directed with words and the application of pressure. Or worse, they put on the convincing act of a bard with genuine care, who is simply trying to achieve the best outcome for the team. These bards can be perceived as car salesmen or politicians. They may say one thing but intend to achieve another, give you only half the facts, or avoid uncomfortable truths.

There aren't many leaders who start off firmly in bard territory, but they do certainly exist. I met a charismatic young man at the 2017 Melbourne International Games Week who I had the pleasure of mentoring while he was on his IGDA Foundation Scholarship. Chima Denzel Ngerem comes from South Africa, having studied law before getting into Games Development. Since then, he's travelled the United States and worked at several large game studios, from Epic Games to Insomniac Studios. And this is in no small part due to his charisma; Chima is the kind of person who walks into a room always carrying the sort of energy that lights it up. Honestly, it makes me a little bit envious.

Chima was an excellent example of an "honest Bard" – genuinely good, caring for the people around him, and wishing to use his skills to improve their circumstances. I think a good deal of this came from his desire to get into Production in particular, as while the Bardic skills benefit a Producer just as they would any other leader in the studio, many Producers start their leadership journey firmly in the area of the Cleric. Without that all important emotional intelligence, Chima could very likely have been a concerningly manipulative and dishonest kind of leader. It was clear that at the start of his journey when I was mentoring him, he'd learned enough and had enough of that natural empathy and care to not begin falling into the traps the bard faces as a leader, manipulating others for individual gain.

It had been some years by the time I had the pleasure of speaking to him again. Interviewing him for his insights having spent some time in the industry now was fascinating. While it was clear when I met him that his real strength was absolutely in the realm of the Bardic arts, he spent a great deal of our time chatting and talking about skills that I saw were much more in line with the Cleric. It was clear that he had reflected upon his experiences in a way that had begun to be reflected in his perspectives on leadership.

While it was clear from the moment I met him that he respected and wished to learn everything about leadership, he had now started living those lessons and begun branching out from his Bardic background into the other archetypes.

The bard taken on its own runs the risk of quite literally being all talk. Without the skills to execute in the way the Warrior does or the wisdom to know how to operate effectively, a bard makes a poor leader. It's somewhat ironic then that the skills the bard exemplifies are so key to the leadership experience that three of them we will discuss were repeatedly referred to as the things that define games industry leadership. The reason this is the case comes down to the fact that communication without content is hollow. You need to be more than the words you say; you need to be the actions you take. Thankfully, as we discussed, it's rare for people to find themselves in leadership positions in the games industry as pure bards to start.

Whether you believe you have started your journey firmly in the skillset of the bard or somewhere else among the archetypes, the bard is somewhat surprising. As mentioned, those skills of influence can be used for great personal gain. But with your abilities so closely tied to the people around you, this can never come without the cost of their trust. And so as we explore the skills of the bard, you will find that there is a great deal of focus here on not just influencing the lives of those around you, but using your influence for their benefit. In fact, the bard may just be the strongest team player of all the archetypes.

Speaking

In my first leadership role, I had two staff. One of them had two large monitors that the office provided, and a third little one that he had bought along from home. And on that third monitor, he just had anime playing. All day, every day. It used to drive me insane. I could not understand how it was possible for him to concentrate. It seemed unprofessional, the fact he always had this entertainment going. It annoyed me. And I just kind of bottled it up for a very long time.

Sometime later my boss at the business came by and saw the anime on his screen. It wasn't anything new, it had been going on for a long time. But the boss ripped into him. And I saw red. I stormed into the boss's office and I gave him an absolute earful for treating one of my staff like that in front of everyone. I told him "This guy is good at his job. He gets his work done." And at some point, I realised I am talking to myself. I realised the fact the anime was annoying me so much had so much more to do with me than it did to do with him or his performance.

So I went and spoke to him about it. I said that I had to admit something, that the anime bothered me for a long time too. But I realised that it doesn't matter so long as you are doing your job and I'm happy with the work you do, you should keep it up, it's awesome. We got to talking, and it turns out that for him the anime is something that is important to him because he grew up in a house where the TV was always on. The background noise helped him focus.

That was the point at which I realised that everyone's lives are intertwined with their work. That everybody has different experiences and, chances are, if somebody's behaviour is something you don't appreciate for some reason? You don't need to necessarily manage the behaviour so much

DOI: 10.1201/9781003431626-9

as managing the person. Chances are if you feel like they are wasting time on their phone, it's because they are dissatisfied with their job, or there's something big going on in their personal life. If you can understand what that thing is, you can empower them to be the best they can be.

– JASON IMMS, HEAD OF QUALITY ASSURANCE,
KEYWORDS STUDIOS

There is a power in words. The right words at the right place allow us to influence or inspire. The right words used by the wrong person can easily be used to manipulate or mislead. Knowing the difference between these things isn't so easy as black and white. When we speak, we want to ensure we respect the power of words and that we are doing so with a strong sense of morals and our personal integrity.

If you are a powerful speaker, people will follow you without question. You must not betray that trust. Your words must be reinforced by your actions: hollow words are a quick way to make yourself seem about as reliable as a car salesman. This is why speaking is about so much more than just communication. Speaking gives us the capacity to influence others to change, but we need to understand who they are. What is it that they need? What drives them? What do they lack?

Communication in leadership is not necessarily the most important skill to learn, but it is one of the most invaluable. Good communication allows us to provide direction and support to the people around us. The alternative is that the members of our team are left trying to guess at our intent or desires. It is essential that we provide them with clarity, so they may understand the what and the why. But we can only provide them with that understanding if we know what they need to hear.

And so key to speaking is actually listening. If you are spending all the time sucking the air out of the room being the one person talking, you are not being an effective leader. It is essential to pause and give others the time to speak so that you can understand them. Speaking is amplified by our understanding of people. The skills of the cleric will amplify our skills as a Bard since there is little use for pretty words without understanding.

We want to speak to influence others to improve our collective circumstances, but a selfish leader can turn their ability to communicate into a means of getting what they want or furthering only their own ambitions.

The ideal use of our ability to speak goes beyond just simple self-interest or even achieving project outcomes. Good leaders use their ability to speak to advocate for change and to communicate with others on their own terms. It's not a matter of just being good at talking in one singular way; it's about being able to speak in the ways that individual people need.

COMMUNICATION

There are few skills as paramount to the leadership experience as Communication is. We cannot lead without communication. The rest of our team must resort to assuming our intent, our desires, where we imagine the project going. It's easy to understand how a failure to communicate leads to innumerable other issues with individuals, with the project, with the work we are doing. Despite its significant importance, it is a skill that many leaders still get wrong.

In all my time working in the games industry, at the core of every issue I saw was really a failure to communicate. It may have been a failure to communicate clearly on just what the expectations for a project were, leading to the team responsible being left to their own devices and finding themselves far off the client's imagined target. Or it may have been a failure to communicate clearly about the values we held and just what those things meant for the team. I've seen small teams fall apart as leadership fails to communicate to them the importance of meeting deadlines and attend meetings.

Communication is not just speaking; it is also listening. I've met some immensely eloquent leaders who only ever managed to hear themselves. They became so convinced of the things they said without hearing anybody else that it would inevitably lead their teams to failure. As leaders, we need those outside voices to help us find the direction in which we are headed and to guide us to the best possible outcomes.

> One of the most important things about being a good lead is having a clarity of communication, of intent, of transparency. Building trust by being honest. And I feel that is a quality that some people just have, but it's also one you can learn.
>
> – OSAMA DORIAS, LEAD GAMEPLAY DESIGNER, BRASS LION ENTERTAINMENT

Clarity and respect are essential to our communication. We must be earnest when we enter a conversation that we are seeking a mutual understanding, even when we are communicating to deliver a message or feedback. This often means being prepared sometimes to negotiate and meet others half-way when there is a disagreement. However, we also cannot become fixated on the idea that communication is somehow about changing the minds of those around us. Sometimes we will need to walk away from a conversation and accept that the person we are speaking to will feel however they feel.

We use communication as leaders in a variety of ways. We communicate our vision to our team. We advocate for them inside and outside of the team. We need to provide clear and easily understood directions. Any feedback we give to others needs to be considered, honest, and empathetic. When we have one-on-one meetings with our direct reports, we need to be curious and prepared to listen, to hear what they need from us. Communication is not just holding a conversation or selling the team on our ideas.

> We have monthly one-on-ones. I'll talk to them about what their personal goals are, where they want to be going, and how they fit within the company. And then Sam will talk to them about project goals, what we need to be doing with the game, that kind of stuff. And then we'll do combination one-on-ones. What do you want to be doing? What do you feel like you are doing really well? What do you need training in?
>
> – ANNA BARHAM, MANAGING DIRECTOR,
> BALANCING MONKEY GAMES

When we communicate with others, we are going through several steps. We do not need to constantly go through these in every conversation, but they help us understand where we may want to improve our communication. Firstly we have messaging, the act of communicating our thoughts. Then we have listening, the act of others communicating their thoughts to us. It's not as simple as the stated words simply being heard; however, they will be interpreted before they are truly received by another person.

Each person in a conversation brings their own unique style to the conversation. They have a way they speak and wish to be spoken to, and they will interpret things differently for us. We can imagine interpretation as a filter each individual person has. Whenever anybody hears or reads something, the statement passes through this interpretation filter and is coloured by a variety of factors, such as their past and their mood on any given day. And then the message finally reaches them, often drastically different from what we stated. We need to understand and respect the individual to communicate with them effectively.

> The instruments you have to help the team require that you understand different communication styles. That person is Matt, and that person is Emily, and they have a preference for this style of communication.
>
> – EMILY MACMAHON, LEADERSHIP CONSULTANT

When we talk about communication breakdowns, it's usually at the interpretive step in the process of communicating with others that the failure has happened. The person we are speaking to has failed to interpret the information we have given them in the way we expected, or we left our information far too open to interpretation. When we have conversations with others, it can be easy to get caught up in the energy of what is being discussed. This can lead to mistakes, as we rely too heavily on our immediate interpretation of something being said or read. And so whenever we are communicating with people, we need to apply another skill: reflecting. This step protects us from our interpretive filters, giving us a bit more time to check the information.

Imagine we are having a conversation with a friend, and they ask if we are interested in doing anything this coming weekend. If we give our friend a simple "no," this hits their interpretive filter, and they are left to interpret the statement. Because we have been so simple and short, perhaps when the message finally reaches them, what they have really heard is actually "no, I don't want to do anything with you." This would easily leave them feeling hurt, and depending on how they chose to respond, it could very easily descend into an argument. So what do we do differently to ensure this does not happen?

> I always come back to communication, that's my field in linguistics. Sometimes how we frame a question really can make a difference. How we approach people. Do we interrupt them? Do we support them? Do we engage two-way communication? Do we demonstrate active listening?
>
> – MARIJA KOPRIVICA LELIĆANIN, SAE INSTITUTE

We cannot control how other people will interpret what we say. What we have control over is ourselves. Rather than trying to correct the skills of others to understand us better, it's important to focus our energy on improving our own skills. So when we look back at this conversation with our friend and analyse what went wrong, we can see that at the point our message met their interpretive filter, they were upset. They didn't really pause to reflect. But we could have just spent a little extra time tailoring the message to avoid this outcome.

We should not pass judgement on the misinterpretation. Take a moment to reflect on what was said. Maybe they have a good reason to feel this way; maybe there is an underlying issue where they have had a bad week and are less inclined to give the benefit of the doubt, or they are feeling undervalued by us. Or perhaps it is in their nature to assume the worst, and we need to be more careful about our choice of words. There's a variety of reasons why they may not have thought about the statement and why it would be interpreted as such.

Trying to change how everybody around us is feeling all the time is a quick way to drive ourselves insane. We must focus that energy instead on improving ourselves and our skills. The easiest solution here is to adjust the message. Instead of telling our friend "no," we say "no, I've been really busy this week and need some time to relax, but thank you for asking." By providing them with enough context, there's less room for their interpretation to run wild. We are always managing ourselves in conversations, not the reactions of others.

> The thing I realised is that everybody at the studio and basically in the industry is interested in creating this wonderful thing. So that's all you really have to tap into in order to relate and communicate. There is a reason why they are doing this, and it's pretty much the same love that everybody has. So all you have to do is just, find the right connector.
>
> – CAMDEN STODDARD, AUDIO DIRECTOR, DOUBLE FINE

Listening is a skill separate from interpretation and reflection. When we are relaxed or excited, we can often listen and jump straight to our next words with little consideration. You may have found yourself in a conversation with somebody in the past where it felt like they were responding more to themselves than they were responding to you, or they were hearing what they wanted to hear out of your replies. We want to avoid this by ensuring that every time we enter a conversation, we are prepared to not just listen but to interpret and reflect on what is being said.

I was introduced to this concept of pausing to reflect when I started speaking more in public at conferences and on podcasts. I found myself listening back on the recordings of my speeches and cringing as I heard myself saying a lot of "um's" and "uh's." I did some reading to find advice on fixing the problem, and after reflecting, I discovered that a lot of it was my own anxiety under those circumstances. Pushing myself so hard to smoothly move from one subject to the next, I was tripping myself up.

The advice I received was to give myself time. To reflect on what I was saying and think about what I was going to say next. What started as an attempt to improve my public speaking extended to my ability to teach and lead as well. By hearing myself, I was able to better communicate with others.

When we have that reflective step, we need to think just beyond the facts. We need to consider how the other person is feeling and how we are feeling. Even if we are incredibly clear with our statement, if we cannot control our emotions at the time of making it, it will very easily not be interpreted the way we would like. And so reflection really breaks down into several more skills on its own, all attached to emotional intelligence. We must first identify what the statement made us feel, why the statement made us feel that way, how the person who made the statement is feeling, and then how we wish to respond to the statement.

This is particularly true when we are providing feedback or having difficult conversations. It is essential in these scenarios that we maintain control of our emotions and our approach. It may be challenging to have these sorts of conversations, but they are essential to our team. They are relying on us for clarity and direction. These conversations need to be focused on discussing a problem to seek a shared solution. We do not want to be perceived as though we are passing judgement. If we are taken the wrong way, take a moment to reflect on what we said and why it may have been interpreted this way.

> You can't be afraid to be uncomfortable. Every time I have failed in leadership, it was because I was not prepared to have uncomfortable conversations.
>
> – JEAN LEGGETT, LEADERSHIP COACH

This is obviously a lot to juggle and consider. Thankfully, in most conversations, we will not need to think so hard about how we are communicating with people. If it is just a casual afternoon conversation, we likely don't need to spend that mental energy on the chat. But certainly, when it comes to those more challenging conversations, or providing people with feedback, these skills are of immense importance and spell the difference between good communicators and great ones.

Our role in each conversation should break down into the following steps:

1. A person makes a statement.

2. We listen to the statement.

3. We interpret the statement.

4. We pause to reflect upon our interpretation of the statement.

    i.   (Optional) How did the statement make us feel?

    ii.   (Optional) Why did the statement make us feel that way?

    iii.   (Optional) How is the person who made the statement feeling?

    iv.   (Optional) How do we want to respond to the statement?

5. We make our own statement.

There are fundamental similarities between this way of thinking about communication and the Socratic Method. Where many of the philosophers of the time primarily practiced the art of rhetoric to bring others around to a different perspective, the Greek philosopher Socrates used an alternate methodology. The key to the Socratic method was a desire to question and understand the perspective of the people being taught and to include them in the conversation. Then, rather than trying to convince them of a perspective, we are working with another person to come to a universal perspective – an agreed-upon truth (Kraut, 2023).

The steps to the Socratic method can be seen to expand upon the steps we have already established. We listen, interpret, and reflect upon the statement of the other person. We accept this perspective but seek to refine the argument. Why is it that they feel that way? Can we identify the underlying belief that brings about that perspective? Now we have a new fundamental understanding that we can use to draw a conclusion from, and we return to the foundational message with a new understanding. Fundamental to this is the need to postpone our judgement of others, as we need to be able to hear and respect their perspectives and understanding of a circumstance so that we can better see it ourselves.

It's important to note, however, that making every conversation a Socratic one is a quick way to exhaust and frustrate the people around us. This style of communication is one we should consider only when we need to understand somebody better, where there is a difference of opinion, and we need to settle upon some sort of shared perspective. This has proven to be something immensely useful to me in my time in game development, even if I did not expressly set out to practice a Socratic dialogue. By respecting the perspectives of others and seeking to understand why they hold that perspective, we provide them with an opportunity to hear our own. We quickly find common ground this way.

Consider the sort of conversations about the viability of a feature on a project. People may argue with immense passion for or against its addition. When we see this kind of passion, we should take a step back. Identify how we feel about the feature, and separate our thoughts from our feelings. Ask the person why they care so deeply about it. Have they identified some sort of flaw in the thing that they have not had the opportunity to share? Do they have some personal attachment to the feature? Is it a feature they specifically worked on designing, and do they really want to see it implemented? Restate their own words and bring it back to the conversation about the viability of the feature. With this new information, does it change our feelings as a group about whether we should move ahead with it?

It's important to note, however, that this sort of conversational style quickly breaks down if there is no trust. If we are speaking with somebody who does not trust us, questioning their motives in their response is a very quick way to frustrate them. Remember, they have their own internal interpretive filter here. When they hear our words questioning them, they will not hear what we are trying to say if they do not trust us. When having these sorts of conversations about vision or direction, trust becomes of foundational importance. It simply does not matter how elegantly we speak or how well we argue if people feel we are untrustworthy.

When we have trust, criticism is a lot easier to give. In "Creativity Inc.," Ed Catmull talks about the importance of candour at Pixar, the act of giving feedback to others that is earnest and honest, even if it is challenging to hear. But there can be no candour if there is no trust. The best feedback comes from people with whom we have mutual trust. This mutual trust often comes from a shared place: the understanding that we are working towards the same shared goals (Catmull, 2014).

> Who are the people in your life? Who do you trust to give you feedback that you're likely to act on? Is it people you don't know? The people you are afraid of? Or is it the people you love? Friends and family love you, and so their feedback is unreliable. But there's this tiny group of people who give you true feedback. And by that, I mean they go through whatever content it is you are producing, they internalise it, and they communicate to you how it could be better.
>
> – JASON IMMS, HEAD OF QUALITY ASSURANCE,
> KEYWORDS STUDIOS

While I was working as a Producer, I had many of these conversations with our technical lead. We had substantial differences of opinion about how the project should go: they wished to see it be the best it could be, and I wished to ensure that it was good and released on time. Our common ground was the project and the fact that we trusted one another to be working towards the same goal: to get the game released and make it as good as it could be.

We would argue most certainly, but it was Socratic in nature. They would state their good intent for polish time or a feature addition and how it would benefit the project, I would acknowledge I saw the value, but then counter with the facts about our time or budgetary constraints. There were no losers in these debates: we found a shared understanding, and nobody was left unhappy. We never would have been able to do that if we did not know we were both just trying to ensure the best possible outcome for the project.

The most important takeaway from all of this is the importance of allowing ourselves time in a conversation to think. We are prone to making mistakes if we fixate on the need to react quickly or avoid awkward pauses. The time it will take for us to briefly consider our feelings and our words is essential to better communication and benefits our ability to truly listen to others. This is only scratching the surface of the importance of communication, however.

Being such an essential skill, there are a huge variety of resources on the subject of communication. Recommendations I often see coming from people in the games industry refer to titles such as "How To

Win Friends and Influence People" by Dale Carnegie (Carnegie, 1982), "Difficult Conversations: How to Discuss What Matters Most" by Douglas Stone, Sheila Heen, and Bruce Patton (Stone, Patton and Heen, 2010), and "Thanks for the Feedback: The Science and Art of Receiving Feedback Well," also by Sheila Heen and Douglas Stone (Stone and Heen, 2014). Much of what I have discussed here barely begins to summarise what is covered in these excellent pieces of literature.

INDIVIDUALITY

There's a concept in teaching about differentiation; the ability to teach the same concept to multiple people by recognising they all learn differently. This isn't just a matter of creating more content for the classroom to consume, but rather to present that content in a variety of ways that everybody can understand and follow along with. In teaching games development, the way this usually surfaces is by introducing the concept we're about to discuss on a slide, discussing the problem with students, and then giving them the opportunity to explore it. While they explore, the facilitator goes to each of them to see where they are and what they understand or do not understand about the problem.

In teaching foundational programming techniques, there are a variety of different levels of experience that will be in the classroom. Those people who saw games development as an opportunity to explore an art that they were passionate about and those who had already started dabbling with development on the side. Differentiation not only recognises this difference but also that among these two groups of students that there'll be different ways that each of them also learn the information they are engaged with. There will be students who see programming as simply being too hard and need to be guided into understanding it and seeing it as less intimidating. There will be others who simply smash through the problem with ease and need new challenges in order to not become bored. And there will be everything in between.

> Some people are better at self-managing than others, no matter their level of seniority. Some will reach out to you if they need it and if they trust you, but those with good self-management still require direction at times and it can be easy to forget to connect with them proactively.
>
> – ALAYNA COLE, DIVERSITY EQUITY AND INCLUSION
> MANAGER, SLEDGEHAMMER GAMES

This was one of the first and most important concepts that I came to understand when I first started teaching. In the classroom, each of our individual students is the "product." We are aiming to create the best possible version of each individual student. The product is not the classroom of students or an output of the classroom of students – that is purely their concern. For teachers it's easy to come to respect differentiation and the need to understand each student to extract the best possible work out of each one. So when we talk about people, we are talking about seeing them as individuals in the same way. We aren't leading a team or leading development on a project; we are leading a group of individuals. And that means differentiating our leadership style for each individual person to guide the best possible results from their work.

The role of leadership is one that is focused on working with groups of human beings, and there comes a degree of unpredictability and challenge whenever working with people. The bard takes this concept one step further, understanding and recognising that the people we work with are individuals with their own lives, preferences, values, and desires. One of the bards superpowers is the ability to work with people as individuals: to help them figure out what they want and need within a team or on a project. And through doing so, build trust and more collaborative teams. So why is understanding the individual so important?

> What are you great at? What can we encourage you to do that you can make the best use of your strengths?
>
> – ANNA BARHAM, MANAGING DIRECTOR,
> BALANCING MONKEY GAMES

It's not enough to just lead people. Each individual person in our team is somebody that we will only be able to lead effectively if we understand them and build our trust with them as individuals. There's a reason that so many game studios have moved to reduce the number of people that leaders manage as direct reports – there's only so many people with whom we can be familiar enough to consider "knowable," with whom we can empathise.

You may have heard of this concept. Proposed by anthropologist Robin Dunbar as "Dunbar's number," it identifies the limit of maintainable social relationships (Dunbar, 1992). Alternatively, you may have heard it referred to as the "monkeysphere," as coined by comedy author David Wong in an article for Cracked.com (Wong, 2007). This number is about 150 people, and includes our friends, family, and colleagues. It can be imagined as concentric rings with us at the centre. The further out we get, the less connected we are to those people – usually as a result of the limited contact we have with them.

Mark Noseworthy talks about this problem in his 2014 GDC talk, discussing how Bungie started to run up against the monkeysphere as a real problem when the studio expanded out to larger scales. Tasks started getting done slower due to the sheer number of contacts that a person would need to manage to implement something that would have only taken a few days during development when the studio was far smaller.

To tackle this problem, Bungie shifted their internal structure to account for smaller teams, which they called "strike teams." These smaller teams would include a producer, designer, artist, programmer – whatever people were necessary to get a specific element of the game completed in a meaningful way. They would be assigned collective responsibility for a user story such as "the grenade I throw blows up the enemies shields with an impressive flash." This small team would then collaborate to solve this problem, doing all the necessary work to achieve their task (Noseworthy, 2014).

David Wong's writing on the subject provides meaningful insights into why this concept is so important to us as leaders. The further out from the centre of our monkeysphere that people get, the harder it becomes to see them as people. If I were to ask you about your close friends, you would be able to imagine faces and names. But what if I were to ask you the name of the person who delivers your mail or makes your coffee?

Imagine we work in the programming department. We are informed of a decision made by an artist to change something about the work we have been doing. As we do not have immediate direct contact with that person, it's easier to be frustrated with them. When we send back that strongly worded e-mail demanding answers, we are similarly that faceless cause of anxiety to them that we took the artist for in the first place.

Group cohesion fails, and the team breaks up into tribes of cliques. It is human nature to "other" the people we are unfamiliar with, putting them in a group separate and different from our own. The programming team are our friends because we know them as individuals in our tribe, but those artists are a group that is strange and unknown to us.

As leaders, we want to move our direct reports as close to the centre of our monkeysphere as we can. These should be the people we see consistently and who we want to grow to understand as individuals. By strengthening our understanding of them as a person, we can foster that bond of trust and work with them to not only achieve the goals of our team and project but also to further their goals as an individual. What do they want? What appeals to them about their job? Maybe they are interested in pursuing something new, and there's an opportunity we can give them to dabble in that task. By understanding what motivates people, it becomes a lot easier to guarantee the best possible work by putting them on tasks or providing them with responsibilities that they are motivated to do.

> A leader needs to have a diversity of knowledge and a diverse approach to the subject matter. They need to understand people's individual limitations and potential.
>
> – ANONYMOUS

This does not require us to befriend every person that we lead. While strengthening bonds and forming meaningful relationships with them as individuals is important, simply working together in the same place should not assume that friendship is a requirement. Instead, it should be a relationship of mutual respect and trust. We consider that person somebody we can rely upon, and they feel the same about us.

If we are leading a team of people who have their own reports, it's unreasonable to expect to be a core part of their monkeyspheres too. Often times, simply making ourselves known consistently and leaving a good impression will be enough. By internally visualising our monkeysphere and the people around us, it'll be easier to identify where we should be investing more or less of our energy. We only have so much to give others before we aren't giving them our very best.

A concept shared with me by my psychologist is this idea about bandwidth. I had a habit of saying "yes" to opportunities often, which resulted in me having very little energy to do any of them – even when I wasn't engaging with them much. Just the weight of those things needing to be done requires bandwidth, and I believe that this also applies to managing others within our monkeysphere. We only have so much social bandwidth to spend on people, which is why it's so important to consider who we invite into our monkeysphere at our place of work. If they aren't somebody we will be working with often, it's okay to only be an acquaintance. I'd go so far as to say it's necessary to draw that line and to decide for yourself where you want to foster relationships and where you are okay with just checking in now and then.

This has been something I've had to spend a great deal of time thinking about during my career as a teacher. I will have multiple groups of students in my care within a year. In order to ensure that they take away the most benefit from my teaching, trust and respect are immensely important. And so in the short time I spend with those students, I invest a great deal of my personal time and energy into fostering that relationship with them so that they feel safe turning to me for my support. But once they move on to their next set of classes, it's essential that I put my energy into the next group of students.

This may sound cold, but it is the unfortunate reality of the circumstances. I would love to follow many of these students through the entirety of their studies and even out to their careers, but doing so comes at a cost to my current students, and so there must be a line drawn about how much further energy I will invest in those students. Of course, there are exceptions – those students with whom I foster genuine friendships or who show exceptional skills that I wish to further mentor. But if we already have 150 people in our monkeysphere – and it is likely that we do in our adult life – then choosing to add somebody new will push out somebody else we desire to care about.

Once we build up those relationships and begin to understand the people around us better, what next? Other than understanding what motivates the people around us, we will also begin to understand more about their needs and their current circumstances. This gives us more opportunities to do good by them and – by extension – the team and the work we are doing. Much of this ties into the concepts of emotional intelligence and empathy that we will discuss once we're discussing the skills of the cleric but consider for a moment that a member of our team suddenly starts performing poorly. With that trust and mutual respect, and by being closer to the centre of their monkeysphere, a conversation about their performance and what's going on suddenly becomes much easier to have.

> I had a boss years ago who gave me a very negative performance review because he felt I was too close to my staff. He said your job isn't to be their friend, your job is to be their boss. I carried that for a long time, I had a lot of internal conflict because my experience said that's not true. Because when I have a problem with their behaviour or their work, and I sit down and go, hey, it's me talking, you need to cut it out. They hear me because we're close. They feel admonished because it's somebody friendly to them telling them a truth.
>
> – JASON IMMS, HEAD OF QUALITY ASSURANCE,
> KEYWORDS STUDIOS

Some people will want more strict guidance and direction. This isn't necessarily due to a lack of confidence or experience, but it could very well be just how they prefer to work. Seek to understand just how much guidance each member of our team requires. Game developers are creatives, and direction is a spectrum. We won't be hovering over their shoulders, telling them how to do their job, but do they need daily task assignments? Do they need greater detail in our expectations of them? Do they desire us to provide them with mentorship?

Once we have this established, we can build an understanding of what they envision for themselves. Where do they want to be, what do they want to do, what do they need that we can provide, how can we help get them there? One-on-ones are a great opportunity to gather this sort of information from our team. With this knowledge, we can begin to answer the question of where each individual fits into the broader scope of the project, the business, and their careers beyond it.

Knowing people also enables us to ensure that they are getting all their needs met. Maslow's hierarchy of needs is a concept proposed by American psychologist Abraham Maslow in his paper on human motivation (Maslow, 1943). The hierarchy of needs is popularly visualised as a pyramid, with a foundation of physiological needs that extends upwards into safety needs, the need for love and belonging, the need for esteem, and the need for self-actualisation at the very peak. As we ascend the pyramid, these needs become more challenging to meet – requiring both external and internal validation. The base tier of the hierarchy of needs is primarily met through wages and employment, which provide the members of our team with those basic physiological needs. As leaders, we are primarily concerned with the top four needs of our teams – safety, belonging, esteem, and self-actualisation.

1. Self-Actualisation – The best we can be.

2. Esteem – Respect, recognition, freedom.

3. Love and Belonging – Friendship, family, connection.

4. Safety Needs – Employment, resources, health.

5. Physiological needs – Food, shelter, sleep.

Safety is the point at which many game development studios inadvertently fail members of their staff. The need for safety is primarily met through security, health, employment, and resources – the income a business provides. These are all things that should be met by the time we are interacting with members of our team, but the unfortunate reality is that we do need to concern ourselves with this tier due to the unpredictability of the games industry. People cannot feel their need for safety is met if they are being thrust from one disaster into the next, which is why our ability to protect them as a Warrior is so important to this need. If the members of our team do not feel safe – either with secure employment or with psychological safety – we will never be able to ensure they are in a position to meet those top-tier needs in the hierarchy.

We will be talking about culture as part of the many other considerations of the bard, but love and belonging can be met through the environment we help to foster within our studio. By building a culture of connection within our teams, people can feel a sense of safety and belonging among their peers – though it's important to recognise that this can never replace true friendship and family. While we should endeavour to ensure that the environment our teams work in is accepting and gratifying places to be, we should be encouraging people to embrace and make connections external to work as well for the sake of their personal health. We cannot allow our teams to be defined solely by their employment.

It's less about finding a career that brings you joy, and more about finding a career that facilitates joy in your life. Because your job is just meant to pay your bills. It isn't meant to fill your cup. So there's a toxicity and danger in a creative indistry like ours where people are looking to their job to be the be all and end all of their identity and their fulfillment.

– JEAN LEGGETT, LEADERSHIP COACH

The need for esteem similarly arises not only out of the culture we foster in our teams, but it can also come more directly from us as leaders. By ensuring that our workplaces are environments in which people respect and recognise one another for their achievements, individuals will be one step closer to having their need for esteem met. The bard is exceptionally good at this, and we'll talk about meeting the need for esteem as part of the chapters on Advocacy and Empowerment.

Finally, the need for self-actualisation is easily the most challenging for the members of our team to achieve and the most challenging for us to help them find. Self-actualisation is about achieving those self-set goals and improving oneself. Described by Maslow as including creativity and problem solving, game development is well positioned to easily provide these needs. However, it often falls short for a variety of reasons. Self-actualisation requires some degree of internal reflection and will usually be easier for those members of our team who have had some more experience and know where they want to go in their careers. By knowing those members of our team who haven't figured out their direction yet, we can work with them to achieve self-actualisation.

Look beyond the value that each person brings to the team in terms of their role or expertise, and work to understand more about who they are. What motivates them, where do they want to go, what do they want to do next, and are there challenges they wish to undertake within the team? If we can learn more about their individual vision for themselves or the project, we have a new way to build trust as we enable them to do their best work.

People need to feel like they have room to grow. That their interests are being considered and looked after.

– ALAYNA COLE, DIVERSITY EQUITY AND INCLUSION
MANAGER, SLEDGEHAMMER GAMES

People are at the core of everything we do as leaders. We work with people, and by working to see them each as a unique individual, it's much easier to see and understand how we can better lead them. This is a concept that bleeds through into everything we discuss in this book. Think back to the previous chapter on vision, and imagine a member of our team who may not see the value in the work we are doing. How have we presented our vision to them? Has it just been a speech, or can we approach the conversation in a different way that appeals more to them as an individual? Is there a part in our vision where they play a specific role, and it overlaps with their vision for where they want to be and how they want to grow as a developer and a person?

This is a turning point in how we talk about leadership. It's no longer just about making great projects but it is also creating great teams. Much like my earlier example about the classroom, I believe that there is value in seeing the people we surround ourselves with as the product we develop as leaders. A great game may just be a fluke, but a great team is positioned for repeat success. Our role as their leader isn't just to ensure that they are doing their best possible work to achieve our goals as a business, but also to ensure that they are enthusiastic and have the trust necessary to do so again in the future.

ADVOCACY

Advocacy is a subject that's difficult to describe, as it is so many things. In political movements, advocacy is all about creating change, usually by bringing to light the needs of underrepresented groups. Leading your teams and advocating for the underrepresented groups and individuals within them is certainly a key goal of advocacy, but that is not where it ends. The rising tide raises all ships. Advocacy is about not only looking out for those individuals to make our studio fair and equitable but also to empower everyone and provide them with opportunities for success. It's about elevating individuals to have the opportunity to learn and grow. It is about enabling the members of the team to be the masters of their own destinies.

There is a great deal of overlap between the concepts of advocacy and the ideas of servant leadership. If enabling the team means that we are stepping back and providing them with the freedom to choose how they work and operate, then advocacy can be seen as a means of providing them with the tools they need to excel. It is using our power to ensure that the people around us are empowered. It could be as simple as advocating for them to get the time off they requested.

All this makes advocacy rather challenging to understand. During my research and interviews, it took me a great deal of time to understand the breadth and depth of ways in which a leader can advocate for their team. But a recurring anecdote in the meetings helped me better understand what it is we are trying to achieve with advocacy. We are not a family, we're a sports team. The sports team has clear objectives: score goals and win games. There is a clear separation between the role of the players and our role as their leader – the coach. We are responsible for looking out for the health and happiness of the members of our team because they are the ones who go out and score the goals.

> I hate it when companies say hey, we're all a family here. The best anal-ogy I've heard is that we're a sports team, and I am the coach. I need to get the most goals out of you all while making sure that you're healthy and happy. If you're unhealthy you're not going to score goals, and if you are unhappy you're going to change teams. I need you to stay on my team, happy and scoring the most goals possible. This isn't a Utopian situation though, because the honest truth is that if you're not able to score goals, then we may need to find another role for you. It's my responsibility to communicate to you what the expectations are honestly and truthfully, with enough time, criteria, and support for you to pivot.
>
> – OSAMA DORIAS, LEAD GAMEPLAY DESIGNER,
> BRASS LION ENTERTAINMENT

I bring this up to discuss advocacy as it's a very useful way to describe and understand what it is exactly that we're doing. As the coach, we are always looking for ways to improve the performance of the members of our team. Having our star player out every game may lead to great short-term success. But if we have players who sit on the sidelines and never get to play, that's a quick way to burn out our star players. It benefits everybody if we give those sidelined players opportunities to improve and allow them to step up and have more time on the field. In Leading So People Will Follow, Erika Andersen refers to this concept as generosity (Andersen, 2012). We are choosing to pass the ball to provide others in our team with the sort of opportunities we wish that we had when we were in their position.

This isn't necessarily as simple as it sounds. It may mean that our star player plays in less games, and we will need to help them understand why that is. We do not want them to be unhappy because we are pulling them from games to protect their health, but we also need to look out for the happiness of others in our team who may feel they have not had a chance to shine. Or perhaps those sidelined players lack confidence and feel like they are being put under a lot of pressure when we ask them to go out onto the field. This isn't about putting them at risk of failure, but about providing them with opportunities where we see that they have a great chance of success and building their personal confidence.

To advocate for individuals effectively in this way, we need to be able to understand them. We need to have a sense of what they want, what drives them, and where they want to be. The star player may like being in every game, but do they manage to be in every game? How are they holding up physically, emotionally? The player on the sidelines may not want to play at all. Why have we hired them then? Why are they here? What do they want to achieve? Sometimes, to ensure that the members of our team can kick goals, they will have to be made a little uncomfortable.

> Sometimes I will throw people in the deep end, but always be transparent with them when I am doing so. It depends on my rapport with the individual, the context of the task, and what they are interested in. But if I am confident that they could handle the task and they just lack the confidence, then I will try to give them those opportunities to show themselves they can do it.
>
> – ALAYNA COLE, DIVERSITY EQUITY AND INCLUSION MANAGER, SLEDGEHAMMER GAMES

Of course making people uncomfortable isn't the goal here. But it is important to not avoid these difficult conversations out of a concern for making people uncomfortable. Much like other skills that we have discussed so far, advocacy benefits a great deal from the skills of the cleric to understand when and how to press people in this way. Taking responsibility for the health and happiness of the team will often mean having to have difficult conversations about their individual contributions. It may require giving them a push to get out on the field, or to take some time to sit on the sidelines and have a breather. We are thinking about their long-term health and happiness.

Thinking about advocacy in this way was what helped me move away from the idea that it was all external. The kind of advocacy one imagines involves convincing stakeholders or senior leadership to give our team or an individual within it the chance to do something interesting. This is certainly part of being an advocate for our team, but it's only a very small part of it. You may be doing more of this if you find yourself dealing with partners at a larger studio or if you are responsible for a small indie team. But for the majority of leaders, their advocacy is usually more team-facing.

As a leader, we have a perspective over the team and connections that give us a greater understanding of everything happening in the business. This perspective gives us the ability to identify opportunities that may align with the needs of our business, the current project, the team, or the individuals that report to us. We want to advocate for these opportunities to go where they would do the most good. So advocacy is at least partially about getting our team members provided with opportunities.

More than just seeking out opportunities, we have the power to create opportunities. Is there a conference in a few months that would greatly benefit the team if they attended it? In our roles, we can advocate for that conference attendance to be available to any member of the business. We are not limited by the existing incentives and opportunities that the business has made available. If we can formulate a good business case for it, then our position as leaders gives us the ability to step into a room with senior leadership and make such a pitch.

You can see examples of such opportunities in the games industry in terms of diversity initiatives. These aren't just about hiring diverse staff or putting them into positions of power. It is about identifying potential biases that exist in hiring practices and advocating for change by highlighting the benefits. Creating a diverse team of developers isn't about denying opportunities; it's about the creation of new ones. And the business case for such a thing is strong: more diverse teams have the capacity to create more diverse games that have a wider appeal if those diverse voices are heard.

Such an initiative isn't about silencing existing voices but elevating the ones that are unheard. In doing so, we want to ensure that all voices in our teams are heard. It's not just about advocating for those who are underrepresented, but ensuring that the way we choose to operate our teams is equitable and moral. That means that no one group is given priority over another. Our advocacy supports the whole team, to give them whatever it is that they require to succeed.

We can definitely do more to advocate for underrepresented people to make sure they have more opportunities, whether that be getting employed by an organisation, getting promoted, or being retained because they have opportunities for professional development. They feel supported and appreciated, those sorts of things. But advocacy is never just about those who are underrepresented. It's making sure that the things we are doing support everybody. That everybody gets these benefits.

– ALAYNA COLE, DIVERSITY EQUITY AND INCLUSION
MANAGER, SLEDGEHAMMER GAMES

These are high-level ways in which we can advocate, but we can also do it on smaller scales. Those low-confidence sidelined players will need us to advocate for them directly. To express our faith in their ability to get the job done and to feel safe should they happen to fail. This is about increasing their confidence, reducing their aversion to risk, and giving them an opportunity to grow into a stronger member of the team. It requires us to have the courage to give them the opportunity so that they may build upon their own courage. This individual-level advocacy is all about empowerment.

It's no secret that game developers suffer from impostor syndrome, comparing themselves to their peers and finding themselves lacking (Langford and Clance, 1993). Empowerment is all about giving individuals the confidence to see their own capacity. It is an immensely powerful way to build trust, as you are choosing to take a chance on somebody who may not see in themselves what you have identified in them. It may take some time for them to build the confidence to really appreciate the opportunity that you gave them, but they will certainly not forget the time that you told them you believed them up to the task.

When I set out to start my own team, one of my key values was empowerment. Our project was small, and our budget was tiny. I expected that there would be motivation issues if people only had a small allocation of funds to a project that they may only work on a few weeks out of the year. And so I started to give the members of my team ownership over their parts of the game. In a sense, I was elevating them to lead positions. Our team is just a handful of developers; it may be easy for them to look to me for my decision on each element of the game. But I made the choice to make them leaders in their own right and to look instead to them for their insights on the things that they do best.

Often this required reinforcing their skills and expressing my trust in them to get the job done and to do it well. I found myself often telling people, "I hired you because you are an expert at this thing, and I am not. Do what you think is right." And people aren't used to that, but it certainly does motivate them. The writing? That's yours now. And when those reviews come in and people say, "this game had an incredible story," that's a success that person owns as an individual. At first I felt this idea of empowering individuals to truly own their work was something I could only really suggest for small teams. But there is little stopping a leader, even in a larger studio, from handing the reigns over to an individual or a small team and telling them, this thing is yours; make it sing.

> Elevating others is the number one priority of a leader. It's to use your experience and your knowledge and the lessons that you've learned to help people avoid making the same mistakes you have made, so that they can grow faster than you did. It's to help them see themselves in a way you never did, depending on the kind of leadership you had around you as you were coming up. So that they can observe their blind spots a little bit sooner than you did, and creating opportunities for them. It's not about hoarding opportunities for yourself because you're the boss or the most experienced person in the room. It's about finding opportunities for others and handing them over willingly. And I think that when you do that you're not taking anything off of your own plate, you're making the plate bigger. Making everybody's plate bigger.
>
> – JASON IMMS, HEAD OF QUALITY ASSURANCE,
> KEYWORDS STUDIOS

Larian Studios, the creators of the critically acclaimed Baldurs Gate 3, made the decision to assign specific writers to specific characters. This decision meant that each writer could become intimately familiar with their character and write them with their own unique voice, their own desires, and their own unique reactions to the games many permutations of events (Clay, 2023). The characters are performed by their actors not just in voice but also in motion capture. The voice actors could similarly become intimately familiar with their characters and the writing and perform them appropriately (Broadwell, 2023).

None of what Larian did on Baldurs Gate 3 is particularly normal in this way. It's highly unusual for the writing process to not be fully collaborative, with writers bouncing around from character to character wherever they are necessary. It's even more unusual for a voice actor to even be a motion capture actor, unless they are a particularly high-profile performer. But the benefits of providing such ownership over character roles in this respect are clear in the result. The names of these individual writers and actors and their roles in the game's success are well known to the fans of the game.

Where it's not possible to give an individual total ownership over the result of a piece of work, we can provide that responsibility to a smaller team. Faced with a swelling studio size that reduced their collaborative ability, Bungie moved to smaller strike teams. These strike teams would include multiple disciplines and be given ownership over a feature of the game (Noseworthy, 2014). This sort of structuring once again allows for small-scale individual empowerment, even in a large-scale studio. While this isn't necessarily likely to result in the same level of celebrity that Baldurs Gate's writers and actors have found, it allows an individual to feel empowered to effect measurable change on a game that is immense in scale.

Empowerment like this is still an opportunity. It is giving the members of our team the power to effect change and have some influence on the outcome of the work that you are creating. As we discussed in the chapter on enabling, nobody in games development has joined this industry to be told how to do their work. They want to take on interesting creative challenges. They want to be able to have the opportunity to flex their creativity and make art. If you do not trust the people that you have hired, or if you are concerned about creative control, it is very easy to hamper their creativity and – by extension – their ownership over the final result.

There are many leaders I have met in my career who have been afraid of providing opportunities for individuals. It usually comes out of a fear of opportunities, growing people beyond their job, or finding other work. It's easy to see how this fear is likely founded on a desire for control or an over-reliance on the output of these team members. But advocating for the individual members of your team demonstrates a care for them that goes beyond the current project or job. It is caring for them as a person. It is enabling them to be the masters of their own destiny.

Hampering the creativity and growth of the members of our team is a quick way to lose their trust. The only reason to fear that a team member may leave as a result of your advocacy is if you are aware that the circumstances of the business or even of your individual leadership are poor enough that there's an expectation of them wishing to leave in the first place. It is usually borne out of a desire for control or an overreliance on the output of a key set of individuals. The reality is that denying the members of your team opportunities in a misguided attempt to keep them around will only achieve the opposite. They will look at our leadership as being what it is – entirely self-serving.

So as you go to advocate for your team, do as the bard does. Sing their praises about them and to them. Inspire them about their own capacity for success, and provide them with the opportunities to better themselves and prove their prowess. Think beyond the current project and even beyond the current business. A good leader advocates for the team to create great games, but a great leader advocates for the team to become great game developers.

Inspiring

One of the biggest factors of my job is nurturing the relationship between the audio team and all the other disciplines. What I've discovered is a lot of other disciplines who work here don't understand audio. It's not their main focus, a lot of the teams here are very visually focused, even programming. So I think communication and perspective of everybody involved is super important. You have to make sure that other disciplines understand why your team is doing what it's doing, what works, and what doesn't.

But that takes a lot of work. You have designers, you have concept artists, you have producers, you have programmers. There's all these different disciplines who are super good at what they do, but they all have different perspectives. So you have to really encourage and grow relationships around those disciplines communicating not only correctly but productively. And that's really hard.

I've done years of work at Double Fine, I actually feel like the studio understands audio now. And we achieved that through location safaris with the other disciplines. We got a bunch of portable recorders, and took along programmers, artists, and Producers out to record sounds on location. We taught them how to record things. That's kinetic learning. When they got back and listened to what they purposefully recorded themselves, it blew up their perspectives.

Our mantra was to make every team the audio team. And it's worked. These are people now thinking about how you could make a game by starting with sound. That was unheard of when I started here. These are people who are always trying to educate themselves, so all I really had to do was show them how this works and make it interesting. And now they cannot get enough of it. It's super collaborative, and it's just because they got a taste for it.

– CAMDEN STODDARD, AUDIO DIRECTOR, DOUBLE FINE

DOI: 10.1201/9781003431626-10

Bards are known for their charisma. Smooth talking and versatile, a bard can really be anything they want to be – or convince you they are something they are not. This skill can be pivotal to avoid a conflict, but speaking can feel far less useful when it's time to get into the thick of it. The truth is that the real power of the bard isn't necessarily about speaking. That's a key skill for them, for sure, but it's not the reason you want a bard leading your team. The thing that makes bards so powerful is their capacity to inspire.

Inspiration is a game-changer. If speaking is about understanding others to persuade them to action, inspiration is providing them with a reason to care. We work in a creative field where we want people to care about the work they do and the people they do it with because they will be doing this thing together for years. The team that genuinely cares about the work and one another will find that there is drastically less friction when challenges inevitably find them.

In moments where hope is waning and all seems lost, the bard can inspire a team back to their feet. They aren't healers; they cannot simply make the pain go away. But they can help a team find their second wind. This isn't about useless optimism in the face of overwhelming odds; it's about helping a party navigate their doubts to find the strength they need to overcome the odds. A bard cannot change the circumstances that put the team in danger. But we can help our team find their capacity to meet challenges head-on.

It's not unusual for the bard leader to be one of the key reasons that people stick around when the situation feels bleak. This isn't our goal necessarily, but a side effect of our influence. We want to foster an environment that is positive and supportive and that people wish to remain in. Our influence has the capacity to inspire others to feel that they are at their best when they are working with the team to solve problems and create something wonderful.

The challenge of inspiration is the fact that we are often only outside observers. We want to provide our teams with the freedom and space to explore, and so we watch over them to ensure they don't stray too far into danger. We cannot create happiness in our studios; it's not as simple as just buying pizza and coming to the office with a smile. And we certainly are not going to create culture; that is something that goes far beyond the actions of an individual. Instead, we watch, and we influence the team with a gentle touch. It would not be inspiration if we forced them to take the actions we wanted to see.

In many ways, inspiring others is the next step to enabling them. Whereas before we may have been simply giving them the space to achieve the work without our influence, now we are bringing our influence back in order to encourage their creativity. We want to see them understand the value of their work, to understand the possibility space we've provided them to work within, and to feel like they are part of a larger whole. It's not enough to simply stand back and let them do the work from a distance; they need to feel that it matters. True inspiration comes from embracing creativity.

VISION

In retail, management is king. Retail revolves around the concept of achieving key performance indicators or KPIs for short. If you have ever worked in a retail environment where achieving KPIs was the goal, you would likely have had one of two experiences: the carrot or the stick. With the carrot, management would reward achieving certain outcomes. If we managed to achieve so many add-ons to our sales, there may be some sort of reward involved. The stick usually involved punishment for not meeting targets, often in the form of reduced hours.

The point of the carrot or the stick is to incentivise behaviour. We don't really care about the reason why, only about what the outcome means to us. Having a team meeting and hearing our manager tell us that they want to see the team increase warranty sales by 20% at the end of the quarter is not vision. We have no reason to care, no reason to be invested in this arbitrary outcome. It's meaningless to us as to why it's so important. Some businesses may try to express a vision in which every customer has a great time, but that simply does not align with the reality of achieving sales targets. So most employees see it as what it is: an attempt to make them care about creating value for the company.

In order to fund my studies I spent some time working in retail. The manager of the store I worked at was a good guy; he cared about the work he did and the performance of the staff at the store. At meetings, he would talk about KPI's, but instead of focusing on the percentages or the employee incentives (which didn't really exist at this business anyway), he focused his energy on selling us on competition. Our store was in competition with the other stores in the chain throughout the country, and we had been recognised for our performance. But now there were other stores that were creeping up on us, and our manager wanted us to get that award.

It got the team enthusiastic, for a time. It eventually became clear that there was really no benefit in it for us. Attendance at the award ceremony was for managers only, who would have their flights and accommodations paid for by the business. When the team won the award, it was the manager who received a trophy. Everybody quickly realised that it wasn't our incentive to win; it was the managers. The new employees tended to work this out pretty quickly and lost interest in the competition just as fast. Why would we care about getting a trophy for somebody else?

A repeated phrase I heard during the research for this book is that the difference between leadership and management is vision. At first it seemed like a strange line to draw, but the more we discussed the subject the clearer the distinction became. A leader may be a manager, but a manager is not necessarily a leader. The difference is in how much people care about our objectives. True vision is achieved only when we can get our team invested and aligned with our goals and then provide them with the freedom to execute on it in the way they see fit. True leadership isn't in KPIs, projects, or math: it's in people. We need people to care about our vision for the future.

> Vision is independent of the project. The four day work week is a topic of vision. You are communicating to people that they are signing up for a more condensed work week. You need to provide clarity around what you believe that looks like for them. That's vision.
>
> – KEITH FULLER, LEADERSHIP CONSULTANT,
> FOUNDER OF GAMEDEVCOACHING.COM

This is why vision is a trait of leaders and not of managers. Managers are focused on measurable outcomes. They are absolutely capable of leadership and expressing vision, but it's a distinction that is lost on many managers. Most managers are primarily interested in the specific steps necessary to reach a destination. They may have a vision for the future, but this isn't shared with the team. They may get a team to care about achieving KPIs as it can be made clear why it matters to them as an individual. But the team does not understand why KPIs matter in the big picture other than to create value for the business.

How do we navigate our way out when we are faced with challenges? A manager may sit down and do the math, plotting out the specific work that needs to get done. They may set performance objectives and direct the team to achieve them. For the team, there's no clear way out of the circumstances. It is business as usual, or perhaps they are being placed under more pressure than they have come to expect. The leader may do the same math, but they explain to the team what they will achieve by reaching the goals. They get the team invested in the outcome. The leader provides the team with a light at the end of the tunnel.

There's leadership and then there's management, and there are different skillsets involved in both - but also a ton of overlap. Vision is a leadership skill, but not a management skill. If you imagine a games development as exploring an unexplored place, management will hack their way through the jungle for others to follow. A leader will climb the nearest tree and check the path ahead, pointing it out for everyone.

– KEITH FULLER, LEADERSHIP CONSULTANT,
FOUNDER OF GAMEDEVCOACHING.COM

While a manager cuts a way through the jungle to create a path for the team, the leader climbs the trees and points in the general direction. Sometimes we need to clear a path for our teams, but there's little room to explore when we do so. Management carves a path to the solution that they need the team to achieve. It is effective at achieving a singular objective when we know the path to take. But if we are to continue discovering exciting new experiences, then we need to incentivise exploration and experimentation within our teams. We need them to feel that they are empowered to find solutions that their leadership has not even begun to imagine.

Vision is direction, adventure, and embracing the unknown. It is choosing a direction and exploring what is found along the way. It's communicating with people so they can see it the way we do, and then empowering them to achieve it. But we cannot inspire people to act if they do not understand why they should care, or what it is they are expected to do. Vision starts with us as individuals, but once shared, it becomes part of the collective. It should grow and change as we share it and explore the possibilities available to us. But it can only be our vision if everybody understands why it matters.

Director roles are individual contributors. They are there to provide direction. They're not there to tell you what they like and don't like about your work. And if they think that's the case, they are the most expensive play testers in the industry. Their role is to provide clarity of direction, a vision, not an idea they had or the things they like. Vision comes with a necessity for clarity on its execution and how it fits into the whole, and if you are not able to provide that, then you are not a director. It's the same if you are a lead. If you're not there to facilitate the work of the team, then you are not a lead. You are just a person who has a position of power over your team.

– OSAMA DORIAS, LEAD GAMEPLAY DESIGNER,
BRASS LION ENTERTAINMENT

For this purpose we need to ensure that we are providing our teams with clarity. They need to understand the why, the how, and the what.

- "What" is about setting expectations, and should communicate to the team just how much freedom they have to explore within that vision.

- "Why" is all about the importance of the mission, it is why the team should care.

- "How" entails making the vision believable, and enabling the team to see their role in getting it done.

Providing clarity of vision requires that we be clear on what things should look like once we are done. Key to this is setting reasonable expectations and being clear on the constraints. When we enable our teams to explore, they need to know what at what point they may have strayed too far from the vision. It is our roles as leaders that we provide them with a space within which they can experiment and know they are still generally headed in the right direction.

Imagine that vision is a direction on a compass. We choose a number of degrees from true North that we wish to head, and we set those as our left and right constraints. We tell the team about the sort of adventures that we expect to have along the way, we pack our things, and we head out together. We want to encourage the team to be willing to take the least tread path, to zig-zag and wander, just not too far out of those set constraints. We always keep a watchful eye, it's up to us to decide how many degrees from our direction that we are happy for the team to explore. There will be a point at which we are required to step in and help our team get back in the direction we want them heading.

> You have to have major clarity, because video games are just so complex. You really have to start out super clear, and sometimes that's not possible. Sometimes it's an indie game jam or it's a basic concept that has a lot of promise, so you can't start with that clarity. But you have to get there fairly quickly, because it's a creative product, but it's also software, and those things are married inextricably.
>
> – CAMDEN STODDARD, AUDIO DIRECTOR, DOUBLE FINE

We need to consider the bigger picture when we are setting our constraints. Are we doing something truly experimental? How much time and money do we have at our disposal to explore? Is there scope for adding tasks? If we are working on a sequel and have limited time to get it done, then it is likely that the amount of creative freedom entrusted to the team will simply be smaller than if they were working on something entirely new. Each circumstance will differ dramatically, and so too will the freedom we should allow for our team to interpret our vision.

Some members of our team may require more or less strict constraints and direction provided to them to be comfortable. There will be members of our team who desire mentorship, which usually comes with a tighter vision and direction. These team members may very likely be uncomfortable with those truly exploratory projects. They may return from exploring a dead end and feel they have nothing to show for it. It's important as leaders that we not only choose the right person for the task but also embrace the value of these more exploratory missions. They allow us to identify paths not worth following and reduce the number of possible solutions to our problem.

What types of failure are blame worthy? We intrinsically think that any failure is bad, but in reality it's a spectrum. There are failures that ar blame worthy. But if we are performing hypothetical experiments that nobody has ever attempted before, and we don't get the result we wanted? Well, now you know more than you did before. That's worthy of celebration. That's the culture at Supercell Games, they celebrate shutting down prototypes. Break out the cake and champagne, we learned something.

– KEITH FULLER, LEADERSHIP CONSULTANT,
FOUNDER OF GAMEDEVCOACHING.COM

We need to embrace the creativity of those team members who are more prone to wandering. When these individuals do go off in directions we did not expect, start by checking their heading. How far from true North are they? Have they gone totally outside of our constraints? If so, then gently remind them of the goal and where we are headed. It's not unusual with this sort of exploratory creativity to find team members fixated on tasks that are not necessarily going to contribute to our end goals. Ideally, we are redirecting these team members before they become so invested in the work that we are abandoning weeks or months' worth of their time.

At the centre of all of this is leadership. We define how far we are willing for the team to wander. We check in with individuals to make sure they are comfortable with the level of freedom and the vision we have set out. We ensure they are protected, have all the things they need for their journey, and watch them go. Creative freedom is a spectrum, and the team still requires constraints to achieve the outcomes we want to see. Giving our team a blank cheque to run off and do whatever they want is something we only really want to do when we are exploring the terrain and are.

The key to vision then is understanding what is close enough. If we struggle to communicate clearly exactly what it is we need, then we are in no place to expect exacting results from the members of our team. It is unfair to our teams to have an expectation of perfect results. Our team is not made up of mind readers, and we cannot explain to them in exacting detail how we expect things to look once they are done. The perfect game does not exist. It might be in development, but it will never leave it so long as its leadership is unwilling to settle on close enough.

If you give anybody a mile wide canvas and say draw a picture, are they going to fill the canvas or will they just draw a stick figure in the corner? There's so much between those two extremes, and if they don't have direction then they'll make anything.

– JONATHAN JENNINGS, GAMEPLAY ENGINEER II, OWLCHEMY LABS

Explaining the why to our teams involves helping them understand the future that we desire to create. This could be the future of our business, our projects, our teams, or even the individuals within those teams. We have a perspective over the project that the members of our team will lack, and this allows us to get a better view of the horizon. From this higher perspective we can get a sense of where we want to go next, where we want to be in the coming months or years. We may express a vision for how part of the project is intended to operate, the way we want our team to operate, or the role we want an individual to step into. Our vision should make the team enthusiastic to follow us, to work with us, and to achieve what we imagine for them. Vision is not a directive; it is creating the inspiration to act.

You may have heard vision referred to as buy-in. When we talk about buy-in, we are typically discussing the act of getting our team invested in the product we are trying to create and the outcomes we are trying to achieve. Achieving buy-in on a project means that the team cares about it and desires to see it do well. It may be easier to see how vision is such a key responsibility of leadership when we express it this way. We don't want a team that does not care about the work that we do. We want to align them with an idea that they can then execute with little influence on our behalf.

Buy-in should be the outcome of our shared vision. Our team is enthusiastically embracing the vision we have shared. The reason we tend to use vision rather than buy-in as a term is because we want to discuss more than just the future of the project with our team. While the terms are interchangeable to some extent, buy-in is typically used in the context of the project and the work we do. We can absolutely get a member of our team to buy-in on their own development, but we only achieve that buy-in by sharing with them a clear vision that matters to them.

We can only truly share a vision with our team after we have invested in the other skills of leadership. Successful vision comes from embracing the courage and vulnerability necessary to allow the team to achieve the results we imagine. It requires that we place trust in the team and allow them to find their own way to the destination that we have defined. We need to understand what drives the individual members of our teams so that we can express our vision in terms that matter to them.

Finally, we need to have a shared understanding of how it will all come together. The question of how is a key part of our vision, though it is also a complicated one. We want to avoid being dictatorial or explaining specifically how a task should be completed. For people to truly believe in our vision, they need to believe that it is possible to be achieved. Not only do they need to believe it is achievable, but they need to feel excited and inspired in trying to find a way to make that vision a reality. It needs to be clear how they may find their way to that imagined future.

> You have to have a really clear big picture. But at the same time you also have to be ready for it to be different. You're going to have a lot of people doing extremely complex work, and they are going to want to have creative power to go in their own direction. More than any other job, I have had to be willing to just let go of what I wanted and recognise the value in what somebody else is bringing me. You have to be able to set aside your own thing.
>
> – CAMDEN STODDARD, AUDIO DIRECTOR, DOUBLE FINE

Say that we are making a new game, and we have imagined a unique art style for it. We communicate to the team why this art style matters, but how do we communicate the how? Going to each member of the art team and telling them how to create specific asset the way we imagine is not great vision. It removes any ability for them to explore and interpret our vision. Instead, we could create a mood board to provide the team as we deliver our vision to them. This enables them clearly understand the sort of space we want to arrive, while also giving them the chance to interpret it in their own way.

Leaders who are only willing to express the why are often visionaries with little technical expertise. They are the kind of leader who is more interested in what a product could do, rather than whether if it is possible to create. It can be challenging to describe the how to a team without feeling as though we are directing them. But without understanding the how a team will either rely entirely on its leadership or discard a vision entirely. It is essential that a team see a viable pathway to success, and that we remove anything that gets in the way.

This unwillingness to share the why that we begin to find examples of evil aligned vision. It often exists in a belief that vision is ours alone. Think about the language you use when you are talking to your team: are they working on "your" game or are they working on "our" game? It may form as a reluctance to hear a vision criticised or to see it changed, which usually leads to a more dictatorial style of leadership. Rather than setting constraints to allow a team to explore, these sorts of leaders demand their vision to be created to their exacting specifications. Faced with an outcome that they do not like, they may also choose to change their vision at the cost of the hard work put in by the team.

When I set out with my team to make a game, I envisioned a project and a team that would enable them to explore and experiment. We built this into our culture and into the core understanding of our first game. We leaned into the idea of the final product we were developing being quirky, weird, and experimental. Members of the team were encouraged to come up with unique and interesting ideas for how to tell the story we wanted to tell, and we gave them ownership over those things. By allowing them to explore the space, they got invested in the final product. They shared my vision. And as a result, they have improved the project beyond the limited thing I had first imagined. Providing them the freedom to explore adds value to our project.

The only reason this was possible was because we were aligned with our shared vision. Alignment isn't something we simply achieve; it's maintained. The process of exploring and seeking outcomes will always be pushing the envelope of what is possible within a studio or on a game. Sometimes we will adjust our expectations to align with the discoveries made by our team in order to embrace these discoveries fully. Most of the time we are adjusting individuals to realign with the rest of the team.

People are like marbles on a table. Everybody drifts, and a leader gathers them back together. The leader reminds people of the common goal and vision. They ensure that the team can reach that goal with the least possible steps, the least amount of resistance. And they do all of that with an understanding of the resources available to them.

– ANONYMOUS

Managerial styles and directives have their purpose when schedules are tight, but we do not need to discard vision in the process. If we find ourselves in circumstances where the work needs to get done quickly and efficiently, we still need to provide our team with a sense of their own personal freedom. As leaders, we are a limited resource. We cannot be looking over the shoulders of every individual to ensure the tasks are done as we expect. What we are really doing is narrowing the constraints of what the team can do and how far they can wander. We need to give them the capacity to get the work done as they see fit, provide a clear and precise vision, and be prepared to negotiate upon the outcome.

Negotiation of vision is necessary during these moments where we are constrained and relying on more managerial styles. At this point, it is no longer about achieving our perfect vision of the future – it is about getting the task done. We are no longer in any position to request minor changes if the outcome we receive does not align with our vision. If we have had to negotiate on the quality of the experience in our workplace, then we must be prepared to negotiate on the quality of the output of that workplace.

When those moments inevitably arise in which we must be quick and directive, it's essential that we also provide them with a vision of the future. While in these places of stress and anxiety, it can be easy to feel like they will remain forever. This can negatively impact on the productivity and morale of our teams if we do not provide them with the reassurance that it is only temporary. Envision a place for them beyond our current circumstances in which they have the capacity to take more time to explore and solve problems with little intervention from us. It is then our responsibility to have the integrity to deliver that envisioned future to our team.

There are times and places where you need to be more directive with people in order to achieve a goal. As long as I communicate to them what it is I am doing now because of these reasons, and we're going to adjust accordingly later. And then you actually do adjust later. My core managing though is setting goals and giving people flexibility within those parameters to do whatever it is that they feel they need to do to get there.

– OSAMA DORIAS, LEAD GAMEPLAY DESIGNER,
BRASS LION ENTERTAINMENT

Vision is something shared with the team. It should be organic, flexible, and open to change. As you begin to work on your vision, it may take some self-reflection to identify what you desire the future to be. And when you do, you will identify both micro- and macro-level goals that you wish to achieve. Once you can identify your vision effectively, you will find that you use it with your team far more often than you may expect. Leadership means having a vision for the future but giving up some degree of control over where we end up.

MORALE

I was told a story about a studio which was going through a long period of upheaval. It had been long and ongoing, but recent events had seemingly brought it to a moment of criticality. The term used around the office was "change fatigue," as every few months there would be some other brand-new way that the team was expected to operate. This only became worse when an announcement came of a restructuring of staff roles that would result in redundancies. Leadership during this time clearly recognised that there was a morale problem within the team, as suddenly there were wellness events organised at the office every few months. These days were full of talks about taking care of one's mental health, it provided access to therapists, and there was a masseuse going around providing massages to stressed staff.

Suffice it to say, the wellness day did not resolve the issue. In fact, it only further contributed to the rapidly spiralling morale of the team. People had rightfully pointed out that rather than taking responsibility for the strain that the team had been put under, leadership had instead provided distractions. Worse, it gave the sense that it was the responsibility of the team to fix the problem for themselves, and that it was their responsibility to get therapy to deal with the underlying issues the studio faced.

What the team wanted was to see an attempt at mitigating the factors that were causing people stress in the first place. The wellness day was treating the symptom, not the cause. It highlighted that leadership were aware of the issues the team were having, but were unwilling to accept responsibility for it or act to change the situation. Leadership were the ones causing the low morale through the constant changes. Instead of contending with the cause, they had made it the responsibility of the staff to cope on their own. Obviously one day of therapy will not help when our work environment is chaotic.

The actions of leadership and the ongoing changes were the root causes of the stress faced by this team. Leadership needed to own this fact. They needed to tell the team they understood that it was causing pressure, and to explain the reason for the rapid and ongoing changes. Clearly there was some sort of vision that was being worked towards, but this needed to be more clearly communicated to the team. Staff needed to be provided with the time and resources to work through the changes, rather than having change thrust upon them. The lack of time and the poor communication created a morale problem not because staff struggled with the changes but because it gave the impression that the leadership did not really understand where they wanted to go or how they were going to get there.

Not all change is bad. But it is the responsibility of leaders to communicate, be transparent, and share a vision for how change will improve a product, business, or team. This is how leadership in this team failed. They created an environment in which the team was left to wonder what was happening and why. People began to question the real motivations behind the changes and why little action was seen to be taken to mitigate the suffering of the members of the team.

Whatever was happening behind the scenes or the reasoning for it, the result was the same. The team's morale was shot. It could have been avoided. Well before this circumstance, people in the team were struggling with trust after months of changes without much guidance or direction. Frustrated by a perceived lack of leadership at multiple levels, the restructuring was simply the peak point at which trust fully eroded among the majority of staff. People already struggling with a lack of trust in leadership saw the situation as ample reason to resign.

It's not hard to see a connection between poor leadership and low morale. But if we have failed to lead our team effectively and build trust to cope with those times of upheaval, even the smallest issue will spiral into a massive morale problem.

Morale is an individual feeling, often a reflection of when people are not having their needs met. Our team is not a hive mind that dictates how everybody should feel at once, after all. An individual in our team struggling with outside influences over their life certainly is suffering from a morale problem, but it would be unfair on both us and them to expect that it is our responsibility to fix these problems. This is not to say that we should not support this person, but rather that it is a different circumstance to consider. It is a matter of tending to the wellbeing of our individual team members.

Morale is solving for local maximum. We're in a life raft, we're at sea, but we have a box of rations. The biggest boost to rations would be to have a feast, eat all the rations up. But that's the local maximum. Long term, what we should be focusing on is reality. So we should be focusing on the minimum number of calories for survival. The long-term experience is more important than the short term one. You can't make people feel a certain way, feelings aren't the be all and end all of what we are after. We have to look further than that. We have to be focused on a longer-term goal.

– KEITH FULLER, LEADERSHIP CONSULTANT,
FOUNDER OF GAMEDEVCOACHING.COM

There does come a point at which those individual morale problems turn into systemic ones. When a majority of our team as a collective fails to see their needs met, low morale will take hold. This is still an individual feeling, but it arises largely due to the failure of the business to provide every member of staff with the basic needs in Maslow's Hierarchy (Maslow, 1943). Following a major restructuring, it's not difficult to see how the members of our team will fear for their basic needs for income and stable employment. They may no longer feel safe in their employment. People will be figuring out their place in the business, they will talk, and the mood throughout the office will spread – particularly if the team lacks trust in us or the motivation behind such a situation.

But the problem need not come from within the business. According to the World Health Organisation, the COVID-19 pandemic resulted in a 25% increase in the prevalence of anxiety and depression worldwide (World Health Organisation, 2022). This undoubtedly led to a systematic morale issue among many game development studios. When a problem impacts on enough of our team that it is no longer just an issue of individual well-being, it has become a systemic morale issue.

Both of these circumstances present substantial challenges to morale, even when we have more control over one than the other. This does not make morale an insurmountable problem. In some cases, the best thing we can do is embrace the suck. We need to embrace that human aspect of how people are feeling and respect and empathise with their emotions.

As awful the situation experienced by many people during the height of the pandemic was, many leaders in the games industry embraced the opportunity for change. Pushed out of their offices, these teams found new strategies and routines to maintain contact. They took the time to care for one another's health. Even though the pandemic had sent them out of the office, it had built trust and camaraderie in the team. While the response in many studios may have been a positive outcome in an otherwise challenging time, it is only really made possible with a foundation of trust between a team and their leadership.

> The ability for your team to trust their leadership, the extent to which they trust them, is going to help them carry on in the absence of good morale.
>
> – KEITH FULLER, LEADERSHIP CONSULTANT,
> FOUNDER OF GAMEDEVCOACHING.COM

Trust is essential for us to deal with periods of low morale. It's immensely challenging to come back from if we find ourselves in a period of low morale without the team's trust that we can guide them through it. It is our responsibility in these challenging times to provide the team with guidance and stability. We are a source of truth for them. They will watch us and how we operate and how we are feeling, and they will use that to get a sense of the current circumstances happening around them. If we seem like we are not in control of the situation we find ourselves in, the team will assume the worst. If we are not in control, it is important to be transparent and honest with the team about that fact. Knowing the truth is almost always better for morale than leaving people in the dark.

We have embraced the chaos as leaders. We are there to be a beacon of stability for our team. They need something they know that they can always rely upon, which is why it is so important that we establish that basis of foundation. We need to help them feel that we will do everything in our power to guide them through it to the light at the end of the tunnel. Our ability to communicate, the energy we bring to the team, and our vision will benefit the team a great deal during these dark periods.

> We're looking at the longer term, and we need to figure out how we're going to solve our current problems. A person training for a marathon has low morale in the morning when they get up, they'd rather be in bed than going for a run. But they are focused on the long term. We're training for the marathon.
>
> – KEITH FULLER, LEADERSHIP CONSULTANT,
> FOUNDER OF GAMEDEVCOACHING.COM

I've met a few leaders in my time who make exceptional bards. They started their journey as leaders with an energy and charisma that made it challenging to feel bad around them. They bring a vitality to the office that just makes us happy to see them and be around them. These leaders use this energy in ways that tend to just turn around the mood of the office.

During one of the most tumultuous times in one of the places I worked, the recently promoted associate manager came to everyone's desk and took their coffee order. They made it their personal business to brighten the days of the people in the office, and it entirely turned around how I was feeling that day. This person was a great leader, and their actions well before this circumstance were reflected in that. It did not fix the morale problem, but it made everybody feel that – even just for a moment – leadership was looking out for them and considering their basic needs. Even if that was just a need for caffeine.

To get to the heart of a morale problem, we need to start by getting perspective from the members of our team. We want to be focused on solutions as much as possible, but sometimes this is simply not within our power. A team suffering in the wake of a restructure or layoff isn't going to be easily led out of that emotion, and that is fine. Some morale problems just need to be morale problems. Don't express empty confidence that it'll end or that the team will overcome the circumstance, as this is something that they are likely to see as empty reassurance. Take it day by day. Respecting their feelings and giving them the space to mourn can alleviate the feeling, but it won't fix it.

For the problems we can solve, we need that perspective to craft a solution that we can communicate to our team. What's the destination we are travelling towards that gets us out of this circumstance? Our responsibility as leaders is to guide our team to see the light at the end of the tunnel. Contending with morale issues is not much different from the periods of time in which we are leading the team or project: the steps we should take should be no different.

This is not to say that we should just ignore the problem, of course. When it comes to contending with low morale, it is essential to understand the root cause of the situation. Much of the leadership advice out there on this topic is incredibly unhelpful in this respect, and I believe that it's important that we start with what not to do when the morale of the team is low.

The first key thing to recognise is that the people around us are intelligent. People see through acts to try and distract from the low morale. This is a point I find particularly frustrating in much of the advice given by leaders in other industries: a family day or a company day trip do not improve morale. They are a distraction, and the team will see it as such. Attempting to bring together the team with empty gestures like this – especially if they have never been done before – is going to be a quick way to lose their trust in us. This is not to say that these events have no value, but choosing to do them during a time like this is the wrong choice.

Our team must see that we have a willingness to contend with the root causes of the low morale. We must act with openness and authenticity to express our understanding of how the team is feeling. Not every problem needs a solution, but if it seems to be something within our power to fix, ask how we can help. What can we do to help alleviate the circumstances? And if it is not in our power, take those proactive actions that make the team feel cared for and respected. Talk with them. Hear how they are feeling. Give them the opportunity to speak and be heard.

Embrace the fact that this is something we are all contending with together. Reinforce the fact that people in the team are not suffering alone and seek out ways to provide support to one another. Many businesses have started to provide mental health and therapy services, and now would be a good time to repeat to our staff about their access to these services.

The key point here is that we should not coddle them with distractions. We make it clear to our team that we recognise the cause of their anxiety and are there to support them. It is important as a leader in this circumstance to be respectful of the mood that our team is feeling. Many well-intentioned bards can fall into the trap of bringing a degree of toxic positivity to this situation: smiling through events that really require more empathy. If the team is facing job losses, reinforcing the team that they are all brilliant and we are sure they are going to land on their feet is hardly going to provide them with much reassurance.

Being a cheerleader as a lead is a mistake. That's not what you want to be. You don't want to be the person to say 'we've got this, it's going great' when it's not, because you're actually going to lose the trust of your people. What you want to have is honesty, transparency, and compassion. Yeah, it sucks, but if we pull together we can do this.

– OSAMA DORIAS, LEAD GAMEPLAY DESIGNER,
BRASS LION ENTERTAINMENT

When we are not in a position to provide the team with solutions, the best thing we can do is embrace the suck. Tell the team that it is a terrible situation and that we will provide them with support however and wherever we are able. But don't fall into the trap that somehow pretending will make it better at all.

But what about the times when we do not have a morale problem? What if our studio is operating exactly as it should be and everybody is content? Just like with contending with those moments of low morale, leadership is not responsible for creating morale in our teams. We contribute to it; we create the circumstances that allow for good morale to take hold. But there is no switch that suddenly makes a studio happy. Creating morale is a process that we contribute to as a collective.

Before we can work on creating good morale in our teams, their basic needs must be met. They must feel secure and safe in their employment. Only then can we begin to work on those higher tiers of Maslow's hierarchy (Maslow, 1943). Good morale comes from the members of our team feeling respected and empowered. They are working in an environment in which they feel they belong, have the capacity to do the things they love, and have the freedom to take some risks. These are things that we can enable them to do in our role as leaders, and they will help to naturally build a sense of joy and belonging in our teams.

Morale is not something that we can buy. It doesn't come from impromptu Nerf battles or barbecues. It comes from the environment around our teams and the ways in which they work with one another. In this respect, morale overlaps a great deal with culture. We aren't creating a sense of joy; we are creating an environment in which our teams can find joy.

CULTURE

The desks at the Valve Corporation have wheels. Founded in 1996 by two former Microsoft employees, Valve was to be an organisation in which people could be valued and provided with the independence to do excellent work. So they chose a unique course for the business: a studio free of hierarchies or bosses. As detailed in Valve's Handbook for New Employees, if you are hired to work at Valve, you have the ability to choose the team you work with, the specifics of the work you do, and the space you work in. Hence, the desks have wheels. The new employee handbook encourages new members of the team to "think of those wheels as a symbolic reminder that you should always be considering where you could move yourself to be more valuable" (Valve Corporation, 2012).

Staff at Valve work in an open-plan office, able to move from location to location depending on the team they have chosen to attach themselves to. The open-plan office has existed since the 1880s, but the concept was truly brought into the mainstream by software developers in Silicon Valley. The idea of the open plan office was to achieve a cultural outcome: increase collaboration by removing the literal barriers to collaborating. Proponents of the open plan office also talked about its capacity to flatten hierarchies and allow more rapid sharing of information.

A century later, research on the open-plan office has revealed that largely none of this has proven accurate. Open-plan offices were found to be a little different than traditional office spaces in encouraging collaboration. In fact, it was found that open-plan offices actually reduced the time that staff spent meeting face-to-face. The lack of privacy and the level of noise negatively impact on job satisfaction. It is a space in which it is hard to concentrate or hold private conversations (Ramsay, 2015; Bernstein and Turban, 2018). The strongest proponents of the open plan office – the managers and bosses – rarely work in one. Walk into any modern open-plan office, and there's a classic office for the person in charge.

Much like the open-plan office, there is a disconnect between what Valve desires and what is achieved in practice. Without dedicated leaders, the role is a lot more fluid. In theory, any person within Valve could lead a project. In practice, a few people become known for their capacity to lead effectively either through care or natural predisposition, while others simply fail or perform poorly. Without the expectation to lead consistently, there is no longer a need to grow the unique set of skills required of leadership. Without people in these roles to protect or empower members of the team, Valve inadvertently promotes a culture that does not encourages the very creativity they want to see. The business rarely makes games any longer.

People practice what they see. Leadership sets the bar. It's up to a leader to say "put this down and we'll pick it up tomorrow." To encourage people to take time off, do the things you enjoy. If the culture rewards overtime, people will work overtime. Leaders need to take time off and do so publicly. They need to take mental health days and do so publicly. It creates that culture and environment through visibility.

– KEITH FULLER, LEADERSHIP CONSULTANT

The idea that culture is some sort of magical problem-solving entity is a misconception at the heart of most game development studios, not just Valve. It is this idea that we can simply dictate what our culture is by writing it down on paper. That saying what matters is the same as exemplifying those ideals. Many studios go out of their way to highlight the things that they do for their teams, and the culture they create through their spending: fully stocked fridges, after-hours meals, a gym, family days. But culture doesn't come from pizza parties, bean bags, or putting wheels on desks.

Culture is the shared values and behaviour of a group of people. It is not enough to have everybody lay their hand on the statement of our teams' values and swear to uphold them. It is something we must hold each other accountable for and help one another achieve. We find it in the feeling we get when we are with our team, the problems we decide to solve, and how we choose to solve them. Culture is our values in action.

A business advertising itself as being a family is something of a cliche. But we may feel like a family when we work together, grow close, build trust, and respect one another. The studios that have a genuine culture where it feels like a family rarely advertise it. It is not written down in their values because it's an outcome of being true to their values. The members of our team see and feel those values, and they will stand up for them because of that fact. When our teams care about our culture, they make it a contract they hold with us and amongst themselves. It becomes the behaviour we live by.

> This place may feel like a family, and there's a lot of people here that I am really close to. But it's a business, and you have to be honest about that.
>
> – CAMDEN STODDARD, AUDIO DIRECTOR, DOUBLE FINE

Many well-meaning leaders inadvertently damage their team culture because they consider themselves to be solely responsible for the creation of it. It is this sense of responsibility that makes pizza parties and beanbags feel like a solution, because they are direct actions we can take. But there is a dramatic disconnect between these things and their theoretical impact on productivity or our staff. Culture is not something we can go out and buy from a store. It is not something we simply achieve or not.

The businesses that buy the beanbags then bemoan the fact that it was a wasted investment because nobody uses them. When the beanbags are purchased, it's because they are something fun. Beanbags make a statement about the style of the workplace and the kind of people in it. Beanbags say "we have fun here" and "everybody has time to relax." If the reality is that people are at their desks 13 hours a day working on their games, the beanbags gather dust. They are marketing, not truth. The culture isn't buying the beanbags, it's the team having the time to use them.

We can see a similar sort of thinking in the wheels Valve puts on their desks. The wheels are there because they want to create an environment in which staff are empowered. The desks are mobile in the same way staff are: they can go where they please and work on whatever they like. But empowerment doesn't come from having access to the tool; it comes from reinforcement of our capacity to use it. We don't make somebody an artist by purchasing paint for them; we empower them to use the paint so that they feel capable of being an artist.

This is a collective responsibility, but leadership is invaluable for their visibility to model and reinforce our values through action. The issue inside Valve appears to be a mismatch between the culture they desire, and the culture that they have created. It is not a culture that thrives on collaboration as much as independence. The company clearly values skill and rewards those who can self-direct. But without any leaders, everybody at Valve needs to become one.

> It's weird to not want the leadership position, because that's what the industry tells you that you should want.
>
> – DAMON REECE, WRITER, YELLOW BRICK GAMES

It is an environment in which the individual must engage with studio politics in order to carve out a space for themselves to exist. A new member of staff joins Valve with little social currency. Starting a new project is unlikely as it is necessary to make connections within the business to get better opportunities. This isn't a pro-hierarchy argument; simply having managers would not necessarily solve this problem. The problem is that this is not what the studio set out to achieve. Their desire was to create a space that empowered all staff equally. The reality is that they created a space in which staff must look for some other measurement of authority. And so people will gravitate towards those in the studio with perceived power.

These sorts of flat-structured studios aren't impossible, but it's important to recognise that they come with their own unique set of problems. Many of these studios founded after experiencing poor games leadership and management. It is a response to lacking leadership that chooses to remove it entirely but may just expose staff to new issues. There is still an important role in these non-hierarchical structures for leadership that ensures the team can do their work without stress or distraction. Being a leader does not mean we are at the top of the hierarchy. Anybody who takes responsibility for people or processes and has the courage to develop them is a leader (Brown, 2018).

Cooperative studio structures also face an issue of scale. Motion Twin, the independent studio originally responsible for the development of Dead Cells, was a co-op structured studio. After Dead Cells found a fan base and became a franchise, the studio grew and recognised that they could no longer make the co-op structure easily work. In a co-op, every member of the team needs to approve and support the direction of the business. This would make it immensely difficult to respond to challenges and make decisions quickly at scale. And so Motion Twin split amicably, with those who wished to continue working on Dead Cells going on to found the (perhaps appropriately named) Evil Empire (Klepek, 2019).

That Motion Twin chose to split like this does not mean they admitted defeat. It is a recognition of the culture that they cultivated within their team. It would be easy to call themselves cooperative and place people in charge who made the tough decisions, but this would no longer be honest to their foundational ideals that everybody would get a say. The choice to split in this way shows us that these different styles of businesses have a place, and they have a purpose. They are a tool. The problem does not arise out of the existence of the tool, but from how we decide to use it.

Which brings me back to Valve. I chose Valve as an example for this chapter because their values are admirable and aspirational. They take risks and value their employees in a way that few other studios do. Where they fail is in their execution of those values. To achieve the cultural vision laid out in Valve's new employee handbook, we need to do more than put it to text. We need people to wholeheartedly believe in and champion our values. We need to train leaders who empower their teams and encourage their collaboration. We discourage dictatorial behaviours. We reinforce our cultural ideals by bringing our teams together often, and valuing their input when we do.

One of the places I worked had a page on their website which listed our values as a business. As a leader within the business, I operated in line with these values as much as I could. I tried to reinforce them and their importance to the people I worked with. That was until the senior leaders of the business made decisions that contradicted the values that they said to stand for. They were willing to ignore these values if doing so would further the pursuit of our commercial goals. This did not kill the culture of the team, but it did create a sense that leadership was not a part of our culture. They were not one of us.

The page of values may have been cliche, but it mattered for visibility and accountability. Everybody on the team should be aware of our values so that they can understand what matters to us. We want our team to be able to hold themselves and others accountable to those values. We have the authority that we can enforce these values if necessary. Enforcement may sound a strong word, but to treat our values with any less respect is to quickly set our team on the path to doubting their importance. Our values must be non-negotiable.

If our team values mutual respect, we absolutely cannot reject a circumstance in which somebody feels treated poorly by their peers. Our authority gives us a responsibility to take that complaint seriously and to ensure that everybody understands how and why that value is so important. We want to be the example that our team looks to for guidance and to gently correct those that stray from our values.

> Stand ups were too formal, I don't work like that. Let's make it fun because it's the end of the day. Everybody has their camera off but I'm going to say fun facts of the day or tell a dad joke, something corny. I'll stick around until I get a laugh, I got you right? And suddenly people start opening up and collaborating. Suddenly stand up is much more about support and collaboration. People put in follow-up requests for assistance when they are blocked. Things get documented.
>
> – CHIMA DENZEL NGEREM, PRODUCER, ZYNGA

We model the culture we want to see through our own actions. If we want to create or improve the culture on our teams, we must be above reproach. This does not mean being infallible, but recognising and being accountable for the moments where we failed to uphold our values. We must be absolutely dedicated to our values and our vision of the future. We need to live those values if we want anybody else to do the same.

There were several recurring values that were shared among interviewees, no matter their place of work. This is likely a reflection of the things that the games industry values broadly and that are important considerations worth bringing to our leadership experience. These values included diversity, psychological safety, mutual respect, and many of the skills typically associated with leadership.

Diversity is not just a diversity of staff, but a diversity of opinion. We want to avoid creating teams whose culture is represented by a singular gender, race, nationality, or role. Research into diversity in the past few decades has identified that while there are not necessarily performance improvements to be gained by diversity, it does increase creativity and innovation – both immensely important considerations for any game development studio (Roberge and van Dick, 2010). More importantly, however, is the moral argument that, as leaders, we have a responsibility to ensure all voices are heard.

To model a culture that values diversity, is not just about ensuring that we hire diverse staff. This is about hearing, respecting, and valuing a diversity of opinions. A culture of diversity ensures that every member of the team has a chance to speak and feels safe doing so. This overlaps a great deal with creating psychological safety in our teams, where they feel they can speak up and be heard without negative repercussions.

A team of diverse hires without the psychological safety to express a difference of opinion is not a truly diverse culture. The members of our team need to feel that they can take risks, make suggestions, and raise concerns without being told they are wrong or to be quiet. This requires a culture of mutual respect, as a difference of opinion should not come at the cost of hearing diverse voices. We may have team members who express frustration at the addition of minority voices; however, enabling diverse opinions and ensuring that everybody is heard can never come at the cost of mutual respect. Such a behaviour needs to be quickly corrected.

> We need to be clear on the difference between psychological safety and trust. Trust is a one-on-one thing. Environment is a key factor of psychological safety and is an organisational characteristic.
>
> – KEITH FULLER, LEADERSHIP CONSULTANT

Finally, we want everybody in our team to understand that they can model and emulate leadership behaviours. The foundational skills of integrity, humility, and accountability are all desirable traits we wish to see in the members of our team. By modelling these behaviours ourselves, we demonstrate to the members of our team the importance of them. It is likely that you can look at any of the skills listed in this book and see the way in which they would be an asset for each member of our team to value as we do. You may wish to model particular behaviours in the hope that the members of your team will do the same.

So our values need to be non-negotiable, and we need to champion them. If our team says that we value "work life balance," then that means we need to call people out when they work late. The moment we say "it's okay under this circumstance as we've got a deadline to meet," we have permanently impacted upon our culture in a way that is difficult to come back from. We have informed our team that the value is actually "work life balance, unless" or "work life balance, except when."

If we wish to create a culture in which our teams collaborate and are empowered, then we must model these behaviours. There are no shortcuts to creating a culture like this; it's not as simple as a trip to buy beanbags or desk wheels. Culture is the reinforcement of values through action and accountability, both individually and collectively. It takes doing the legwork to model the behaviours we want to see and showing the members of our teams why these things should matter to them as well. We must share our values, live the culture we want to see, and the members of our team will follow.

4.0

The Cleric

The cleric is misunderstood. Wielding a shield, it can be easy to perceive them as defenders that step in front of the team to protect everybody else in a similar way to the Warrior. But the cleric lacks the necessary Constitution to place themselves in the line of danger in the same way. They are typically perceived as a support class, tending to the people around them in a similar way to the bard. But the cleric lacks the charisma to really rally or influence the people around them in a meaningful way.

While the Warrior is focused on the project and the bard is focused on the collective, the cleric is interested in the self. Defined by their wisdom, they understand what triggers their emotions or how they are feeling in the moment. In this way, the cleric is better able to predict and understand how and why another person may feel a certain way in a situation.

Early in the journey of being a cleric, it may feel like you spend most of your time inside of your own head: pondering about the going-on around you or within you. Fortunate are the leaders who have a team of peers who are on a similar journey, able to share their thoughts and build a greater understanding of themselves and others through collaboration and communication. There are great benefits to encouraging a culture that does this within your own team, as it will only benefit your own development in the skills of the cleric.

Don't mistake this sort of cerebral description of the cleric to be something that makes them entirely useless. Rather, the cleric is easily the most versatile of the Archetypes, while also being the most challenging to teach

DOI: 10.1201/9781003431626-11

and learn. Starting your journey as a cleric can make much the rest of the journey dramatically easier, as you are already starting with the skills that most leaders in the Games Industry lack. When we talk about leaders and refer to the mind, heart, and mouth, the cleric is through and through the heart. They are self-aware, empathetic, and keen to take care of the people around them. The cleric is the person on the team who is easy to talk to, who listens, who makes you feel heard, and endeavours to ensure you have the support you need to succeed.

Starting the journey of a cleric is one of self-reflection and introspection. You look inward and question your actions, the meaning of the things happening around you, the influence you have over events, and how you might better begin to improve upon them. This sort of intangible nature to their skills is a good reason why people never really start their journey here: you don't really go to study and leave with the skills to be a great Cleric. It's something that usually begins as deeply personal for an individual. Most people who start their journey here instead start it as a result of the lives they lived well before they began their adventure in game development: time spent within their own heads, perhaps.

That was the case for me, at least. I started my journey in game development having reflected upon the challenges I faced in my life, and at one point I had considered getting into psychology. Having supported my mother through immense depression and suffered with it myself, I developed a sense of emotional intelligence that made it easier to manage my feelings and identify feelings in others. But the pull of creativity had been constant throughout my life, and so I ended up in game development. What I had intended as a career in art, however, turned into one focused more on production and project management as I discovered I had a strong sense of time management, but more than that, I could talk to and empathise with members of the team in any department.

Epitomising the ideas of selflessness and sacrifice, it's not unusual to see clerics burn out fast in the Games Industry just as I did early in my journey. So focused on tending to and caring for my team, I often neglected myself. It took going to therapy and unravelling my desire to serve others to really see the risks involved in putting the team above all else – including yourself. This is the darker side of the Archetype; seeing the clerics shield as one used to defend others when you have not invested in the necessary Constitution to be able to remain standing. To understand that you are just as much a member of the team in need of care, protection, and tending. If your leadership is not tending to you, then you need to be sure that you are tending to yourself – not just to the people around you. And this is why the attribute of the cleric is wisdom. The wise cleric understands when they can take the hit and when they need to stand aside.

With this sort of understanding of yourself, you find that you begin to better understand the others around you. It becomes easier to place yourself in their shoes and to empathise with their plight. This is much of the reason for the Cleric's often self-destructive tendencies, but also the source of their greatest strength. The people that you lead are just that: people. But in a business, it can be so easy to reduce them down to a role. A failure becomes the result of 'that Programmer', leading many leaders to cold interventions without an attempt to treat the root of the problem. The cleric – by knowing themselves – doesn't need much time to begin to understand others.

It's important however to quickly crush any perception of the cleric as a healer. This was another mistake I made when I was early in my journey as a young leader. As you begin to build your skill and understanding of the Cleric, you will quickly come to understand why many of the leaders interviewed for this book resent that idea. There are trained professionals outside of the Games Industry who are the people that you need to tend to your mental and physical health: it's likely that if you have a cleric on your team, they will remind you to go and tend to it. But they are not responsible for patching up your wounds or tending to your feelings. They are to help you recognise when YOU need to tend to your wounds or feelings, and to encourage you to seek that help.

This may all sound great, but there is, of course, the risk of an evil-aligned Cleric. It may sound counter-intuitive given the human-focused nature of the class, but this is what makes it so dangerous. Where an evil-aligned bard can mislead, an evil-aligned cleric can manipulate. You can look into yourself and understand how you feel and act, and use this knowledge to manipulate how others feel and act. You can put on performative acts of caring, leading the team to wrongly believe that you are choosing their best interests. You can speak and act as somebody who cares without truly meaning it. It's for this reason that we as leaders need to invest genuinely in the people around us and respect our duty of care for them as individuals.

At the heart of it, the cleric is about the leader and the people around them. It's about understanding the separation of these things: where boundaries need to be drawn to protect your well-being and the well-being of others. It's about having the empathy to understand why people may feel and act the way they do, and to embrace their individuality and right to self-determination. It's about having the wisdom to accept that you are unable to change people, only to lead and attempt to guide them towards better solutions. The Warrior may be able to stay in the fight for long periods, but knowing when to retreat takes wisdom. The bard may be able to communicate and bring people around to their mode of thinking easily, but knowing when to have that conversation takes wisdom.

This is why the cleric may seem so inactive from the outside when you lack the understanding of just what the class does. Investing into the skills of the cleric means investing into a force multiplier for your other skills. It makes you a better Warrior and a better bard by investing in yourself and the people around you. The skill and investment to do that can be somewhat invisible as a result, as it entails just doing those existing skills better in a variety of easily missed ways. Good Clerics are all about making great teams, and it can be very easy to miss just how the cleric achieves this when they aren't really doing much differently.

Throughout this book, we've referred to this idea of making decisions that minimise the human cost of making great games. The cleric puts this sort of decision-making front and centre, with its focus on the people around them. As you read through the different skills of the cleric, I encourage you to think back onto the previous chapters and think about the impact these skills have on those that we've already covered. Consider the ways in which this focus on the other people in the team and upon ourselves makes a lot of these skills more effective. This is the point of the Cleric. It's not just about achieving success; it's about lowering the human cost of achieving success.

Feeling

At that point I had been there for roughly three years as an associate. In addition to doing the work I was assigned to, I'd also been taking on extra tasks to support the team. I was like, hey, I've done this for three years now, I'd like to discuss the potential for a promotion. What do I need to do? And my manager was just not forthcoming at all. No action items, nothing.

When my manager joined the team one of the first thing she told us was something like "I'm a mum. You can tell me anything, you can trust me." I was already on my guard after the lack of assistance for my request for information about a promotion. But then I was told by one of the other managers about another meeting she was in. She told everyone present that I was underperforming. I've never under-performed in my life! So I requested a meeting with her and asked her directly, do you think I am underperforming? She told me, yes, I think you might be. So I asked her how, can you give me something to work on? And she tells me no, I just have this feeling. What do you mean you have a feeling?!

If you have evidence that I am underperforming, then it needs to be on my performance improvement plan. But it's not. It was clear she was not being authentic; she had some issue with me she wasn't willing to talk about. So I start applying for other jobs because I'm like, I know how this story goes, I know how it ends. Before it gets to that point, I am going to jump ship. So I applied to a whole bunch of other places.

– ANONYMOUS

DOI: 10.1201/9781003431626-12

We all have good days and bad days. Feeling is human. In a role so people focused as leadership, it is of immense importance for us to be able to empathise with our staff at the very least. We want to be able to understand and respect ourselves when we also have those days with strong feelings, so that we can manage our emotions and our behaviour. Without these skills, we will cause harm to the people that we are working with, often unknowingly. None of this should seem overly surprising, but the skills of feeling are some of the most lacking among leaders in the games industry.

It can be easy for many leaders to feel that they need to hold themselves above emotion. They put on a strong face or act in such a way as to distance themselves from their feelings. Much of this can often arise out of a focus on those creative and technical skills in the time that often precedes promotion to leadership. It can be easy to believe that feeling and managing one's emotions don't really benefit us all that much in those fields where we are simply responsible for executing tasks and creating art. For those who feel this way, they bring that belief to their leadership.

But being able to feel is of immense importance not only to our roles as leaders but also to our capacity to create art. Feeling allows us to tend to our health and well-being and to be able to identify when the people around us are in similar need of support. By developing our emotional intelligence, we can not only empathise with the people around us better but also understand ourselves. It makes us mindful of our own feelings and needs in a way that benefits the people around us. In our position as leaders, we have the capacity to provide the members of our team with a healthy example.

The usefulness of this skill comes down to a singular, indisputable fact: that making games is hard. We will be faced with difficult decisions that will test us and our peers. We are surrounded by people who are passionate about their work and bring a myriad of different perspectives – cultural, artistic, and technical. Aligning so many different views will often feel like an insurmountable task. It is stressful for us as leaders and for those within our teams. Without the capacity to recognise that stress, people will find themselves hurt. It is then essential to embrace the need to feel.

We all want to feel safe and secure and to be able to act and operate in a way that makes us comfortable. Feeling is all about being able to create this safety through a greater understanding of ourselves and those around us. Feeling isn't just about expressing emotion; it's reflective; it's authentic. The people around us need to feel safe in their ability to be themselves, just as we do. We can create that sort of safety just by taking a few moments to reflect on our actions and our emotions. We cannot operate just based on our feelings alone; we need to understand and be able to explain why.

Feeling is particularly personal. The way that you feel will be inspired by your own perspectives, your own experiences, and the events surrounding your present circumstances. But by being able to develop a greater understanding of your own feelings, you can better understand those around you. Everybody feels, and so developing mindfulness of your own emotions can help you better understand the feelings of those around you. Ask yourself why you feel the way you feel, or why you acted that way. Ask yourself the same questions as those around you. Sometimes all it takes is a little curiosity.

EMOTIONAL INTELLIGENCE

One of the games I worked on did not meet its sales targets. It's not an unusual story, particularly not when you work in indie games. The mood in the studio after the games release was complicated, with members of the team blaming themselves for a variety of reasons. One of the team leads, however, was adamant that the responsibility was theirs alone, that nobody else in the studio should have any doubt about the validity of their contributions. But there was a problem.

Throughout the whole time this person took responsibility, they were clearly agitated. The more they came into the office, the clearer it became that they were really tearing themselves up over what had taken place. In a private conversation, some members of the team expressed frustration. The impression they were being left with was that their contributions to the project and its failure did not matter. The person leading the team saw it as their singular responsibility to make it successful. It was not their intent, of course, but it left some people within the studio feeling more like their contributions did not matter.

The mood of this person constantly soured to the point that they were talking about leaving the industry over the failing. Rather than absorbing the blow for the loss, their behaviour made it uncomfortable to be in the office. Holding themselves responsible as they did impact upon not only their mood, but the mood of the people around them. Without knowing exactly what they were thinking, I can only assume they felt it was their responsibility as a leader to absorb the blow. But unprepared to do so, it may hit them harder than they expected.

Thankfully, they would move on from this event as better leaders. The next time a failure took place within the studio, they took responsibility and made themselves accountable for remedying it. In many ways, their behaviour changed what would have been an otherwise immensely challenging time into a far easier one to cope with inside the studio. The key thing that had changed was that they had begun developing their emotional intelligence.

A lot of leaders can be quite questioning when something doesn't fit into a structure. And peoples emotions don't necessarily fit into neat packages.

EMILY MACMAHON, LEADERSHIP CONSULTANT

When a studio experiences failure, it is not unusual for blame and doubt to find their way into our teams. It's the responsibility of leadership to step up and take responsibility when such failures occur. It may not be entirely our fault, but we are the ones who issued the orders, who understood the risks, and who must be responsible for remedying the issue. The leader who steps up and takes responsibility for a failure like this is admirable. But to do so, we need to have some self-awareness and the confidence required to bounce back.

Taking responsibility does not mean that we make it all about us. It also does not prevent the team from feeling what they are going to feel. An inexperienced team may be inclined to point fingers or blame one another, we want to prevent that by taking responsibility ourselves. We are not and should not be trying to protect them from feeling sad when things go wrong, but we want to remove any doubt from their mind who is responsible for fixing the issue.

When we talk about emotional intelligence, it may be easy to assume that what we are talking about is empathy. Emotional intelligence is the ability to understand how and why others feel the way they feel. This alone, however, would not have been enough to prevent the circumstances I described. Bottling up our emotions so we don't risk people around us feeling bad is only going to cause them to explode out later. Emotional intelligence is not just about understanding the feelings of others, it's also about understanding our own feelings.

Emotional intelligence is critical to great leadership. We are working with people who have their own individual experiences, and who live their own lives outside of the workplace, who will undoubtedly bring their feelings into and out of the workplace. Ideally, everybody in our studio has some degree of emotional intelligence so that we might understand and empathise with one another as we face challenges together. There is a cultural consideration to being able to empathise with and understand others, as it reinforces for them the value of building their own capacity to do the same.

There are many models for understanding emotional intelligence. The most prevalent among leaders to assist in understanding the role of emotional intelligence to leading teams is the research done by Daniel Goleman (Goleman, Boyatzis and McKee, 2002). This model breaks emotional intelligence down into four quadrants:

- Self-Awareness, understanding ourselves.

- Self-Management, controlling ourselves.

- Social Awareness, understanding others.

- Social Management, influencing others.

Within Goleman's model of emotional intelligence, everything starts with self-awareness. We can only understand others once we are able to accurately assess and understand our own feelings and emotions. By developing this emotional awareness, we are able to build upon our self-confidence and start to develop strategies to motivate ourselves. This enables us to begin working on self-management, to control our emotions, and to take the initiative. We become active rather than reactive to our feelings.

As we develop our self-awareness, we will also be able to develop our social awareness. By being able to better understand and identify our own emotions and triggers, we will be able to understand those of the people around us. But before we can begin to effectively manage the emotions of others, we need to first be able to manage ourselves. Both self-management and social awareness are necessary to be able to engage in social management well. Nobody has their emotions managed well by somebody incapable of self-control.

> If someones behaviour is something you don't appreciate for some reason, you don't necessarily need to manage the behaviour as much as you need to try and manage the whole person. Get to know them better.
>
> – JASON IMMS, HEAD OF QUALITY ASSURANCE, KEYWORDS STUDIOS

Few skills have the capacity to elevate everything we do as leader the way Emotional Intelligence does. Social awareness allows us to better communicate with and understand the individual needs of a person. What motivates a person? Is there a reason that their performance has been reduced this week? How can we reduce conflicts between them and others? As we begin to move from awareness into regulating the way others feel, we can start to use our understanding of people to inspire them, influence them, build trust with them, and collaborate with them much more effectively.

Where emotional intelligence really shines is in our application of it to ourselves. Self-awareness allows us to reflect upon our actions, our successes, and our failures and to embrace continuous improvement more easily as leaders. We can identify and take responsibility for our part in a failure while maintaining a focus on what matters: solutions and ensuring it does not happen again. Through self-awareness, accountability and integrity become much easier to maintain.

People who lack self-awareness have a lack of self-confidence, or worse: an overly bloated sense of self-worth. People lacking this important skill then go on to have a lack of ability to regulate themselves, easily becoming emotional or failing to understand how their feelings may impact upon those around them. Without self-awareness we are prone to dwelling on failures. It creates the sense that the leader is at the centre of the team's universe. This is why everything starts with the development of our self-awareness.

Building our emotional intelligence is a skill just like any other. The perception that it is an innate trait or too difficult to develop may come out of the soft and squishy nature of emotion and feelings, particularly in an industry so focused on hard and actionable skills. Game studios are much more interested in technical expertise by their very nature, making the ability to work with others often a much lower priority. Thankfully, this is something that has been changing in recent years, but it continues to be a challenging subject.

> There's a fixation on the work, the tasks, which undervalues the skills required to coordinate others. To lead with empathy. The industry does not do a good job of hiring empathetic people, or educating people to be empathetic. There's this mindset that anything that takes me away from the technical work is something you are asking me to do on top of my job.
>
> – KEITH FULLER, LEADERSHIP CONSULTANT, FOUNDER OF GAMEDEVCOACHING.COM

To develop our emotional intelligence, we need to start by understanding that it is a behaviour rather than a trait or passive skill. Emotional intelligence in the moment is a choice that we must make, and as such, there are actions that we can take to reinforce the skill. These behaviours and actions may become more passive with time as we settle into an understanding of ourselves, but to start, we want to be specifically aware of what we are doing and why.

We begin the journey by developing our self-awareness. Doing this is helped by having others provide us with honest feedback and insight, people we can trust to hold us accountable. Mentorship is invaluable, but we want a group of people who are around us often and willing to tell us plainly how we are acting. Therapy and training from a leadership coach would be preferable here, but we could also get assistance from the members of our team, our family, or our friends. The key thing we need from them is honesty.

This starts with a conversation that makes it clear to them that we are looking to develop our emotional intelligence, and we want their insight and opinion. If they are uncomfortable, it may help to have the process made anonymous. Whoever is helping us here must feel safe to give us entirely honest feedback. We ask them to monitor our behaviour, how we carry ourselves in conversation, and what they would like to see us do differently. Taking this feedback, we reflect and consider how we want to progress. The key thing we are looking for is any surprises, those behaviours that we are not aware of.

While we are gathering this feedback from others, it is also useful to keep a journal. This s a great way to help organise our thoughts each day and reflect on our feelings about the events that have taken place around us.

It allows us to work the same muscles that we will use when we are self-aware in much the same way that going for a jog can help us prepare for a marathon. It also has the added benefit of allowing us to compare our journal against the feedback we receive from our peers.

Just like the times we first took up the pencil or wrote our first line of code, this will absolutely feel awkward at first. When we are in conversation with somebody, pause after they speak. Take a moment to consider our feelings, words, phrasing, and how others may react. Then we allow ourselves to speak. As we develop our self-awareness and begin to work on our empathy, we will be focusing such thoughts on how the people around us are feeing instead. People who exercise their emotional intelligence take the time to reflect on their feelings and the feelings of others in every conversation, we just do not notice it.

Emotional intelligence is not just about holding conversation, of course. This understanding of others and their feelings allows us to understand what motivates the team around us, what interests them, to manage conflict, to help them see our vision, and to align their values with our own. If we can first understand how a person tends to feel or think, then we can prepare appropriately to reduce their anxiety and help ease otherwise challenging conversations.

> It's people you are dealing with. Your emotions and expectations, their emotions and expectations. There's that constant change, that flux. It's always going to be there.
>
> – AMY LOUISE DOHERTY, CREATIVE DIRECTOR, ARCH REBELS

Consider for a moment that we need to inform an employee that they are being fired. There's no way to make this conversation easy, but by taking a moment to consider the person themselves and approaching the conversation in a way that appreciates how they feel, we can make the whole experience a lot less painful. How does this person act when we see them? Do they often tense their shoulders, do they have a tendency to assume the worst? We may have identified that they have a rather anxious personality.

The question then becomes how to start a conversation without further exacerbating their anxieties. The worst possible thing we could do is send this person a meeting request in an e-mail titled "we need to talk." Every moment in the lead-up to our meeting with them will be filled with their anxiety and stress about what is to occur. It will put questions in their mind why their boss needs to talk to them and only make an unpleasant experience that much worse.

Having established trust will often do more to reduce anxiety for others, just by virtue of the fact that people understand that we are going to take care of them. In this example alone we are talking about needing to use communication, individuality, authenticity, and expectations. The reality is that all of these skills – while absolutely skills unto themselves – are somewhat empty without the emotional intelligence to back them up. Telling this individual "hey, do you have a moment to chat? Unfortunately, it's not good news" may really be the best we are going to get if we have not developed a positive rapport otherwise.

This journey does not need to end with us, as we can work to improve the emotional intelligence within our teams. We want them to be able to interact with one another with as few barriers as possible, even those that they may inadvertently put up themselves. A team that can openly and respectfully interact with each other is able to collaborate with one another more effectively. These things build better workplaces as they create trust and a culture of empathy. We are brought closer together through an understanding of one another. In order to develop the emotional intelligence of our teams, we need to work on normalising awareness and regulation of emotions.

There are a variety of strategies to develop emotional intelligence in our teams. To assist us in doing this, I recommend reading Building the Emotional Intelligence of Groups. In this paper, Vanessa Urch Druskat and Steven B Wolff identify the ways in which group emotional intelligence can be achieved. Much like improving our own emotional intelligence, this is done with behaviours that encourage reflection and accountability.

In this paper, the authors note that developing the self-awareness of our teams involves those behaviours that encourage reflection. Ask how everybody is doing at the start of a meeting. Make the time to get input from everyone and have a conversation about the current mood in the team. When members of the team are quiet, ask them what they think. Tell them what you are thinking and feeling, and ask them for the same. Do not shy away from the politics at the studio and ask the team what they think of its culture.

They also argue that regulation of the teams' emotions requires a willingness to both confront and care. Where there are issues with behaviour we must hold people accountable. Set and enforce ground rules and expected behaviours within the office. We also want to support them when they need assistance, to validate them, and respect their individuality. Find ways to relieve stress and tension during challenging moments, and express an acceptance for the feelings others have. Maintain our vision and focus on problem solving (Druskat and Wolff, 2001).

We can also extend our processes beyond considerations of the project. Take the time to acknowledge the people in our team. Typical stand-up procedures are to ask what people have done, what they plan to do, and if they are having any problems. We could add to this and ask how they are feeling, do they feel confident about getting the work done? Retrospectives and postmortems are excellent tools to have the team reflect on what is transpiring and what they could do differently, and these too can be extended to the team's emotions.

Every skill and tool we use as leaders is uplifted by our emotional intelligence, and so too is the work of our teams. Our work is incredibly challenging, and emotions will inevitably become charged. The complexity and challenge of our work are reduced if we can develop a culture of empathy and accountability within ourselves and our teams. It removes one thing that can hinder our creativity and success. We must do the necessary work on ourselves to help guide the team to improve as well. This way, we may focus as a collective on those things that really matter: the project and the people around us.

AUTHENTICITY

We have all had that leader who is cold, who turns up to the office and never interacts with the team. They are there to do a job, and they keep the people around them at arm's length. You may have had the experience with them where they suddenly became friendly at work functions, and this is one way in which when and how you choose to be authentic may actually negatively impact on the impression you give others of your person.

This leader choosing to be friendly at the staff Christmas party knows how to be authentic. They have simply made the choice as to when and how they are authentic. It does not make sense to go to a party and then act at arms-reach from those in attendance, and so for the sake of team building, they suddenly find their ability to be human. The irony of this kind of performative authenticity is that this leader actually appears less authentic as a result. The people they lead come to see this person as unwilling to be themselves when it's hard, and so every action this leader takes is scrutinised. During meetings where this leader then expresses sympathy or sadness, it is taken to be performative and inauthentic.

It's important to recognise, however, that this type of performative authenticity does not need to arise out of a desire to do harm. In my experience, these sorts of leaders who struggle to be authentic in the workplace are quite socially awkward or struggle with the idea of showing weakness. There are, of course, examples of this kind of leader who simply desires for their staff to do the work and does not need to become personally involved with them to get the job done. They act more like a manager than a leader, focused on outcomes instead of people. This isn't necessarily authenticity without integrity; it is just a poor example of a leader.

However, there are ways in which authenticity can become aligned with evil. Like the previous example, this type of performative authenticity is not limited to staff parties. It is characterised by ongoing manipulative behaviour in which a person acts the way that they believe others want or expect them to act. This type of leader often presents himself as friendly and charismatic but does not act in the best interests of others. Their priorities are to outcomes, and their performative authenticity is used to extract value from others. Their kindness extends only so far as it benefits them: expressing sadness that the team must crunch, while having done nothing to explore alternatives.

> We hired some new people who, for some reason, I just couldn't work with. For the longest time, I didn't know what was up, but I just had a gut feeling about them. Eventually, I would find out that the individual wasn't being an authentic person, or even a nice person. They were talking about people being their back. Not speaking to the person about their problem, just going straight to their manager. It creates an environment that's no longer collaborative and friendly.
>
> – CHIMA DENZEL NGEREM, PRODUCER, ZYNGA

Evil-aligned authenticity is not authenticity at all, not really. But the way in which the behaviour matches up with the expectations of authenticity makes it easily missed. This isn't so simple as a betrayal of one's integrity. Betraying your values is easily noticed, and the evil-aligned leader is more subtle than that. They are often characterised by the dark triad of personality types: psychopathy, narcissism and particularly the self-interested and manipulative traits of Machiavellianism (Paulhus and Williams, 2002). Upon understanding authenticity and the power of it, the self-aware leader needs to tread carefully in how they express it if they are to avoid irreparably damaging the trust of their team.

Being inauthentic may seem relatively harmless on the scale of damaging behaviours, but it is one of the most specifically personal and human ways in which we may betray our team. To be caught pretending to be authentic is to be caught pretending to act human. It creates an environment in which our every action will be scrutinised. People who have experienced such leadership often have difficulty trusting future leadership that is genuinely authentic due to the sense of emotional betrayal that comes with performative authenticity.

Politicians, lawyers, law enforcement: depending on your location and the experience of people over a long enough period of time, there may be a well-earned distrust of authority. Enough inauthentic behaviour in a role can be so damaging that the expectation becomes that such people are simply not trustworthy at all. Executives in the games industry have developed such a reputation for themselves such that many have simply dropped the act, focusing entirely on creating shareholder value than leading great teams. But it's not a problem that ends at the executive team. I have spoken with enough people that have expressed distrust in Producers for it to have become clear that they have had experience with somebody in the role who was more interested in getting the project done on time and under budget, than doing it safely and sustainably.

Authenticity as a skill is one that can be a bit challenging to understand. Think about the meaning of the word, the quality of being genuine or real. If somebody is being inauthentic, they are pretending to be something else. So then authenticity is bringing truth and honesty to our leadership. It is understanding that being a better leader means being a better version of ourselves. We aren't just putting on the leadership mask and pretending to be a leader or a good person. We are a leader; we are choosing to exercise leadership. The person we are when we are with the team is not some fictionalised version of ourselves; we are authentic when we are with them.

There is a complex intersection of other concepts that we've discussed so far that contribute to our authenticity. It's about integrity. It is self-aware action that reinforces our values. It is our emotional intelligence informing a greater understanding of ourselves, what we desire, and what we feel. It requires reflection on our feelings, and we bring this reflective ability to conversations. It is knowing ourselves, our strengths, and our weaknesses. It is exercising discipline. By knowing ourselves, we can truly know what we value, and we can lead with purpose. Authenticity is about us, and it is one of the most powerful ways to build trust and relationships. It is also the fastest way to destroy those same things.

When we choose to be authentic, it needs to be true to the idea of authenticity. That we are being ourselves for no gain, that we are choosing to operate in this way to allow people to see us for ourselves. This means accepting some personal exposure, and it can be immensely challenging. But as a way to build trust and to influence the culture of our team, the first steps towards authenticity can create dramatic and positive changes in the people around us. By being willing to accept our feelings and to show vulnerability, we set an example that our team might follow.

Practising vulnerability and transparency when things are easy makes doing those things instinctual when things are not so easy.

– ALAYNA COLE, DIVERSITY EQUITY AND INCLUSION MANAGER, SLEDGEHAMMER GAMES

Much like the other skills that we practice, authenticity must be exercised with intent. Authenticity requires that we accept some exposure, that we make ourselves more known to the team. But do not mistake authenticity for the need to be emotional or overshare. We may reflect on our circumstances and feelings and identify that we are frustrated, yes. Authenticity does not mean that we allow ourselves to stomp around the office because that is how we feel. We want to be honest that we are feeling frustrated about our current circumstances so that the team understands that their frustrations are shared. But we still have control over our emotions, and a focus on finding solutions.

Nobody benefits if our mode of authenticity is being constantly angry or frustrated, which is why emotional intelligence is essential to healthy authenticity. We are self-aware, we identify, and we acknowledge the feeling. Then we consider the approach to sharing and – more importantly – resolving the emotion.

If you have a newborn that has kept you up all night, you can tell on your way to work that you are feeling short-tempered. Do not go to the morning; stand up and say, "hey everyone, I feel pretty grouchy today so don't test my patience." Maybe you offer an apology in advance, but it is essential to maintain that awareness of your emotions throughout the day.

Or maybe you find yourself in a position in which you have been told to direct your team to complete additional tasks ahead of the coming milestone. You may disagree with the directive, you may argue passionately against the move. But once the directive is given and the meeting is done, you cannot allow yourself to become fixated on blame or anger. When you share the news with the team, express your frustration and move on. Turn your focus to finding solutions.

Authenticity requires that we be disciplined and exercise self-control. We need to help guide the team such that they do not become fixated on their own anger and frustration, and we do this by managing our own.

A focus on solutions is essential to positive authenticity. We must understand what is outside of our control as an individual and set a good example to our team about management of mental health. We cannot by any means become fixated on dwelling upon our negative emotions or the problems we are unable to fix. These things impact upon the morale and culture of our team and fly in the face of our other leadership responsibilities. Dwelling on the problem languishes in the circumstance. We need to seek solutions and express a vision for the path out of the present situation to our team.

Rather than dwelling upon the problems, spend this energy focused on solutions. This allows us to share our frustrations with the team to encourage them to similarly open up to us about how they are feeling. It also sets the expectation for why we do this sharing: we can only fix the problems we are experiencing if we know what they are. Without a focus on solutions we set an expectation that giving up or accepting defeat are viable options.

I think there is often a kind of misguided attempt to stay positive in the hope that it is contagious. Sometimes it works, but sometimes you just want somebody to be up at the front of the entire group like, this game isn't what we want it to be, but it's fine, and we've got to get it out the door.

– ALAYNA COLE, DIVERSITY EQUITY AND INCLUSION
MANAGER, SLEDGEHAMMER GAMES

A focus on solutions does not mean that we are constantly optimistic. As we discussed on the subject of morale, sometimes a situation just sucks. You may be a more optimistic personality, and then perhaps the authentic behaviour is to respond as such to the circumstances you find yourself in. That's fine, and certainly preferable over pessimism and resistance to every changing circumstance. But we must allow people to feel the way they feel without any expectation they feel the same as we do. Their feelings are just as legitimate as our own. Empathise with them, accept their feelings, and help guide them through those emotions by setting a good example.

One of the worst things we can do as leaders is avoid circumstances that make us uncomfortable. We postpone the inevitable challenges and risk exacerbating problems. But by choosing to be authentic, we can take some of the sting out of these moments. It can be immensely hard to fire an employee, for them and for us. In these moments (and with a foundation of trust), we can open up and be authentic with the person. We can express that there's no easy way to have this conversation and that we are sorry that they are going to inevitably feel hurt because of it. We make these conversations more human and less corporate as a result.

> There's a phrase we like that is "be comfortable with being uncomfortable." And that has this kind of dual meaning as it pertains to dealing with the unknown, like putting yourself in positions or assignments, or volunteering for assignments you don't know how to do just to learn.
>
> – CAPTAIN BRANDEN BUFFALO, NATIONAL SPACE DEFENCE CENTRE, UNITED STATES SPACE FORCE

Understanding ourselves also benefits our understanding of how to lead others. We do not decide on a leadership style to define ourselves by, but we do develop a better understanding of the ways in which we naturally lead others. We can identify the strengths and weaknesses of our personal leadership style, and supplement it as necessary. For example, I find myself gravitating to servant leadership. I like to enable members of my team to participate in decision making, and allow them the freedom to do their best work. But this may not work for everybody, some people may desire more coaching or direction. If I rely too much upon the team to make decisions, we may never decide upon anything.

By understanding that this is the way I lead people, it means that I can begin to identify these blind spots. I can trust that they feel I am supporting their effort and spend more of my energy looking for opportunities to coach or direct if it's clear it is needed. I can identify when it's time for a decision to be made, and if we have not settled upon a single direction, I can take ownership of the decision – and the negative repercussions of it, if necessary. Being authentic about it means being able to acknowledge and share those blind spots with my team so that they can help provide me with the feedback I need to improve.

Your own leadership style will differ, and you will need to take that time to reflect upon your own strengths and weaknesses. If you are an extremely technical leader, then you may tend towards more directive styles of leadership. You may naturally want to direct people, so how can you create opportunities for people to self-direct? You can then share with others the awareness of this being your leadership style, and ask for opportunities to help them self-direct. Bringing this awareness to your daily leadership, you can begin to identify where you have that desire to direct others, consider if there is an alternative and, more importantly, consider if that's what this person needs.

Authenticity also develops a greater understanding of our goals and purpose as a leader. What is it we want to achieve in our role as a leader? How do we want to impact upon our teams, our projects, our businesses, and the players of our games? Purpose is found in our values and beliefs; it is communicated to our team as vision; and it lives or dies based on our actions. Telling our team that we envision a studio environment in which they have the flexibility to work from home is great. Asking the staff to come into the office an extra day every week defeats our purpose.

Only if we are authentic in our actions can we hold others accountable for theirs. We see this often in the push to return to the office. Executive leadership encourages leadership back to offices that they are rarely ever seen in. We care a lot more when it's the people we have direct contact with who take the action. If we desire to see the members of our team in the office, we need to start by modelling the behaviour. We model the behaviours that we desire to see in our workplace. The team will not necessarily follow so easily, but how can we expect them to do anything we aren't willing to do ourselves?

> Learn from the vulnerability, transparency, and the experiences of others. Show that you aren't perfect and infallible. Model things like taking responsibility for failure, taking sick days, taking leave, and not working overtime.
>
> – ANTHONY SWEET, PRINCIPAL DESIGNER, LEAGUE OF GEEKS

Choosing authenticity means bringing our whole self into the workplace and accepting the vulnerability that comes with that. But only through embracing our feelings and our humanity can we truly begin to build genuine trust in our teams. The people around us need to feel confident that we are not just pretending to care about them, or that we have their best interests at heart. It's only if they trust that our care is not performative that they will hear us when we need them to most.

WELLBEING

In my early career as a Producer, time difference was a major hurdle. Based in Western Australia, we were working with publishing partners like Sony and Microsoft who tended to be on either European or American time zones. Knowing that it would likely require weird hours and wanting to look out for the well-being of the team, I raised my hand to take care of those meetings. As we developed our game and got closer to release those meetings became more frequent. Some days I would have a meeting at 2 AM, another at 5 AM, and then be work from 9 AM to 7 PM while the programmers worked on polishing a build to send in.

Nobody asked me to do this, the fact that my hours were so ridiculous was a fault entirely of my own design. I felt that it was my responsibility to take this on. If I didn't do that, it was likely somebody else would have to, and I wouldn't wish that on anyone. Of course, there could have been one of us doing 2 AM meetings and another doing 5 AM meetings, it didn't all need to be me. But it felt unfair to ask anybody else to take on those meetings as their own responsibility. I was protecting the team, but it was coming at the cost of myself.

When things in the studio got especially bad, and the team was clearly suffering, I felt responsible for trying to fix that. I empathised with them, I cared about how they were feeling. I made myself solely responsible for fixing the problems they faced out of a sense of duty, and I sacrificed myself to try and achieve it. Looking out for the well-being of our team means looking out for our own well-being, too. We're a part of the team! Protecting them means protecting ourselves.

It was clear in hindsight that I should have set boundaries and asked for assistance. I thought what I was doing was what good leadership looked like. I didn't understand it at the time, but the core of my misunderstanding was a perception of the roles of the cleric and the warrior. It's easy to imagine both classes wielding a shield to protect the team, but it's not that simple. With shield in hand, the warrior has the constitution to keep on protecting the team. The cleric has the wisdom to know when they need to lift the shield to protect themselves.

I didn't fully understand the importance of my own well-being to the quality of my leadership until I saw a psychologist. Other leaders I spoke with shared their own stories of the moment of revelation that came to them through their own therapy or conversation with other developers. Three concepts flowed through the stories that we shared: the need to take care of ourselves, to prioritise where we choose to spend our energy, and to create healthy boundaries.

The first thing we need to understand about well-being is that we can only truly tend to it once our team's most base needs are met. A team that lacks the safety and security at the basest points of Maslow's hierarchy is never going to truly feel healthy (Maslow, 1943). Until those most base needs are met by the business, much of what we provide as leaders will be band-aids on a bullet wound. If there is a morale issue within our team because of their most basic needs not being met, it is a mistake to assume this is a well-being issue. It's a failure of the business to provide the most basic expectations of employment.

Tending to our own well-being requires that we start with the concept of mindfulness. Originating from Hindu and Buddhist teachings, the idea of mindfulness is an ability to see all things as they are. Clinical psychology would begin using mindfulness meditation techniques in the treatment of a variety of contexts (Kabat-Zinn and Hanh, 2009; Galante et al., 2021). In modern society, the idea of mindfulness has become over-saturated to the point of being considered unhelpful (Purser, 2019). It's many different things to many different people.

Where I want to focus on the idea of mindfulness is in its clinical context, and in the context of us as individuals. It may benefit us to meditate, but it is not necessary for mindfulness so long as we have the emotional intelligence to be self-aware. In this way, mindfulness is an extension upon our emotional intelligence. It is the wisdom to know ourselves, the situation we presently find ourselves in, and how it is impacting upon us (Mindful.org, 2020).

I was struggling with anxiety about my dog. He had got off his lead and ran at one point, crossing four lanes of traffic to get back home. It was an experience that rattled me more than I expected, as I find myself worried about him getting away from me again or escaping whenever the gate was open. I would tell myself it was silly when I had these anxious bouts, but that didn't make the anxiety pass. When I started practising mindfulness I would realise I was feeling anxious, check on my dog, see he was fine, and carry on with my day.

Yes, anxiety about a pet helped me be a better leader. It made me understand the way in which I would act. That I had these protective tendencies and a habit of worrying about things that had not happened and may not happen. By working through these anxieties and understanding when they occurred, I could see myself better. The emotions I felt that were less strong but still had an impact upon me or my day to day became easier to manage. It was by working through this anxiety that I got the traction I needed to improve my mindfulness in other ways.

By understanding our feelings and anxieties, suddenly those skills that seem hard become so much easier to exercise. It could be that we find the courage to let the team loose when we finally realise that we fear losing control. Maybe we embrace the individuality of a member of our team and let them watch anime in the office because we realise we need to manage the person and not the behaviour. Or perhaps we realise that we are avoiding a difficult conversation with a team member because the idea of it makes us uncomfortable. The way we behave and how mindful we are of our own feelings impacts upon everybody around us. Using mindfulness in our day-to-day changes everything about how we approach well-being.

How you find your ability to be mindful will be a journey unique to you. It might be that you find a way to mindfulness through meditation, an app, or therapy. The important thing is not to give up on it. It is challenging. Sometimes it is even confronting, as you may learn truths about yourself that you were previously unaware of. But it is not some innate talent or born trait, it is a learned skill. Give yourself the time to learn it, and continue to practice it. Having the wisdom to know yourself through mindfulness will raise your leadership to another level.

When we can better understand our feelings and act accordingly, the next step is to understand where we need to draw the line. One of the clearest misconceptions about the cleric and tending to the well-being of the team is the idea that this means healing them. We are not trained therapists; we cannot tend to the members of our team in this way. We want to care for them, for them to feel comfortable talking to us, and to help them where we can. But we need to understand where people need assistance that goes beyond us, and this is where boundaries are important.

> I have really strong opinions about when people say Producers are like the team therapists, or the team mum. Gendered nonsense aside, I'm not qualified to be your therapist. I'm not here to be your industry trauma dumping ground. That's not my job.
>
> – DR. JC LAU, SENIOR ADVANCED PRODUCER,
> PROBABLYMONSTERS

Well-being isn't about healing; it is about supporting the health of the team ourselves. If we are close to members of our team that going out for coffee, sitting, and listening to them vent about their home life would benefit them, then absolutely, we should feel comfortable doing that. But we can support and tend to the well-being of our team without needing to become friends with every individual, or expecting them to trust us enough to talk about their personal lives. We need to respect that their work is not their life. Where an individual's life impacts their work, we should absolutely support them where we can. But we cannot position ourselves as being the individual responsible for fixing the problem.

> My supervisor would ask the students, 'Are you responsible for them, or are you responsible to them?' Understanding the difference is a huge implication, because then you can understand what your role is and the way other people's emotions factor into it. You are responsible for doing your job in-line with the key indicators of success, but in regard to the people who report to us, we have a responsibility to them - to help them do their part to achieve the goals.
>
> – DR RAFFAEL BOCCAMAZZO, CLINICAL DIRECTOR, TAKE THIS

I believe that this is another key distinction between leaders and managers. A manager may feel they are responsible for the output of their team.

They push their team to achieve those key productivity indicators that the business finds valuable. As leaders, we need to embrace this idea that we are responsible for the workplace and its output. We achieve that output by having a responsibility to the people around us. We are not responsible for the people around us; we cannot take responsibility for every mediocre asset or every bad day they have in the office.

Being responsible to the people around us means reducing the friction they have in the workplace. We must enable them to do the best work they can by creating an environment they can thrive within. We are not responsible for the well-being of the members of our team, we are responsible to it. The distinction here is that we are not going to everyone to tend to their well-being as individuals, but that it is our responsibility as leaders to create an environment in which they can live and work healthily.

Our objective is and should always be to protect the well-being of the members of our team. There are simple actions we can take to see to that well-being that are in line with the ideals of protection. Consider the things that would negatively impact upon the well-being of our team and seek positive change where possible. Consider what is within our power that is not also going to negatively impact upon our own well-being. Endeavour to prevent those things that will create an unhealthy environment for the members of our team. Protection now is well-being in the future.

> Preventing burnout and crunch is only part of making a place a sustainable business. These are symptoms of unsustainable practices, not the cause.
>
> – KEITH FULLER, LEADERSHIP CONSULTANT

Which brings us back to boundaries. We are not accountable as leaders to the individual well-being of our teams, but to their collective well-being. This does not mean that we do not tend to the well-being of individuals, but that we need to recognise the source. If it is the workplace that is causing negative impacts on their well-being, then we should act and provide them with whatever support they need. But if the problem goes deeper than that, if it is a personal issue or the source is external to the place of work, then it comes down to us and our level of comfort as individuals.

Boundaries aren't about having a point at which we simply stop caring about people. It is about knowing the point at which we are no longer comfortable or able to provide support. We want the members of our team to feel comfortable coming to us for support. To talk to us when they are struggling with a task or having a bad day. But if the source of their bad day is an abusive relationship at home or the passing of a loved one, it would benefit both us and the member of our team to help them find more professional care than we can provide.

> We need to mitigate the impact on peoples' wellbeing. Understand the responsibility of the business in providing the first two levels of Maslowe's Hierachy of Needs. When it fails to provide for people, then business closure may be an acceptable scenario to consider.
>
> – KEITH FULLER, LEADERSHIP CONSULTANT

Boundaries are not a static thing, however. Every day will bring with it new challenges in our jobs and our lives; we will have more or less capacity to contend with the issues surrounding us. The spoon theory is a metaphor proposed by writer Christine Miserandino in a 2003 article, in which she describes the challenges of living with Lupus. She talks about sitting in a diner with a friend who asks about what it was like to live with Lupus, and Christine goes on to explain by using a collection of the spoons at the dinner table. She explains that every task she needs to do in a day requires spoons. If she wants to go for a walk or have a shower, those things take a number of spoons that she may only have a limited amount of. Each day becomes a careful exchange of resources to achieve even small tasks (Miserandino, 2013).

While the example that Christine gave was specifically with regards to living with chronic illness, it is a concept that I believe is important to understand for our own mental health and well-being. These small tasks are things that require an amount of energy that people without chronic disease or disability take for granted. Living with these sort of illnesses gives us a mindfulness of the energy cost of even small actions that other people often lack. With this sort of mindfulness, it's not difficult to look at how we are feeling in a given day and understand if we have more or less spoons.

We all feel those low energy days, where it's hard to get out of bed and we just feel unmotivated. Sometimes it can be really challenging to understand why, but being able to recognise these feelings can guide our performance for the day ahead. We will have the priorities that we need to tend to relating to our duties within the business, but we may need to create boundaries about the other issues that may come up throughout the day. If we are not going to be able to wholeheartedly tackle a problem that requires us at our best, then we need to put it aside until a better time if possible.

Being able to understand how we are feeling and how many spoons we have in a given day does benefit our team. Just being able to tell the members of our team that we are having a rough day and require their help to get through it builds trust as the team can experience some authenticity from us. If they approach us with the need to talk about their rough day, it may be opportunity to share our own feelings with them. If we feel ourselves on the edge of losing our temper, we know already then to excuse ourselves from the conversation.

This doesn't just benefit the people immediately around us, but sends a message to the members of our team. We care about respecting the people around us through an awareness of ourselves. It makes well-being something that we value as part of our culture, and sets a positive example to our team. Empathising with our team and sharing our own feelings with them will validate and encourage their own openness.

By sharing in this way, we contribute to a culture of psychological safety within our teams. We contribute to the cultivation of that psychological safety by accepting and protecting others when they open up or take a risk, and by doing the same ourselves. We need to ensure we enforce boundaries here, as we want people to feel they can open up and express concern about the situation without becoming fixated on complaints. We must not lose sight of the need to seek solutions. But it's imperative that we cultivate an environment in which people feel safe to feel.

The final thing about to understand about well-being is the need to put your oxygen mask on first. If you have ever been flying you will have heard this instruction during the flight safety video. If there is an emergency on a flight and the oxygen masks are deployed, you are directed to put your mask on before helping others. It may seem selfish, particularly if you are prone to feeling that you are responsible for protecting the members of your team. But without the oxygen you need to sustain you during an emergency, we put others who may need our assistance at risk.

You can't get your team right until you've got yourself right.

– EMILY MACMAHON, LEADERSHIP CONSULTANT

It was this advice that made me realise that I had been doing my job poorly. I had been putting others before myself to the point that I was suffocating. How many issues had I missed or simply lacked the energy to contend with as a result of not taking care of myself? The advice took some time to really sink in and start to action, but the longer I led others the clearer it became why it was so important. The more stressed I was, the more prone I was to making mistakes or missing issues.

Tending to your own mental health will benefit your team in ways you cannot begin to imagine. Your self-awareness plays a huge part in the team's perception of you, in addition to their own emotional and mental state. Taking the time to work on protecting or improving on my mental health improved my self-awareness and benefitted the teams I work with by extension. Thinking about many of the negative experiences I've had with leaders I've had in past, so much of what we experienced as a team would have been an entirely different experience had our leadership been receiving therapy at the time.

Obviously, it is not as simple as just going out and getting therapy. Healthcare around the world differs dramatically, so it is unfair to suggest that it is that simple. If you live in a place where it is expensive, I suggest making some time every week to sit and journal. It's much easier to identify why you may be feeling a certain way if you can look back at your words. Alternatively, there are mindfulness apps out there, though I have had mixed success in my experience with many of them. If the main thing holding you back is some perception of yourself as not requiring it, ask yourself why. If the answer is that it would be too challenging or that you are above the need for support, then you absolutely would benefit from therapy.

Our jobs as leaders are stressful. Even if you believe that you cope with the issues well, you need some kind of support mechanism through which you can work through your emotions and stress. We deal with circumstances that change and differ dramatically from those that our peers will have dealt with. Therapy helps us to work through the emotional impact to ourselves, while coaching helps to guide us and check our solutions with people who have experienced similar circumstances. Leadership is not a journey that should be travelled alone.

Knowing

I was in a studio at one point where I was assigned a junior game designer. And honestly as a junior she was one of if not the most brilliant juniors I've ever worked with. Her work was above most seniors. She was a superstar, firing on all cylinders, just really really good. And so I made the mistake of giving her full ownership over her tasks and barely spending time with her. Just checking in a little bit and saying, great, good job! And I thought that this was the right thing to do with somebody performing at this level.

But then I realised, I don't think she's happy. I'm very unsure why, something must be going wrong with her personal life. So I scheduled a one on one and I said, I think something is wrong, is it okay if I ask what it is? Eventually she told me that she felt adrift. She didn't know how well she was doing. And I was like, are you kidding me? I've been telling you non-stop that you are doing an amazing job! I'm barely able to give you feedback! And she said, yes, that's the problem. She saw me spending so much time with other people and so little time with her, and she didn't know how to interpret that.

That was the record scratch moment. I'm like, my god, I need to communicate better with everybody across the board and really understand situational leadership. I went and got training that leveled me up big time so that I'm better able to catch these situations. I make other mistakes, of course – you are always going to make mistakes. But this is one mistake I rarely make anymore.

– OSAMA DORIAS, LEAD GAMEPLAY DESIGNER,
BRASS LION ENTERTAINMENT

DOI: 10.1201/9781003431626-13

I only know one thing, and that is I know nothing. This popular quote is attributed to the Greek philosopher Socrates, and captures the essence of knowing. The skills of knowing are some of the most challenging to do right because there is often no real correct answer on how to do them. There is not necessarily any process or framework that makes these things easier to do, or guarantees success even most of the time. To truly express the skills of knowing requires two things: that you reflect upon the outcome of your choices, and that you are prepared to change and grow.

Throughout the skills we've discussed, we have highlighted the balancing act that is often required of them. This is only amplified with those skills relating to knowing, as we start to dabble with forces and decisions that are often outside of our potential to influence or control. We have been gradually moving away from the things that we have some direct power over, and now find ourselves firmly in the territory of the things we can control the least: other people. Where feeling gives us some ability to understand, knowing requires embracing the fact that we cannot control how others will react, only how we choose to act.

You will be faced with challenging decisions throughout your career. The sort of choices that do not have an easy answer. There will be an expectation of us as leaders to make the difficult decision, even when it hurts. The team may never know the challenging choices we had to make, and they may not even thank us for choosing the least bad option out of a selection of worse ones. This is simply part of the burden of leadership.

How much information should we share with our teams? Should they be made aware of each conversation, and each circumstance that we're having to contend with? Should they be aware of the circumstances of our funding and just how many months we believe we have remaining before we may shut down the business? If we give them that information, do we also not possibly risk our capacity to bounce back if people choose to leave and find work in a business that isn't at risk of closure?

This is only one example of an infinite number of possible challenges we could face in the course of our careers. There is no reasonable way to provide guidance that suits every single circumstance we could face. Seeking outside support for mentorship and guidance is absolutely invaluable whenever we face such challenges, but we can prepare for these moments by knowing ourselves. If we can build a better understanding of ourselves in this way, we can begin to make more informed decisions about these moments of challenge.

Knowing is about your experience, yes. But more importantly, it's about your values, your morals, and the principles you choose to lead by. What are our strengths, our weaknesses, and our blind spots. We may not be able to know the correct answer to every circumstance we may be faced with, but we can know ourselves. If we can do that and act with integrity about what we stand for, we will be able to make the best decision available to us.

TRANSPARENCY

I was told a story some time ago about a studio which took pride in its transparency. Leaders at this team had rightfully acknowledged the lack of transparency at bigger studios, and so they chose to set up a digital ticker within the studio. This ticker displayed the amount of funds the studio had remaining in their bank accounts to spend on the project. It was updated at the moment, meaning you could see that money in the accounts was moved around to pay for the studio's many expenses.

Imagine being a developer in this place. Every day you come into the office, and you look up at that ticker. Would you be able to stop yourself from doing some quick math in your head? How many years of pay does that money offer if it's just for you? If it's a team of 80 or so people being paid the same as you, how many years of development does that support? And that's not including the money needed for every other expense the studio has that you would be unaware of.

Suffice it to say, it did not go well. Leadership, not understanding just what their team wanted when they asked for transparency, went out of their way to make things so transparent that anxiety in the studio peaked. People doing the math and figuring that they had less than three years of pay available to them started looking for work elsewhere, and the studio experienced an unexpectedly high number of departures. It is just one of the many game-development horror stories I've heard shared over drinks at conferences.

> Sometimes you need to tell the team "listen, I would love very much to tell you about this, but unfortunately I cannot share this information with you." Treat people as adults.
>
> – OSAMA DORIAS, LEAD GAMEPLAY DESIGNER,
> BRASS LION ENTERTAINMENT

There are plenty of examples of studios that failed to provide transparency when it was necessary to do so. When Telltale Games shut down in October of 2018, they had made new hires only a week prior who had relocated to work at the business. It's highly likely that leadership was aware of the potential for their financial failure, but this was kept from the team until everybody was told in a shock all staff meeting that they were now out of a job (Gach, 2018). Hearing this story and the many others like it, it's not unusual for well-intended leaders to go in the entirely opposite direction. The reality is that good transparency management sits somewhere between under-sharing and oversharing.

The reality of the situation is that we need to make difficult choices about what we do or do not share with the members of our teams. We want to provide transparency; this story should not discourage us from sharing information with our coworkers. The question rather is, what information? What is necessary for our teams to know? What information will cause them to become overwhelmed? How much context do they require to avoid unnecessary anxiety? There is a point where transparency becomes a distraction from the work. We want to create an environment that enables the well-being of our teams.

It's safe to say that every person I spoke with valued "transparency, but." It's challenging to articulate the specific point at which transparency turns from an asset to a liability, but we see examples all through the games industry where leaders simply fail at transparency. For the most part, this failure is in not sharing necessary information with the members of their teams until it is too late. But there are those rare examples like the financial ticker where the problem goes in the entirely opposite direction. People want transparency until they don't. We need to understand where that point resides for our team.

> There are always going to be things you cannot tell the people that report to you, because they are not going to have the necessary context. There's a lot of nuance.
>
> – LIANA RUPPERT, COMMUNITY MANAGER, PREVIOUSLY OF BUNGIE

In an interview with Jason Schreier for one of his books, leadership at Obisidian Studios describes a circumstance in which they faced the potential closure of their studio. After the loss of funding for a project resulted in the firing of 70 members of staff, leadership at Obsidian was put in a position where they could no longer guarantee the ongoing survival of their studio. Just months away from closure, they had to make a decision about whether or not to take a risk on crowdfunding to try and keep themselves afloat (Schreier, 2017).

Crowdfunding is not exactly a reliable source of income. The decision to develop a title to take to a crowdfunding platform is risky, not just because it may not pay off but because the studio needed something fast. It could result in weeks or months of unpaid work or overtime. Even if the crowdfunding campaign was successful, they would need further publisher support to finish the job. The remaining funds available to the business could possibly be allocated somewhere else to get some funding. Or perhaps it was a sign that the business was simply not working, and closure should be a consideration.

Of course at the time of writing, Obsidian is still open and running. You may not know the specific details of this story, but you already know the outcome. Inspired by the success of Double Fine Adventure, the team at Obsidian chose to take the risk of crowdfunding. They put the facts before the team and allowed them to make up their own minds. Would they stay with them and take a risk, or would they play it safe and find work elsewhere? The gamble paid off, and the Pillars of Eternity crowdfunding campaign managed to raise over $4 million for its development (Purchese, 2012).

I presented the facts of the situation with Obsidian to industry leaders and asked them how they would approach such a circumstance themselves. Rather than having one clear pathway to success or one clear answer, every person I interviewed instead asked questions. How long have I been working with these people? Are we close? How long can we continue to operate without the funding? Do we need to pull people from other projects to create a prototype? Have we market tested the game that we want to get funding for?

While Jason Schreier's book gives us some fascinating insights, these are questions that we will probably never have the answers to. We can only hypothesise what the mood would be like in the studio after taking a risk like this. The reason these questions matter is because the level of transparency and even the choice itself are informed by the culture, the mood, and the success of the studio. A studio of people who lack trust are going to be less willing to take risks when presented with harsh facts.

Providing people with transparency in such an environment may kill our chances to save everybody's jobs as people choose to leave to find more stable work.

> One business had just two or three months before their coffers would run dry. We had to discuss and figure out what to do to resolve the problem. Being transparent with the team could risk losing ten percent of them, and at that point it would mean they couldn't land another contract. The whole company would be closed. So do you tell everybody? If you don't, people may just miss out on a paycheque and choose to move on anyway. Leaders need to be exposed to the stories of other teams so that they can understand what to be prepared for. The military probably looks at the outcome of battles to train, but doesn't present a scenario where the solution is 'the' solution. It's important to go through big picture questions, not just some rote process in circumstances like these.
>
> – KEITH FULLER, LEADERSHIP CONSULTANT, FOUNDER OF GAMEDEVCOACHING.COM

Undoubtedly, the circumstances caused a great deal of anxiety within the studio, but sharing the facts was an ethical necessity. If Obsidian only had months or even a year of runway with which to keep their staff employed, that is a fact their staff needed to be made aware of. People with families and mortgages needed the opportunity to start looking for work elsewhere, and to be able to do so without judgement from their peers.

The way we choose to present such information is also important. Telling them the facts will not be enough. We will always bring some of our own personal bias to such a circumstance, even just presenting the reality of the situation. Do we feel confident in the ability of the studio to be saved by crowdfunding? Do the people in this team trust us to make the right decision for them? Are we trying to sell them on this plan just because it is our plan?

We have a responsibility to the team and to the business we work for. These are not fully separate entities: our teams are reliant upon the success of our business to make a living, and our businesses are reliant upon the members of our team to make money. In presenting the facts to our team, we need to consider and balance the impacts upon them and upon the studio itself. Any action that damages one also causes harm to the other. The connection can often be challenging or tenuous to see, but it is a symbiotic relationship. We are always balancing these two things, not choosing one over the other.

This makes it nearly impossible to provide good or consistent advice on when and how to be transparent with our team. Transparency could make people's work easier or prepare them for the worst. It could also cause unnecessary anxiety for them or harm to the business. Transparency must be about sharing information that minimises harm and maximises good within our studio. Sharing our studio budget from minute to minute does not minimise harm, but informing the team of dwindling funding or potential job losses in the coming months does. Sometimes the right amount of information to share is enough just to reduce the team's anxiety.

> So the people managers in our team were being tanked. They weren't aware of some of the bigger strategic conversations happening around the team and our direction. By bringing them into the room and letting them have some transparency on the situation, suddenly the conversation changed quite a bit. Now when the rank and filed developers have questions, their managers are actually clued in. Sometimes you need to do it where you are being transparent with the whole team. But other times it's making sure the managers are equipped to have those one-on-one, anxiety settling conversations in private.
>
> – LUKE DICKEN, SENIOR DIRECTOR OF APPLIED AI, ZYNGA

There's no formula for when and how we provide transparency. Generally, we want to avoid oversharing. The two key considerations about what constitutes necessary information are the time and impact. When we are talking about transparency at a macro level – the kind of issues that impact a whole team – we are usually considering the impact on the foundational needs of the team as defined in Maslow's Hierarchy (Maslow, 1943). Does it pose a risk to their employment, their security, or their safety? If so, then the next question is: how much time do they have before it becomes a risk. An issue they may face in the coming weeks is critical to share, but something a year away may be far less important to share.

However, these are macro-level considerations for transparency. These sorts of stories provide a good example of how we need to think about transparency, but most of the time we need to think about transparency at a more individual, micro level. These conversations tend to be easier when it comes to making decisions about what to share or not. Individual transparency is usually more about providing feedback that has less impact in the long term. It's usually about providing the team with news about their performance, even when it may be uncomfortable to share. There are very few conversations here where I believe it is worth hesitating for a long time.

These are the sorts of conversations in which we must give people honest insight about their performance. Depending on your upbringing and experiences in life, you may find it harder to give one type of feedback or another. Providing people with positive feedback can present a challenge for some leaders, though generally negative feedback is the more challenging to provide. Whether the feedback is good or bad, the critically important aspect of transparency for this individual is communication and individuality.

While nobody generally likes to be criticised, there is such a thing as hollow praise. We must be able to provide clarity through our words by considering how the person we are speaking to desires to interact. Those individuals who desire to improve upon their work and look up to us as mentors will want us to provide them with feedback that can clearly describe the things we like and what we do not like, to enable them to understand how they need to improve. If we need to provide negative feedback, it's imperative to direct it at the behaviour or the work, not the individual.

> Our job is to identify the faults in other people's work. And people can take that personally if we're not very kind. Building trust is about building good communication skills in the QA team. It's about removing the people from our observations. So when I'm testing something that you've produced, I don't say you messed up again and there's a bug here. I would say we were expecting the feature to behave in these ways based on these sources of truth, and these are our observations.
>
> – JASON IMMS, HEAD OF QUALITY ASSURANCE, KEYWORDS STUDIOS

People underperform or may even execute a job poorly. When they do, we must provide feedback about the output and not the person doing the work. It is much simpler to have an honest conversation about improvement when what we are discussing is the work done and not the way in which it was done. Find the work lacking, but never the person. Unless we are fully aware of what is happening in their lives, it's very likely that poor performance reflects some other issue they are experiencing. When we criticise the output, follow up with a question: what can I do to help?

When we present an individual as the problem, the need to improve is placed squarely on their shoulders. By presenting the work as a problem, it becomes an issue that can be solved as a team. This once again reinforces that trust: that we want them to get the job done, and that we want to work with them to get the best possible outcome. Avoid presenting our way as the ideal or only way to solve a problem. We want to help lead our team to better results, not direct them to it. By collaborating with them to achieve results their way, we reinforce their ownership over the problem and its solution. Take the time to identify the problem with them, and then help guide them to a solution that works for everybody.

We want to build teams that value honesty and candour. Teams that recognise that criticism is levelled at the work, not the individual (Bennis, Goleman and O'Toole, 2010). In Creativity Inc, Ed Catmull paints a picture of Pixar as a studio in which candour is encouraged at all levels. To ensure the quality of their animated movies, Pixar had established what it called the Braintrust. A group of other Pixar employees would watch and then provide constructive criticism and advice to the film's director. By giving one another honest and genuine feedback – even when it may be negative feedback – the studio is able to develop the skills of its staff. However, it is not just enough to encourage feedback. Candour is only truly enabled through mutual trust, respect, and an understanding that every member of the team is striving to achieve the best possible outcome.

In one chapter of "Creativity Inc.," Catmull talks about the development of Up. After watching an early cut of the film, the Braintrust really focused on the number of plot threads that were being juggled. At this early stage in its development, Up had a complicated and winding story about getting old, lost love, a rare bird, talking dogs, and the fountain of youth. The other members of the Braintrust criticised the density of the film, suggesting plot threads that should be changed or removed.

In the end, the film's director created a plot hole that few people caught. The film had spent a great deal of time explaining how its antagonist had not aged as much as its protagonist by adding a side story about the fountain of youth – or rather, eggs laid by the rare bird that had fountain of youth-like effects. Despite the creation of the plot hole, fans and critics were as satisfied as the Braintrust were in the final version of the film (Catmull, 2014). It's safe to say that without the Braintrust and transparency of feedback, Up would have been a very different and likely much less successful film.

Of course, sometimes we are not criticising the work. Sometimes we need to have difficult conversations with people whose behaviour needs adjustment. This is always a more challenging conversation to have and will require a lot of patience and trust when our objective is to correct it and not simply just fire the individual responsible. A conversation like this is much more about us as leaders being able to step out of our comfort zone to lay down some hard truths to people when their behaviour negatively affects the other members of our teams. We still want to maintain that focus on solutions, but people need to understand how and why their behaviour is unacceptable.

None of this is possible without trust. A team member who does not trust our leadership will never truly absorb or consider our words when we provide them with this feedback, no matter how critical or clearly it is presented. It is much easier for us to deflect criticism from somebody we do not trust, after all. If we find that the members of our team are not really taking our words to heart when we provide them with this honest feedback, we may find that we have a trust issue within our team.

Transparency makes leaders uncomfortable. We often must make choices about what information we do or do not share or how we are going to make people aware of hard truths. In many ways, understanding the information that our team should be made aware of is only half the problem. The other half is about knowing ourselves well enough to recognise when we are making excuses to avoid difficult conversations. Practising transparency means embracing discomfort sometimes.

EXPECTATIONS

What behaviours are acceptable at your game studio? In July 2021, Activision Blizzard Entertainment made news headlines across the games industry when it was accused of having what was described as a "frat boy culture." Female members of staff reported being subjected to sexual harassment, unequal pay, and retaliation if they were to speak out. Stories from members of staff at the time accused the studio of not taking action to protect staff and ignored complaints that were shared with HR. At least one member of Blizzard's executive leadership team was implicated in the accusations as a perpetrator (Allsup, 2021; Liao, 2021; Hollister, 2021).

The response from studio leadership was to deny the accusations. Activision Blizzard would issue a statement denying the allegations, asserting that they did not reflect the company's culture (Plunkett, 2021). However, an open letter signed by over 800 staff at the company would argue that the response damaged attempts at creating equality and perpetuated an atmosphere at the company that doubted victims (Clark, 2021).

Building the sort of culture that we want to see in our teams requires that we set and enforce clear boundaries. A decision to not correct behaviours that make an environment dangerous for some of our staff sets a boundary through inaction. A failure to condemn such behaviour sends the message that it is condoned. The accusations levelled at Activision Blizzard are extreme, but a failure to act when the issue is small can rapidly grow a problem to such catastrophic proportions.

Managing expectations is a key responsibility in our role as leaders. When we talk about expectations, there are two terms they often use: boundaries and limitations. When we are talking about boundaries, we are talking about the interpersonal. They are the expectations that we as a leader and as a team have of our people. Limitations are more about the work. It is the way in which we desire as a collective to see the work get completed. There is another third thing, however, and that is the expectations the team has for us as their leadership.

Boundaries are the outer limits of our cultural contracts. When somebody shouts at another member of the team, this should represent a failure to uphold our contract. It's a boundary we do not cross if we want to create a culture in which everybody feels respected and heard. When things get hard, it's not unusual for temperatures to become flared. But that does not excuse the lack of respect that is implied by shouting at one another. It does not matter if it is leadership shouting at a member of staff – arguably it's worse, as it sets a high example for our team.

Often, a team will have a code of conduct that dictates behavioural standards for the team, but these are not the same thing as boundaries. A code of conduct is an excellent tool for setting the basic enforceable expectations about behaviour in a team, but it is still just a piece of paper. Boundaries are organic, they represent the kind of culture that we are cultivating within our teams. They may be written down in a code of conduct or expressed through our values, but they are only truly made real when we act upon them.

Boundaries are similar to social norms in that they are informal guides to our behaviour. The difference is only that we are setting them at individual and team levels. It is a social norm that people will flush the toilet after they are finished in the bathroom. It is a culture that people turn up to meetings five minutes early. It is a boundary that we do not shout at our peers. The difference here is one thing is that culture defines our desirable behaviours as a collective, and boundaries are the things that fall outside of acceptable norms as a collective or as individuals.

We need to be able to respect the boundaries of others if we want them to respect our own. Every day that we come into the office, we may have varying tolerances for certain behaviours. We may ask people to keep the volume down because we've got a particularly bad headache that day. We still want people to respect such a request, even if it is only in the short term. We would be rightfully annoyed if somebody broke the contract and ignored such a simple request, and so it's our responsibility as leaders to ensure that everybody is respecting the boundaries.

The message we want to be sending our teams is that we listen to and respect each other's needs, no matter how small they may be. As leaders it's especially important that we pay attention to and respect these boundaries, as we are setting an example for our teams that we treat others the way we want to be treated. We also have the authority to hold others accountable if they cross the boundaries of others, and we must do so. It's not enough to only enforce our personal boundaries. If we expect our needs to be respected, then respect must be shown to the needs of all.

When boundaries are more long-term, they are a cultural contract. For example, ask people to keep the staff kitchen tidy. It may not happen right away, and people will require a gentle nudge. It may be best phrased as a request, "do you mind cleaning up your mess?" We reinforce the boundary by making people accountable. This cultural contract is mutual, however: if we request that others keep the staff kitchen tidy, it's expected we will do the same. Breaking the contract gives everybody permission to make a mess of the kitchen.

Sometimes boundaries will change, and that's fine. The informal, organic nature of them compared to our cultural values means that there can be a difference between those non-negotiable boundaries and the more flexible ones. Cracking jokes and treating things as lighthearted may be encouraged until the circumstances are dire. At that stage, it may be necessary to reinforce a higher degree of empathy for one another if people are being rubbed the wrong way by the jokes. When we adjust these behaviours, it needs to be clear why and done without accusation. People may not even realise that the contract has been altered.

Enforcing boundaries often requires difficult conversations, and it's this fact that makes many studios stumble. Without training, many leaders simply avoid having the conversation, and so the behaviour is perpetrated to the point that the boundary no longer matters. It's not unusual for people to become defensive when told that their behaviour is out of line or needs adjustment, even when the failure is minor. Going into these conversations always needs to be done thoughtfully and with respect to the individual, even if the boundary that has been crossed is dire.

> Set expectations, and make sure that you're checking in with people when deliverables aren't being met. But also have the courage to be firm, because it's one thing to set your boundary, but another to enforce the boundary.
>
> – JEAN LEGGETT, LEADERSHIP COACH

For example, we talked about somebody shouting at a coworker earlier. Shouting is a symptom of a larger problem. If people are so frustrated or angry that the only way they feel they can be heard is to shout, then clearly there is something wrong. Is there something happening in the studio to motivate it? Or is it something happening in this person's private life?

The worst thing we can do in this circumstance is shout down the person doing the shouting. It only undermines any boundaries we set about mutual respect. Instead, setting boundaries with this person looks like a gentle conversation after the event. Pulling them aside to say, hey, we don't do that here; you were out of line. Once we reinforce those boundaries, we can start to dig into the core of why they felt it was necessary in the first place and then remedy the source of the fault.

> Businesses should set explicit expectations of people leaders. It should be documented, and then shared with the team so that they understand what to expect from their leadership. What they are responsible for and accountable to.
>
> – KEITH FULLER, LEADERSHIP CONSULTANT, FOUNDER OF
> GAMEDEVCOACHING.COM

It is also important that we draw boundaries for our leadership. Our teams will have existing expectations about what a leader does, and these may not necessarily align with how we intend to operate. There is value in providing your teams with documentation laying out your responsibilities as it relates to them and their work, most certainly. But how we act and what we choose to invest our energy in also sends a message to our team about what they can expect from us.

For example, there is a propensity among leaders who are particularly strong clerics to be perceived as therapists. A particularly effective cleric may leave their team with the impression that they are open to discuss difficult issues because they are so personable. When we support our teams, this does not necessarily mean personal support with mental health or well-being. We are there to provide support for the circumstances experienced within our studios. And so we must set clear boundaries and expectations about what we will and will not support our team through.

> Being a people leader, you want to give people space to be open and create that psychological safety. So they will talk to you about whatever, but I think it's important to draw boundaries. I'm not here to solve all your problems, because I cannot solve your personal, emotional problems. That's not my skill set. Early in my career I was just like, everyone come talk to me. It's fine. And it just became my job to remove everyone's anxiety from the team, which is great. But then I'm carrying all that anxiety. What do I do with it? I'm fortunate, I have a therapist. But not everyone has that, right?
>
> – DR. JC LAU, SENIOR ADVANCED PRODUCER,
> PROBABLYMONSTERS

This may not sound so bad, depending on the kind of person you are and the relationship you have with your team. You need to know yourself well enough to know where you are satisfied with drawing the boundary with your team members. You may be the kind of leader who is happy to sit and hear their problems. You may want to maintain a perfectly professional relationship. It is a fact that you will fluctuate between these two extremes, even if you intend to make yourself available as much as possible to hear your team. You are always communicating these boundaries each day; you need to be clear with yourself on where the line is.

Where boundaries define the individual social expectations we have with one another, limitations are about the work and how we do it. That we do not turn up late to meetings is a boundary: we are breaking a social contract we hold with our peers. Not working on projects after hours is a limitation: it is a constraint set on the work and specifically enforced by leadership.

The games industry is always pushing to create bigger and greater games. We can see this particularly in the size of maps. Studios would proudly market how their map was so many times larger than the map from their previous games, and these sizes would just keep on growing. When Bethesda Game Studios released Skyrim in 2011, it boasted a massive 14.5 mi² (37.5 km²) wide map. Ubisoft's Assassins Creed Odyssey released just seven years later in 2018 and is over six times larger at 90.7 mi² (234.91 km²) (Phillpott-Kenny, 2020). Today, games like No Man's Sky now boast near infinite map sizes.

In 2023, Bethesda Game Studios released Starfield. Starfield is a game similar in many ways to Skyrim, it is an open-world RPG. But its scale is immense in comparison, encompassing a full 1000 planets. Analysts, executives, and developers all warned in interviews that Bethesda needed to be careful about overpromising what they can deliver (Browning and Stevens, 2023). Just because technological advancements have been made to enable such scale, does not mean it will be exciting.

When Starfield was finally released, players quickly found that the majority of the thousand promised worlds were barren. Unique worlds with unusual creatures only comprised ten percent of the planets promised by Starfield. One developer defended the choice, explaining that the planets were empty because that is just the reality of space exploration (Simelane, 2023). There is a clear disconnect between the expectations of its developers and the reality of what matters to the game's players. Infinity starts to look awfully boring after you see another world shaped just like the last one you visited.

Studios that are passionate about technical and artistic achievement can often become so fixated on the how that they lose track of the why. As our games get larger, they become more and more challenging to polish and maintain the level of quality that we would (hopefully) like to maintain. This creates a disconnect between many game developers and the players of their games. These technological feats sound impressive but are in many ways largely meaningless to the average player beyond a snappy line of marketing.

This may be why limitation is often perceived as the enemy of passion in the games industry. Passion is a powerful force, and it is through passion for the work that the development of our games can become similarly out of hand. Even among those studios that value creating more healthy places to work, passion can lead to ruin. Limitations are not about hampering passion but about setting clear expectations about how we develop our games.

> If I were to wave a magic wand to change one thing at Double Fine, it would be for people to recognise the value of constraint. Sometimes when we're sketching or doing work on a game, we almost look at constraint as an enemy. When you're creating art, it's pretty essential. You have to have some boundaries.
>
> – CAMDEN STODDARD, AUDIO DIRECTOR, DOUBLE FINE

Our team may decide that work is to be done between certain hours. These are the left and right limits of our workday, and the team needs to respect them. More importantly, leadership needs to respect them. Consistently working late hours at the office sends the message to the team that these hours are merely a suggestion and not a limitation. If the team is consistently working excessive hours to achieve their tasks, we will inevitably become dysfunctional. It means that any sort of estimations about how quickly work can be completed will become inaccurate: we don't know how much more the team is consistently needing to work outside of our established hours.

Say for example that a member of our team estimates that it will take two weeks for them to complete a task. If they are working additional hours outside of our stated start and end times for work, we can no longer say that the task they are working on takes only two weeks. Not only does this make any sort of accurate future estimation impossible, but it also means that anybody replacing this individual would have a preexisting expectation to work excessive hours.

But this is only the business and project arguments for setting such limitations. The more important fact here is that we have a responsibility to ensure the well-being of our teams. By allowing a single team member to work excessive hours, we are setting a precedent. It sends a message to the members of our team that we value their passion and their output over their health. A choice to work overtime never just impacts a singular person, which is why it is so important to intervene. Just like how we would establish and enforce boundaries with the members of our team, we need to enforce these same limitations to ensure the health and well-being of everybody.

Wherever it is possible in our role as leaders, we also want to set limitations on the scope of work. While we may not have direct responsibility for setting the scope, we can make well-informed arguments that advocate for the team wherever proposed work is excessive. To do this, we want to make sure that we are having conversations with our team to understand what they see as being possible within our current constraints.

The challenge about enforcing limitations is that they can quickly fall into those evil aligned dictatorial tendencies. Demanding that team members follow a particular process or use a particular tool is not a good use of our ability to set limitations. For what reason is that process important? What benefits does the tool have for the members of our team? We want to ensure that we are setting healthy limitations for our team that are well reasoned and clear. They need to understand why the limitation exists.

It is for this reason that expectations exist firmly in the skill of knowing. Nobody can tell us specifically what healthy limitations our place of work should have. If the hours of work at our studio are flexible, that team member who is working late hours may just be a night owl. We do not want our limitations to hamper the creativity or the passion of our team, but to protect their well-being. We balance limitations with flexibility in everything that we do in terms of ensuring the project work gets done.

Whether it is setting boundaries or limitations, we must clearly communicate and model our expectations for our teams. It's not enough to just speak to these things; we need to talk our talk. Integrity and accountability are essential for us to set expectations that our team is meant to follow. They are looking to us as the baseline for what their behaviour is allowed to be or how they are allowed to work. Lead the way you expect your team to follow.

ACTIVE INTROSPECTION

Every single person I spoke with during the research for this book shared one thing in common: an inward focus. They looked at their performance and considered how better to improve the outcomes for their projects and for the people on the teams they lead. For many of the leaders with whom I spoke, it was a constant consideration: how were they performing, how they were going to approach this next conversation, and what they could have done differently on the last project to avoid an issue.

I went through several attempts to try and capture this concept in a few words, to describe just what it looked like. I considered reflection, curiosity, vigilance, or thoughtfulness. I ran these ideas by the people I interviewed, and the general consensus was that these are all relatively passive words. The process that they were doing was something they specifically chose to do. It was active; it was considered. They would think about the potential outcomes of their actions or the outcomes that had occurred as a result of their actions.

Eventually, we would settle on the concept of active introspection. It is reflective, thoughtful, vigilant, and curious. We think and reflect on our actions and feelings. We are vigilant about the potential problems we are currently facing, could face, or will inevitably face. We are curious in seeking ways to improve our circumstances or prevent worse ones. It is not necessarily the most important skill, but it is very likely the most powerful one. If you fail at every other skill that we've discussed throughout this book but succeed at active introspection, you will inevitably improve on your leadership.

> If you are going to be a really great leader, then you need to have done a big more digging around in yourself. Have a very clear understanding of what you're here to do in terms of your leadership. What's meant to come about through your leadership? What is your purpose? And at the same time, you've got to know all of your Achilles heels. All the things that freak you out or terrify you, and all the reasons you probably shouldn't say that thing you really want to say. You've got to be aware of all of those parts of yourself that arise, and then you'll need to know all the strategies to manage all of that.
>
> – EMILY MACMAHON, LEADERSHIP CONSULTANT

The concept of active introspection is unique from those of reflection, thoughtfulness, or vigilance alone as it encapsulates no specific point in time. Both concepts are about informing our actions in the present: reflection looks to the past, thoughtfulness considers the people in our present, and vigilance protects us from being surprised by our future. Curiosity encourages us not to just get stuck inside of our own heads thinking about these things, but to seek input from others as well.

Reflect on the past.

Thoughtful in the present.

Vigilant to the future.

Curious about our performance.

Reflection is the foundation for active introspection. Donald Schön's "The Reflective Practitioner" examines the ways in which professions such as engineering, psychology, and management would improvise. These individuals would be faced with unique challenges that could not simply be solved using learning from a textbook or a framework passed onto them by a teacher. By improvising in the moment and then taking the time to stop and reflect upon the outcome afterwards, these individuals could help inform their future practice.

The act of improvisation is immensely important to us as leaders in the games industry. Improvisation in leadership may sound dirty, but it is the reality of our role. We are dealing with constant chaos; the industry is constantly changing. The software changes, the processes change, and people – the core element of our job – are unpredictable. We have core values that we act upon, and by this point, you should understand the importance of integrity to make decisions that align with your values. But we are still always improvising within that space.

We will at some point in our career need to improvise and make a decision that is based entirely on our individual experiences and ideals. We can (and should) seek outside input for such choices, but the people we receive our mentorship from will lack the singular expertise we have in our unique position. This does not mean we disregard their insights, but that no matter how well informed we are about the decisions we make, none of them will be based on a simple formula or similar experience. Our experiences are entirely unique. Every studio, every team, and every game is different.

While it may be challenging if it is not something you have engaged with before, reflection is a concept embraced by game developers. It is the way in which we embrace continuous learning. As an industry, we take the time to consider the usefulness of a tool or process, and we use that information to inform our future decision-making. I would go so far as to say that every talk we see at game development conferences is the result of reflection in this way. A studio or individual has improvised a new process or technology, reflected upon the outcome, and decided to present the things that worked or not.

What the games industry tends to fail at doing is reflecting on the impact of choices on people. As leaders, we want to extend our reflection from just the tools and processes. We must use our emotional intelligence as we reflect on the impacts of our actions on the people that we work with.

This is why curiosity is so important to the act of active introspection, as we cannot simply stop at assumptions about how our teams are feeling. Even if we feel certain, we must seek to gather insight from the people around us. We need to understand how our leadership impacts others from their perspective, not just our own.

> If you have a problem with something I'm doing, let me know. I don't want to do anything that makes our working together difficult, and I know it's challenging, but you have got to let me know so I have a chance to adjust my behaviour. If you go straight to the manager level, they ask why you didn't change this behaviour. Well, nobody told me they wanted this to be done like that.
>
> – CHIMA DENZEL NGEREM, PRODUCER, ZYNGA

Beyond just thinking about the past, we also want to think about the future. When we are vigilant, we are considering the potential outcomes of our actions and those actions outside of our control. We may have to make decisions or contend with challenges that arise because of the team, project, or business. If reflection is about asking why, then vigilance is about asking what if. It allows us to prepare for circumstances and how we may want to contend with them.

It's important, however, that we do not become so fixated on what ifs that we lose sight of what is important. I've met many leaders during my career who spent the entirety of their career in the land of what if. Being a space in which we may not have all the facts or even need to imagine the outcomes completely, it can be easy to get caught up thinking about the future. The risk of vigilance is that it can make us risk averse, or even stressed about things that may not ever happen. We must strike a healthy balance here, as it is our responsibility to consider the implications of the future on the decision-making we do in the present.

The key to healthy vigilance is a matter of scale and control. Let's consider an example in which we need to fire a member of our staff. We want to go into this conversation thoughtfully and with empathy; It is going to be challenging for them and for us. But even if we handle it perfectly, that does not guarantee how they will feel about it after the fact. It is possible that they will feel hurt or even betrayed in that moment. Nobody is helped by us stressing about what somebody might think of us in several months. The most we can do is control our actions and feelings in the moment; we have minimal control over the outcome.

However, if we are making decisions that impact the long-term viability of our business, then we need to be extremely vigilant and set our sights far on the horizon. Rather than a singular firing, what if we are forced to perform layoffs? This is a choice that impacts everybody within the studio in the present; it has the potential to change our culture, we may struggle to find new hires, and it could negatively impact upon the public perception of the business. This is a decision which requires extreme vigilance because we have a high degree of control over the outcome, and there are drastic long-term implications involved in the decision we are making.

Reflection and vigilance inform our decision-making guided by thoughtfulness. Thoughtfulness is about others. It is about having the empathy and compassion to consider the impacts of our choices on others. Just because we are faced with having to make difficult decisions, does not mean that we can abandon compassion for those around us. It is about understanding that we should not hold it against the person who feels betrayed by us firing them, even if we did everything we could to soften that blow. Nobody ever has a good experience being fired, but there's no reason for us to be thoughtless and make it harder just because it was going to be hard anyway.

Through reflection, we have already chosen to embrace continuous learning, but it does not need to be completely internalised. This is why we are curious, seeking out feedback and insights from others. Curiosity is less about us as individuals and more about us as leaders. We want to get perspective on how our team feels about our decision-making and performance, to ask the sort of questions that result in them telling us, "it's not what I would have done." We can dig into such answers to get some important perspective on what we could be doing differently.

My teams liked me, because they saw that I had good intentions. But I made a lot of mistakes, and it took a while before I even realised because one of the problems with your team liking you is that they forgive your mistakes. They don't raise them as flags. So I got better at communicating and asking people questions. Making it safe for them to give this feedback by building trust and being more vulnerable.

– OSAMA DORIAS, LEAD GAMEPLAY DESIGNER,
BRASS LION ENTERTAINMENT

This is not to say we should not ask people to comment on our behaviour. If we have the sort of relationship with a member of our team who will call us out on bad behaviours, then it is absolutely worth asking them for that input. The challenge with seeking and giving input about how we act as individuals is that it can be quite confronting, and it is not the responsibility of our team to improve our leadership and the way we act as a person. It can often be easier to find this feedback from a superior or through therapy.

All these concepts are not without their risks. Early in my career I was introspective, but not necessarily actively. I would reflect on every conversation and consider every possible outcome without much mindfulness. It impacted on my well-being. Every conversation felt like walking through a minefield of my own design as I tried to consider how best to approach it. The fact I was not actively reflecting meant it was passive – mostly in the back of my mind.

It felt like a superpower to me, and in many ways it was. I would often find myself worrying about possible outcomes for a given circumstance, and put actions in place to prevent the most negative of outcomes. The team appreciated the effort I put into everything we did and ensuring their safety. But there was a physical and emotional toll that I took for granted for the longest time, thinking that it was really just all part of the job. It was my responsibility to worry about those things, so that nobody else had to.

Years later when I went to therapy, I found out that what I was experiencing was actually hypervigilance. I had a fixation on potential threats and avoided them wherever possible. It was not overly surprising to discover that many of the people I was interviewing for this book found themselves diagnosed with the same anxiety. Much like me, however, the awareness of this anxiety had made it easier to manage and turn it back into that superpower again. Hypervigilance is dangerous, yes. But vigilance is an asset if we can be mindful of our feelings and how we choose to act on our internal thought processes.

We avoid hypervigilance through the active part of active introspection. We approach this introspection with awareness and purpose, pushing the thoughts from the subconscious into our conscious mind. If you have worked in a studio which has performed postmortems or retrospectives, choosing to actively be introspective is the same. We take the time to pull ourselves aside and ask ourselves: what went right, what went wrong, what should change, what should stay the same, what would I do differently next time?

Active introspection differs from retrospectives and postmortems in that it is personal to you as an individual. We are not just thinking about or reflecting on the past or the future, but also about ourselves and the people around us. It's not just projects, but feelings and emotions. It isn't a documented process. Perhaps if it were big event, this would be a worthwhile process, in which case I encourage you to document it. But the priority here is for us to interrogate the outcome of an action and our role in it. It is not unlikely that we will make the wrong call in those moments, and that is okay. Whether things end well or not, it is essential that we stop and take that moment to reflect on the outcome.

Often we won't really understand our role in a failure until we have taken the opportunity to reflect on the outcome. When we do understand how we fail, we need to own it. We need to come back to our responsibility to hold ourselves accountable if we are truly going to embrace improving and growing as leaders. Accountabichachlity is not a step in the act of performing active introspection, but it is a step on the path to becoming a better leader. Only by owning out failures are we ever truly able to learn from them and move on from them.

> Being above reproach implies that you can't make any mistakes. And that's so incredibly not true. The most trustworthy people I know are people who own their own mess. People who make a mistake and then say, hey, I see how the decision I made or the way I acted or the thing I said or whatever it was, I can see it hurt you. And that's my fault. Here's how I am going to do better, because I'm a work in progress. I'm going to do better tomorrow than I did today. That's what being above reproach is about.
>
> – JASON IMMS, HEAD OF QUALITY ASSURANCE,
> KEYWORDS STUDIOS

Through active introspection, you eventually come to the same realisation that everybody I spoke with came to: there is no such thing as a good leader. There are leaders who performed well on a project, or were deemed good by their peers during that period of time under those circumstances. But on a different project, under separate circumstances, with a different set of people, the same leadership could easily have fallen short of the needs of the project or the team. The leader who practices active introspection is a leader who recognises that the only way they will ever be considered truly good by their teams is if they are constantly changing and improving themselves, the project, and the people around them.

We all have good leadership days and bad leadership days. Even the most patient individual has lost their patience at some point in time. This isn't a reflection of the quality of our leadership, but a reflection of us on that given day. Pushed far enough by other factors, we may find ourselves snapping at a coworker for not getting a task done when they said it would be done. That's not okay, but we can recognise why it happened and make amends in a positive way only if we take the time to consider what happened and provide ourselves with some grace to be imperfect. We can only ever improve if we can identify what triggered the moment, apologise for the outburst, and work to prevent it from happening again.

Active introspection doesn't guarantee good leadership, but it helps us find our way. Leadership is a lot like vision in that it is not a destination but a direction we are travelling in. There is no magical location that you arrive at where you become a good leader and never have to consider these things again. It is a journey, a practice, and you will always be striving to keep your skills fresh. We will have days where we will stray further from our desired direction than we would like, and that's fine. Just as is the case with any skill, a single bad day does not define our leadership. It is a deviation from our desired path. Take the time to pause and check your compass.

Epilogue

I didn't choose to be a leader. During my early studies, I worked with a group of other games students on our major project. We had been given an XBOX 360 development kit and the task of creating an XBOX Live indie title. We started by electing ourselves for the roles we wanted to be responsible for. I had chosen to work on what I was most familiar with, which was technical art.

Being typical students, most of my peers were more interested in using the campus network to play Warcraft 3. But there were a handful of us dedicated to the task, and in my role as the technical artist, I found myself acting as a translator between the art and programming teams. Over time, I earned the trust of my peers, and they voted for me to take over the responsibilities of the team's previous Producer.

I did not get a choice in the matter.

Wanting to ensure that I was prepared for the role, I set out to do my research. I had no idea what a Producer was responsible for. Being a fairly quiet and mousey teenager, I felt that I lacked the confidence to be a true leader. Up to that point, my only leadership experience had been with friends playing World of Warcraft, and even then, I had to be convinced to take up the mantle. The responsibility involved with leading a team on a game – even a student project – felt like more than I was capable of.

A single GDC talk changed my mind, "Building Your Airplane While Flying: Production at Bungie" by Allen Murray. In this talk, Murray describes the transition the studio made between Halo: Combat Evolved and Halo 2. How they had multiplied the number of producers in studio in order to better protect the team and manage the scope of work (Murray, 2009).

I was inspired. When I got into studying game development, it was not out of any particular love for any specific videogame. I loved the idea of creating something, be it graphics or code, and so I had been exploring different creative and technical industries to see what clicked. Watching that talk by Allen Murray was the moment at which my interest in game

DOI: 10.1201/9781003431626-14

development turned into a passion for it. I chose at that moment to pursue a career in game production.

As I built my skills as a leader and a producer over the years, I continued to refer to Murray's talk. I was already a fan of the Halo games, but now I was also a fan of Bungie. I followed their games well after they moved on from Halo to developing Destiny. I absorbed every insight I could into the studio, as I admired the kind of culture they projected. I aspired to work in a place that seemed to have so much love and care for its developers.

> There's this quote, start how you mean to continue. If we look at the history of a lot of studios that started the way Blizzard or Valve did, there's this idea that they were going to do more risky stuff. But they were also going to give people their time to do that, to make their weird thing, and maybe it will work, maybe it doesn't. It didn't matter. We're here to create something. That's how their studio started, and then fast forward several decades later, and their studio is having trouble and starting to show cracks. Because they started one way, and continued a different way. You need to pivot and adapt, sure, but that's your prime philosophy that you built your company upon.
>
> – ZENUEL, INDEPENDENT DEVELOPER,
> PREVIOUSLY OF STRANGE SCAFFOLD

Then, in late 2023, Bungie laid off dozens of members of its staff. It was a layoff like any other that took place over 2023: equal to most in its lack of empathy or care expressed by executive leadership throughout the whole process. But as the studio that had inspired me to lead in the first place, the news hurt in a way that I had not expected. There were a few hours in which I genuinely considered if this book was even worth writing any longer. If a studio I had once considered to be aspirational could cause such harm to the people it had once identified as being its heart, was there any hope for the industry to change at all?

I had an interview with Keith Fuller the same day I heard the news. I've been lucky to call Keith a mentor over the last decade of my time in the industry, and his voice of reason was exactly what I needed to hear. Without knowing the circumstances at the studio or the choices the leadership had at its disposal, it is challenging to pass judgement. Leadership at Bungie is accountable to the members of their team, and it is clear that executive leadership betrayed the team's trust. Even if the layoffs at Bungie were completely unavoidable, one thing could have been different: the way the layoffs were handled in the first place.

A few months after Bungie laid off over 100 staff, League of Geeks needed to lay off 31 of their own. The way in which leadership at these two studios chose to handle the aftermath speaks volumes. Following their very public layoffs, Bungie CEO Pete Parsons took to X (formerly Twitter) to lament the loss as a sad day at the studio (Carpenter, 2023a). Trent Kusters, co-founder of League of Geeks, made it clear in an interview with GamesIndustry.biz that the failure was entirely owned by the directors of the company (Dealessandri, 2023).

It is hard to imagine that Kuster's words provided much solace to the developers who lost their jobs. But it is made clear how the failure came to happen, and it relieves those who lost their employment of any responsibility. Kusters and the other directors demonstrate a willingness to accept responsibility and plot a path forward. League of Geeks is not a publicly owned company and can freely choose to share such information without repercussions. However, while Bungie may be a company that needs to answer to shareholders, Parsons reflection upon the events lacks much emotion at all. It comes across as a sanitised corporate response to the loss of colleagues and accepts no responsibility for the role executive leadership played in events.

Undoubtedly, the circumstances within the League of Geeks following the loss of their colleagues feel dire. But it seems likely that leadership has retained the trust of the developers that remained at the studio as a result of their willingness to take ownership of the situation. In the months following the layoffs at Bungie, developers within the studio have described the atmosphere as "soul-crushing." All trust in leadership has been lost, with one person going so far as to say that the developers remaining within the studio feel it has become a situation of "us vs them" between leadership and workers (Valentine, 2023).

A recurring theme throughout this book is the need for leadership to accept the circumstances that are outside of our control. The way in which we choose to treat our teams during the times in which things are hardest is some of the most telling about the quality of our leadership. If our empathy and concern for the well-being of our teams is limited only to when we are at our best as a collective, what does that say about us as leaders?

When circumstances are dire, our leadership is even more important. We need to provide our teams with a pathway out. We express a vision for the future and demonstrate to them how we can still succeed. But we also must be authentic and transparent in the presentation of the facts. It may not be easy, and maybe the chances of success aren't great. But we simply cannot maintain trust in these moments unless we are willing to drop the corporate double speak and talk directly to the members of our team as one of them.

It had been my intent when writing this book to ensure it was time-less. To avoid direct references to the years in which it was written. But it is impossible to ignore the events that have occurred in the industry between 2023 and 2024. So much has changed between the moment I first put words down and the point at which I write this epilogue. The loss of talent in the industry is genuinely inconceivable.

And yet, I cannot help but be hopeful for the future. I attended the Game Developers Conference in 2018, when Game Workers Unite first made their push to see the games industry unionise. Resistance within the industry at the time spanned from influential leaders within the industry's largest professional association to developers in the trenches concerned about the stability of their employment. Dozens of studios have established their own unions since then, many of them in response to a crisis or scandal.

> Things are going to be fine. Yeah, we're experiencing some severe growing pains. But I think, ultimately, the one thing you cannot remove from the human spirit is the desire to create something. Whether it's something empowered by society and culture and the systems we live under, it won't matter. Because humans still want to make things. The industry might look different, but it's not going anywhere.
>
> – ZENUEL, INDEPENDENT DEVELOPER,
> PREVIOUSLY OF STRANGE SCAFFOLD

In Games of Empire: Global Capitalism and Videogames, its authors discuss the concept of cognitive capitalism, a method of production in which knowledge plays an integral role. The mind of the workers is the machinery of production, generating profit for the business owners. While speaking with developers to gain a greater understanding of the content they were covering, they had the opportunity to speak with an executive from the studio they had visited. During their conversation, the executive explained how they perceived the role of the worker at their business. "Our machinery is the mind of all these people who come up with these great ideas. Our collateral walks out the door every night... You just hope like heck that they show up on Monday" (Dyer-Witheford and Peuter, 2009).

Business leadership in the games industry understands the value of the staff working for them. At present, the balance of power is heavily skewed in favour of those in executive positions in the industry. But so long as the industry and its leadership refuse to be accountable for their role in the crises we face, union membership will continue to rise. As it does so, the balance of power in the industry will begin to shift.

There will be moments throughout your leadership journey that will define the kind of leader you are. How do you wish to be remembered by the members of your team, present or future? Will they remember you as the leader who put the development of a scrapped feature over their needs as an individual? Or will they remember you as the leader who gave them the time to be with their family when it mattered the most? What is it that you desire your legacy to be?

> We have a duty and a responsibility to hold ourselves to a higher standard.
>
> – JEAN LEGGETT, LEADERSHIP COACH

Videogames come and go, but those experiences we create with the people around us are forever. There is no reason we cannot have both. We can make great games while caring for great people, it does not need to be one or the other. The only way for that to truly be possible is through a willingness to embrace the people on our teams as essential to the process of making games. To see them as experienced contributors in their own right and empower them to do the best work of their careers.

We only really get to that point if we are willing to acknowledge the moments in which we will inevitably fail them. No matter your personal feelings on the role of unionisation in the games industry, great leaders are willing to be held accountable. They desire their teams to tell them when and how they have failed. To give them feedback and direction on how they need to improve. This is a behaviour that only arises from empowered teams that trust their leaders desire to improve.

> You will get it wrong, and that's okay. You are still learning. When I started getting into these roles I panicked because I don't know everything, it was this weird version of imposter syndrome. But there's also something about it being a people manager that's like, god, what if I ruin this person's career and they leave the games industry? And one of the things that helped was people telling me that people don't leave companies, they leave bad managers.
>
> – DR. JC LAU, SENIOR ADVANCED PRODUCER, PROBABLYMONSTERS

For us to improve as individuals and as an industry, we must be willing to accept and interrogate the ways in which we have failed. No matter how pure our intent or desire to be great leaders or a great industry, failure is an inevitability. We need to move forward with open minds and open hearts, willing to ask what we could be doing differently. It is not enough just to hear the answer. We also need to understand why it matters and choose to make a change.

Acceptance of failure must be followed by a willingness to grow, even if it hurts. If we are to build trust with our teams – or to rebuild trust with developers as an industry – we need to show that we desire to make this a better place for everyone to be. Empty words and promises simply are not enough. They never were, but they are especially not enough any longer.

Multiclassing isn't just about developing the tools necessary to work with people and accepting change. It is the development of a breadth of skills necessary to lead effectively through change and uncertainty. But more importantly, it is the knowledge to accept that we will never be able to exemplify all of it. We may level up and build our skills as a Warrior, a Bard, and a Cleric. But we will never be perfect at all of them; no leader ever can. If there is one thing I hope you take away from this book, it is the value that comes from embracing the need to continue learning and growing.

The years ahead for the games industry are uncertain, but it needs great leaders more than ever. Great leaders operate in those uncertain spaces in their day-to-day, and still find ways to provide clarity and support the teams they have a responsibility to. This is still a business, and great products still need to be made. We will never be able to be informed of every permutation of a situation that we will be faced with in our roles as leaders. In order to ensure that we are able to continuously grow and develop, we need to accept that we are still learning. We will fail along the way, and that is okay. It's to be expected.

That can only truly be possible with teams that feel safe and empowered to do their best work. The reality is that we need them more than they need us. Only with the help of a great team can we navigate our way to being great leaders. Tomorrow presents new opportunities to be the leader we desire to be.

The best version of ourselves will never be what we bring to the team today, but what we choose to bring to them tomorrow.

References

Allsup, M. (2021) *Activision Blizzard Sued Over 'Frat Boy' Culture, Harassment.* Available at: https://news.bloomberglaw.com/daily-labor-report/activision-blizzard-sued-by-california-over-frat-boy-culture.

Andersen, E. (2012) *Leading So People Will Follow.* John Wiley & Sons.

APA Dictionary of Psychology. (2023) *APA Dictionary of Psychology.* Available at: https://dictionary.apa.org/.

Bennis, W., Goleman, D. and O'Toole, J. (2010) *Transparency: How Leaders Create a Culture of Candor.* John Wiley & Sons.

Bernstein, E.S. and Turban, S. (2018) 'The impact of the "open" workspace on human collaboration', *Philosophical Transactions of the Royal Society B: Biological Sciences,* 373(1753), p. 20170239. Available at: https://doi.org/10.1098/rstb.2017.0239.

Blanchard, K., Zigarmi, P. and Zigarmi, D. (2013) *Leadership and the One Minute Manager Updated Ed: Increasing Effectiveness Through Situational Leadership II.* HarperCollins.

Boccamazzo, R. et al. (2023) 'Occupational Burnout in Games: Causes, Impact, and Solutions'. Game Developers Conference. Available at: https://www.gdcvault.com/play/1029254/Occupational-Burnout-in-Games-Causes.

Broadwell, J. (2023) 'Baldur's Gate 3 voice actors also did all their own motion capture', *For The Win,* 28 August. Available at: https://ftw.usatoday.com/2023/08/baldurs-gate-3-voice-actors-also-did-all-their-own-motion-capture.

Brown, B. (2018) *Dare to Lead: Brave Work. Tough Conversations. Whole Hearts.* Random House.

Browning, K. and Stevens, M. (2023) 'Starfield's 1,000 Planets May Be One Giant Leap for Game Design', *The New York Times,* 31 August. Available at: https://www.nytimes.com/2023/08/31/arts/starfield-bethesda-microsoft-xbox.html (Accessed: 26 January 2024).

Carnegie, D. (1982) *How To Win Friends And Influence People.* Simon and Schuster.

Carpenter, N. (2023a) 'Destiny 2 developer Bungie lays off dozens of staff', *Polygon,* 30 October. Available at: https://www.polygon.com/23939245/bungie-layoffs-destiny-2-final-shape-delay.

Carpenter, N. (2023b) 'The game studios changing the industry by unionizing', *Polygon,* 8 January. Available at: https://www.polygon.com/gaming/23538801/video-game-studio-union-microsoft-activision-blizzard.

Catmull, E. (2014) *Creativity, Inc.. Overcoming the Unseen Forces That Stand in the Way of True Inspiration*. Random House.

Clark, M. (2021) 'Nearly a thousand Activision Blizzard employees slam its response to harassment suit', *The Verge*. Available at: https://www.theverge.com/2021/7/26/22594882/activision-blizzard-employees-open-letter-management-california-sexual-harassment-lawsuit.

Clay, K. (2023) 'Why Baldur's Gate 3 is a masterclass in game writing', *KAT CLAY*, 3 December. Available at: https://www.katclay.com/why-baldurs-gate-3-is-a-masterclass-in-game-writing/.

Collins, J.C. (2001) *Good to Great: Why Some Companies Make the Leap – and Others Don't*. Random House.

Dealessandri, M. (2023) *League of Geeks: 'We'll fight till the last breath'*, *GamesIndustry.biz*. Available at: https://www.gamesindustry.biz/league-of-geeks-well-fight-till-the-last-breath.

Druskat, V.U. and Wolff, S.B. (2001) 'Building the emotional intelligence of groups', *Harvard Business Review*, 79(3), pp. 80–90, 164.

Dunbar, R.I.M. (1992) 'Neocortex size as a constraint on group size in primates', *Journal of Human Evolution*, 22(6), pp. 469–493. Available at: https://doi.org/10.1016/0047-2484(92)90081-J.

Dyer-Witheford, N. and Peuter, G.D. (2009) *Games of Empire: Global Capitalism and Video Games*. University of Minnesota Press.

Gach, E. (2018) *Telltale Employees Left Stunned By Company Closure, No Severance [Update]*, *Kotaku*. Available at: https://kotaku.com/telltale-employees-left-stunned-by-company-closure-no-1829272139.

Galante, J. et al. (2021) 'Mindfulness-based programmes for mental health promotion in adults in nonclinical settings: A systematic review and meta-analysis of randomised controlled trials', *PLOS Medicine*, 18(1), p. e1003481. Available at: https://doi.org/10.1371/journal.pmed.1003481.

Goleman, D., Boyatzis, R.E. and McKee, A. (2002) *Primal Leadership: Realizing the Power of Emotional Intelligence*. Harvard Business School Press.

Grayson, N. (2022) 'Bungie leadership assures employees Sony deal will not result in layoffs, restructuring', *Washington Post*, 1 February. Available at: https://www.washingtonpost.com/video-games/2022/02/01/bungie-sony-buyout-destiny-2-developers/.

Greenleaf, R.K. (1970) *The Servant as Leader*. Center for Applied Studies.

Hoffman, E. (2004) 'EA: The Human Story'. Available at: https://ea-spouse.livejournal.com/274.html.

Hollister, S. (2021) California sues Activision Blizzard over a culture of 'constant sexual harassment', *The Verge*. Available at: https://www.theverge.com/2021/7/22/22588215/activision-blizzard-lawsuit-sexual-harassment-discrimination-pay.

Homer. (1991) *The Iliad of Homer*. Oxford University Press.

International Game Developers Association. (2021) '*Developer Satisfaction Survey (DSS) – IGDA*'. International Game Developers Association. Available at: https://igda-website.s3.us-east-2.amazonaws.com/wp-content/uploads/2021/10/18113901/IGDA-DSS-2021_SummaryReport_2021.pdf.

Johnson, L.K.D. (2018) *The Light Triad Scale: Developing and Validating a Preliminary Measure of Prosocial Orientation.* Available at: https://ir.lib.uwo.ca/cgi/viewcontent.cgi?article=7588&context=etd.

Kabat-Zinn, J. and Hanh, T.N. (2009) *Full Catastrophe Living: Using the Wisdom of Your Body and Mind to Face Stress, Pain, and Illness.* Random House Publishing Group.

Karunamuni, N. and Weerasekera, R. (2024) 'Theoretical foundations to guide mindfulness meditation: A path to wisdom'. Available at: https://doi.org/10.31231/osf.io/mfs63.

Klepek, P. (2019) 'The ambitious future of "dead cells" is ditching co-ops for capitalism', *Vice,* 30 October. Available at: https://www.vice.com/en/article/3kxed3/the-ambitious-future-of-dead-cells-is-ditching-co-ops-for-capitalism.

Kocurek, C.A. (2015) *Coin-operated Americans: Rebooting Boyhood at the Video Game Arcade.* University of Minnesota Press.

Kraut, R. (2023) '*Socratic method | Definition, Socrates, Examples, & Facts | Britannica*'. Available at: https://www.britannica.com/topic/Socratic-method.

Langford, J. and Clance, P.R. (1993) 'The imposter phenomenon: Recent research findings regarding dynamics, personality and family patterns and their implications for treatment', *Psychotherapy: Theory, Research, Practice, Training,* 30(3), pp. 495–501. Available at: https://doi.org/10.1037/0033-3204.30.3.495.

Lencioni, P.M. (2012) *The Advantage: Why Organizational Health Trumps Everything Else In Business.* John Wiley & Sons.

Liao, S. (2021) 'At Blizzard, groping, free-flowing booze and fear of retaliation tainted "magical" workplace', *Washington Post,* 6 August. Available at: https://www.washingtonpost.com/video-games/2021/08/06/blizzard-culture-sexual-harassment-alcohol/.

Markovits, D. (2015) 'Theories of the common law of contracts'. Available at: https://plato.stanford.edu/archIves/sum2020/entries/contracts-theories/index.html.

Maslach, C. (1998) 'A multidimensional theory of burnout', in *Theories of Organisational Stress.* Oxford University Press, pp. 68–85. Available at: https://doi.org/10.1093/oso/9780198522799.003.0004.

Maslow, A.H. (1943) 'A theory of human motivation', *Psychological Review,* 50(4), pp. 370–396. Available at: https://doi.org/10.1037/h0054346.

Mindful.org. (2020) *What is Mindfulness?, Mindful.* Available at: https://www.mindful.org/what-is-mindfulness/.

Miserandino, C. (2013) 'The Spoon Theory written by Christine Miserandino', *But You Dont Look Sick? support for those with invisible illness or chronic illness,* 25 April. Available at: https://butyoudontlooksick.com/articles/written-by-christine/the-spoon-theory/.

Murray, A. (2009) *Building Your Airplane While Flying: Production at Bungie.* Available at: https://www.gdcvault.com/play/1284/Building-Your-Airplane-While-Flying.

Murray, G. and Green, J. (2021) *After Covid-19, Aviation Faces A Pilot Shortage* Available at: https://www.oliverwyman.com/our-expertise/insights/2021/mar/after-covid-19-aviation-faces-a-pilot-shortage.html.

Newfield, A. (2020) *Oops, I Became a Manager: Managing the Veterinary Hospital Team by Finding Unicorns.*

Noor, F. (2024) *2024 – Game Industry Layoffs – Obsidian Publish.* Available at: https://publish.obsidian.md/vg-layoffs/Archive/2024.

Noseworthy, M. (2014) 'Evolving Bungie's production practices for a Brave New World'. *Game Developers Conference.* Available at: https://www.gdcvault.com/play/1020597/Evolving-Bungie-s-Production-Practices.

Paulhus, D.L. and Williams, K.M. (2002) 'The Dark Triad of personality: Narcissism, Machiavellianism, and psychopathy', *Journal of Research in Personality*, 36(6), pp. 556–563. Available at: https://doi.org/10.1016/S0092-6566(02)00505-6.

Peeters, B. (2004) 'Tall poppies and egalitarianism in Australian discourse: From key word to cultural value', *English World-Wide*, 25(1), pp. 1–25. Available at: https://doi.org/10.1075/eww.25.1.02pee.

Peters, J. (2022) 'Sony officially closes $3.6 billion acquisition of Bungie'. *The Verge.* Available at: https://www.theverge.com/2022/7/15/23220335/bungie-sony-acquisition-complete-official-done.

Phillpott-Kenny, I. (2020) *Comparing Skyrim's Map Size to Assassin's Creed Odyssey, Game Rant.* Available at: https://gamerant.com/skyrim-map-size-assassins-creed-odyssey/.

Plunkett, L. (2021) *Activision Blizzard Sued By California Over Widespread Harassment Of Women, Kotaku.* Available at: https://kotaku.com/activision-blizzard-sued-by-california-over-widespread-1847339746.

PsychOdyssey. (2022). Available at: https://www.doublefine.com/dftv/psychodyssey.

Purchese, R. (2012) *A Project Eternity recap: what $4 million has funded | Eurogamer. net.* Available at: https://www.eurogamer.net/a-project-eternity-recap-what-usd4-million-has-funded.

Purser, R. (2019) 'The mindfulness conspiracy', *The Guardian*, 14 June. Available at: https://www.theguardian.com/lifeandstyle/2019/jun/14/the-mindfulness-conspiracy-capitalist-spirituality.

Ramsay, D. (2015) *Open Office Plans: Advantages, Disadvantages, & Research, Adventure Associates.* Available at: https://www.adventureassoc.com/open-office-plans-the-advantages-disadvantages-and-research/.

Roberge, M.-É. and van Dick, R. (2010) 'Recognizing the benefits of diversity: When and how does diversity increase group performance?', *Human Resource Management Review*, 20(4), pp. 295–308. Available at: https://doi.org/10.1016/j.hrmr.2009.09.002.

Sawyer, C. (2003) *Chris Sawyer Software Development.* Available at: https://www.chrissawyergames.com/faq3.htm.

Schreier, J. (2017) *The Story Behind Mass Effect: Andromeda's Troubled Five-Year Development, Kotaku.* Available at: https://kotaku.com/the-story-behind-mass-effect-andromedas-troubled-five-1795886428.

Schreier, J. (2019) *How BioWare's Anthem Went Wrong, Kotaku.* Available at: https://kotaku.com/how-biowares-anthem-went-wrong-1833731964.

Schreier, J. (2021) *Cyberpunk 2077: What Caused the Video Game's Disastrous Rollout – Bloomberg.* Available at: https://www.bloomberg.com/news/articles/2021-01-16/cyberpunk-2077-what-caused-the-video-game-s-disastrous-rollout.

Simelane, S. (2023) *Starfield developer explains why planets are 'meant to be empty by design' – Destructoid.* Available at: https://www.destructoid.com/starfield-developer-explains-why-planets-are-meant-to-be-empty-by-design/.

Spellecy, R. (2003) 'Reviving Ulysses Contracts', *Kennedy Institute of Ethics Journal*, 13(4), pp. 373–392.

Stone, D. and Heen, S. (2014) *Thanks for the Feedback: The Science and Art of Receiving Feedback Well.* Penguin UK.

Stone, D., Patton, B. and Heen, S. (2010) *Difficult Conversations: How to Discuss What Matters Most.* Penguin Publishing Group.

Taylor, D.B. (2020) 'Sony Pulls Cyberpunk 2077 From PlayStation Store and Will Offer Refunds'. *The New York Times.* Available at: https://www.nytimes.com/2020/12/18/technology/cyberpunk-2077-refund.html.

Valentine, R. (2023) *Bungie Devs Say Atmosphere Is 'Soul-Crushing' Amid Layoffs, Cuts, and Fear of Total Sony Takeover, IGN.* Available at: https://www.ign.com/articles/bungie-devs-say-atmosphere-is-soul-crushing-amid-layoffs-cuts-and-fear-of-total-sony-takeover.

Valve Corporation. (2012) 'Valve's Handbook for New Employees'. Available at: https://cdn.cloudflare.steamstatic.com/apps/valve/Valve_NewEmployeeHandbook.pdf.

Wilcox, K. (2021) *Webb's Deployments Most Complex Ever Attempted | APPEL Knowledge Services.* Available at: https://appel.nasa.gov/2021/11/24/webbs-deployments-most-complex-ever-attempted/.

Wong, D. (2007) *What is the Monkeysphere? | Cracked.com.* Available at: https://www.cracked.com/article_14990_what-monkeysphere.html.

World Health Organisation. (2022) *COVID-19 Pandemic Triggers 25% Increase in Prevalence of Anxiety and Depression Worldwide.* Available at: https://www.who.int/news/item/02-03-2022-covid-19-pandemic-triggers-25-increase-in-prevalence-of-anxiety-and-depression-worldwide.

Zara, C. (2012) *Tortured Artists: From Picasso and Monroe to Warhol and Winehouse, the Twisted Secrets of the World's Most Creative Minds.* Simon and Schuster.

Index

For Product Safety Concerns and Information please contact our EU
representative GPSR@taylorandfrancis.com Taylor & Francis Verlag GmbH,
Kaufingerstraße 24, 80331 München, Germany

Printed and bound by CPI Group (UK) Ltd, Croydon, CR0 4YY
08/06/2025
01897003-0013